CULTURESCOPE

GRADE SCHOOL EDITION

THE PRINCETON REVIEW

Guide to an Informed Mind

CULTURESCOPE

GRADE SCHOOL EDITION

THE PRINCETON REVIEW

*Guide to an
Informed Mind*

RANDOM HOUSE, INC. NEW YORK 1995

LIZ BUFFA

Buffa, Liz

The Princeton review culturescope.   Grade school edition/Liz Buffa–1st ed.

    p.   ca.

    Includes bibliographical references and index.

    ISBN 0-679-75365-6 $18.00

    1. Handbooks. vade-mecums, etc.—Juvenile Literature   I. Title

II. Title: Culturescope

AG105.B93   95-8497

1995

31.02–dc20

ACKNOWLEDGMENTS

A lot of people went into the making of this book, starting with the parents who shared their concerns about education, teachers who spent time talking about curriculum, and friends who helped with all sorts of great ideas. Special mention must be made of the help the author received from James Bradley, for his wonderful research, Mike Freedman and Marcia Lerner, for their unflagging moral support, and Dominick, David and Paul, for agreeing to read through the final manuscript.

Almost from the start of this project it became clear that a book that hoped to encompass all of the information included between these covers was more than a one person job. Thanks are not enough for Chris Kensler, Maria Russo, Lee Elliott, Kristin Fayne-Mulroy, and PJ Waters, creative editing team extraordinnaire. Together they oversaw armies of researchers, they requisitioned and selected the hundreds of photos adorning these pages, and, most importantly, they contributed and added material to this book where it was needed. Their contributions were instrumental to the creation of this book. And were it not for the design team of Heather Kern, Adam Hurwitz, Meher Khambata, and Julian Ham, these myriad elements would not have come together so harmoniously. Hats off to John Bergdahl for his outstanding illustrations. Kudos must go out to the production team of Adam Hurwitz, Heather Kern, Dinica Quesada, Glen Pannell, Chris Thomas, Chris Scott, Joe Cavallaro, Lisa Ruyter, Kim Jack Riley, JiSun Chang, Zachary Knower, Joseph McPartland, Sara Kane, Illeny Maaza, Carol Slominski, Peter Jung, Jessica Brockington, Julian Heath, Russel Murray, Michael Recorvits, Dave Romeo, and Ray Suhler, who worked long hours creating the illustrations, trimming photos, and tweaking the design for what must have seemed an eternity. This book is as much theirs as anybody's.

The editors would like to thank Bruno Butler and Joe Peletier for their insights and help in gathering the materials we needed, Kate Lardner for making sure we weren't lying, Judy Lyon Davis for her indexing genius, and The Bettmann Archive for their incredible assistance and resources.

TABLE OF CONTENTS

WHAT IS *CULTURESCOPE*?

This book is about making connections. *Culturescope* tells you what a child should know at each grade level and encourages kids to tie together the different subjects they learn about. We think an "informed mind" is one that is not only full of crucial knowledge but also agile and excited about learning. We've designed the book in a kid-friendly way, so that even "traditional" subjects like math and science will be accessible and inviting to them.

Culturescope is also designed to foster connections between you and your child; to involve you in your child's learning process as much as possible. After this introduction, the rest of the book is aimed at kids, but parents should take an active role as kids work their way through—reading to smaller children at times, reading

Paste

along with older children, helping out with the projects we suggest, and keeping an eye out for the books, records, CD-ROMs, and movies we recommend.

WHAT SHOULD A KID KNOW?

Before we wrote this book, we gathered together grade school curricula from several states and compared them to find out what kids across the country are expected to know at each grade level. While we found a good deal of curricular differences from state to state, there were still quite a few commonalities. One reason for these shared curricular standards is the developmental stages common to all children. Whether they're from Connecticut or California, children are generally ready to learn certain things at certain ages. First grade, for example, is the best time, developmentally, for a child to learn how to read. Some children begin earlier, some later, but most start real reading at this grade level.

Education also builds on itself. You cannot learn multiplication without learning addition. So, if a child is expected to start doing multiplication in second or third grade, she had better master the concept of addition by first grade.

In addition to analyzing the state curricula, we studied the test prep material geared to students taking the Iowa, Stanford, California, and Metropolitan Achievement Tests. From the shared standards of these very different standardized tests we got some more insight into what today's kids are expected to know.

WHAT ELSE?

Luckily for kids, there is a good deal more to education than reading, writing, and arithmetic. A child needs to play, to think about the world, to explore other cultures, and to be aware of music and art. A child also needs some help with the basic rules of living and getting along with others. To satisfy these "whole education" demands we ransacked children's sections of bookstores, spent time in children's libraries, and surfed the Internet to see what sort of books are being published to help children get a complete education. We gathered hundreds of sources, many of which are recommended of this book.

QUIZ TIME

We took all this information—state curricula, standardized test questions, and published material—and made lists of "checkpoints" for each grade level. These lists eventually became the six *Culturescope* Quizzes, one for each grade level, that you'll find at the beginning of *Culturescope*. Each quiz covers the full range of *Culturescope* subjects at a particular grade level.

The quizzes test concepts your child should be comfortable with by the end of each grade. If an incoming fourth grader takes the fourth grade quiz, he shouldn't be expected to answer most questions correctly. He would be better off taking the third grade quiz first, then the fourth grade quiz to see what kind of head start he may have. And for heaven's sake, if your child misses a question, don't panic! That's what the other 400 pages in the book are for. You need only turn to the page given on the answer key for a full explanation of the concepts being addressed in any given question.

HOW TO READ THIS BOOK

Culturescope is meant to be fun. Encourage your child to keep the book around and open it up whenever she thinks of it. After a kid takes her quiz, she should look up the questions she got wrong, then just dive right into the subject that interests her most. There are six chapters in *Culturescope*, arranged in alphabetical order:

> English
> Fun and Games
> Humanities
> Math
> Science
> Social Studies

Each chapter is organized by grade level, starting with first grade questions and ending with sixth grade questions. The grade level of each question is noted in the margin with the number in the big circle like this:

It's important to remember that just because a question is for a higher grade than your child's, it isn't necessarily off limits. In some areas, such as Math, it may be impossible for your child to understand concepts meant for higher grades. In other areas, you may want to be sure to read with a younger child questions meant for higher grades on topics such as sexual reproduction and AIDS. But in general, a little curiosity about what lies ahead is a good thing. This is especially true since books, movies, music, and other recommendations often appeal across grade levels.

Your Child Should Be Jumpy!

To facilitate "jumping around" from one chapter to another, we cross-reference topics in a very special way. A kid may be reading a section in the Humanities chapter about newspapers and come across this:

> First and most important, a newspaper is where you can read to find out about what is happening around you—from the big fire downtown to what the president (p.296) is doing to run the country.

The purple word president is accompanied by a page number. When the child turns to page 296, she will find a full discussion on just what the president of our country does. These cross-references help the reader find the information she needs to fully understand any given topic.

The Sidebars

Along with the main text, there are hundreds of sidebars in *Culturescope*. Your child will find lots of fun facts, games, trivia, and definitions in the sidebars on each page. The sidebars come in seven categories:

1. The Culturescope Sidebar

YOUR NOSTRILS TAKE TURNS!

That's right—they take turns every three hours or so—one breathes and smells while the other takes a rest.

This is our "normal" sidebar. It further illuminates the main text, adds interesting bits of trivia, and rounds out the discussion.

2. Definition

definition

superlative
(soo PER luh tiv) *adj.*, the best, the most supreme; above everything else.

*Mr. Potboiler said Clyde's essay on cockroaches was **superlative**, then he fainted when Clyde showed him his pet roach, Louie.*

There are definition boxes for important, but not always hard, words. Each box contains our trademark Princeton Review phonetic spelling, the definition, and a sample sentence that uses the word.

3. What to See

We make all kinds of recommendations for movies, TV shows, and videocassettes that relate to the subject being discussed. These sidebars, as well the music and book recommendations, provide great ideas for additional exploration of topics in which your child is particularly interested.

4. What to Read

Check these sidebars out for interesting books and magazines on each particular topic.

5. What to Hear

We recommend songs and albums throughout *Culturescope* that relate to the topics. Sometimes the relationship is a bit of a stretch, but this is grade school, not rocket science! Go with the flow.

6. What to Access

To keep your kid at the cutting edge, we also recommend CD-ROM programs and various resources available on the Internet.

7. Arts and Crafts

Sometimes doing an experiment or drawing a picture will make a concept easier to understand. Lots of activities are suggested throughout the book, from drawing a "community helping hand" to making an intricate paper "fortune teller."

THE APPENDICES

There are three appendices in *Culturescope*. The first two are lists of all the presidents and all the states and state capitals. Your kid can use them to help study for those horrid "Name the Fifty States and Their Capitals" tests and those even more dreadful "Name the Forty-two Presidents and Their Vice-Presidents" tests.

The third appendix is really fun. It has all of our book, music, and movie recommendations. We put polls up on the Internet asking teachers, parents, college students, and kids themselves what children's books they enjoyed, what movies they loved, and what music they listened to. We also considered critics' choices and recent winners of prestigious awards in children's literature.

The movies we've chosen are appropriate for the whole family—adults too. The music can be enjoyed together as well. While we have not included book series like *The Hardy Boys*, *Nancy Drew*, *Baby-Sitters Club*, and *R.L. Stine Mysteries*, we want to make it clear that that is not an indictment of those popular genres. Reading is reading is reading. Don't discourage your child from reading anything. If he enjoys *The Hardy Boys*, let him read *The Hardy Boys* to his heart's content. But you might want to be standing in the wings with *Hatchet* by Gary Paulsen to slip into his hands when he's getting a little sick of the adventures of Joe and Frank.

KEEP ON LEARNING!

Culturescope is meant to help you keep an eye on your child's progress, to remind you how to explain something, and to provide your child with interesting and accessible information. It is not meant to stress out any member of your family. Remember, education is fun. Try to expand on this theme yourself. Check out local museums. Watch for movie revivals. Look in the Classics section of the video store. Take the kids on trips to farms or funky buildings or whatever interesting things are around you. There's something to be learned everywhere.

The Culturescope Quizzes

FIRST GRADE

First grade is an exciting and challenging time for your child. This is the first year in which he has a real structure and discipline to his study. Important concepts are introduced in first grade. An understanding, but not necessarily a mastery, of them is needed.

MATH

Single digit addition, subtraction, shapes, grouping and patterns are the important concepts in first grade. Your child should have a general idea of what these things mean. Let her start doing addition problems on paper, without using her hands to count out. Encourage estimation—an important concept for all mathematical thought. If your child can begin to get this kind of a "feel" for math, she'll be in good shape. Time is introduced in first grade.

SOCIAL STUDIES

The concepts of community, rights, responsibilities and services are introduced in first grade. Getting the basics here allows a child to understand United States government in later grades. Some basic facts of history are important—who the president is, who the first president was, for example.

SCIENCE

In science, your child will probably be studying animals, planets, stars, nature. This is a time of great curiosity about the world—his immediate world and the world beyond. Capitalize on that curiosity with observation—look at leaves, collect rocks, just think about different shapes and sizes and textures. Careful observation constitute the beginning of scientific inquiry.

ENGLISH

Your child should be starting to read—"decoding" words and recognizing the sounds that letters make. The level of reading varies greatly. Keep exposing your child to books, and keep reading to them. Books are the best way to learn how to read. It's a lot easier to decode a word that has a picture above it. Tell your child to use these hints to figure out what she is reading. The concepts of rhyming, opposites, and alphabetical order are all important to enforce early reading skills. Sequencing words to make sentences and sentences to tell stories are important early writing skills.

HUMANITIES

Rhymes are a lot of fun in first grade. So is taking your child to a museum, probably a natural history museum (art museums may still be a few years away).

GENERAL

The calendar, holidays, family relationships, north and south, and nutrition are all ideas to start thinking about. We've also included some great outdoor games for first graders. Don't forget the importance of running around, learning rules and playing.

FIRST GRADE QUIZ

1. **Name three planets in our solar system.**

   _____

   _____

   _____

2. **How is Paul's mother's brother related to Paul?**

   (A) He is Paul's grandfather.
   (B) He is Paul's brother.
   (C) He is Paul's uncle.

3. **What time is it?**

   (A) 6:00
   (B) 6:30
   (C) 7:30

4. **3 + 4 =**

   (A) 6
   (B) 7
   (C) 8

5. **What does gravity do?**

   (A) It makes things go fast.
   (B) It pulls smaller objects towards larger objects.
   (C) It makes things stronger.

6. **What will a kitten be when it grows up?**

   (A) A dog
   (B) A guinea pig
   (C) A cat

7. **Which of these things does your community do for you?**

   (A) It does your homework.
   (B) It walks your dog.
   (C) It puts up street signs.

8. **Which of these is not a state?**

   (A) Texas
   (B) Chicago
   (C) Delaware

9. Who is the President of the United States?

   (A) George Bush
   (B) Michael Jackson
   (C) Bill Clinton

10. Which word has a long "o" sound?

    (A) Chicken
    (B) Toe
    (C) Clock

11. If Mary has 12 donuts and eats 3, how many will she have left?

    (A) 12
    (B) 15
    (C) 9

12. Put the following words in A-B-C order:

    hat
    ball
    orange

    (A) hat, ball, orange
    (B) ball, hat, orange
    (C) orange, hat, ball

13. Which of the following things uses electricity?

    (A) A bicycle
    (B) A book
    (C) A lamp

14. Put the following sentences in order:

    (1) She bought some bread.
    (2) She made a sandwich.
    (3) Jenna went to the store.
    (4) She brought it home.

    (A) 3, 1, 4, 2
    (B) 3, 4, 1, 2
    (C) 1, 3, 1, 4

15. What are the people who make up a country called?

    (A) Elves
    (B) Citizens
    (C) Panda bears

16. What is the opposite of sad?

    (A) Lazy
    (B) Heavy
    (C) Happy

17. Juan and Peter are playing tag, Juan is "it" and he tags Peter. What happens to Peter?

(A) Peter eats a pumpkin.
(B) Peter is "it".
(C) Peter must go home.

18. How many crayons are there?

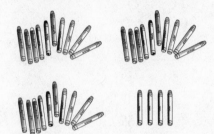

(A) 24
(B) 34
(C) 7

19. What word rhymes with house?

(A) book
(B) mouse
(C) glass

20. Where's the best place to see paintings and sculptures?

(A) Art museum
(B) Video arcade
(C) Library

21. Put the following words into the best sentence order:

goes store to the Jill

(A) Jill to the store goes.
(B) To the store Jill goes.
(C) Jill goes to the store.

22. What are the next two numbers in this pattern? 52, 54, 56, 58, 60, __, __

(A) 61, 62
(B) 65, 70
(C) 62, 64

23. What happens when you heat up ice?

(A) It becomes water, then steam
(B) It becomes steam, then water
(C) It becomes a Snickers bar

24. Which word has a long "o" sound?

(A) Chicken
(B) Clock
(C) Toe

25.   24
       +17

(A) 41
(B) 37
(C) 31

CULTURESCOPE

ANSWERS TO THE FIRST GRADE QUIZ

QUESTION NUMBER	CORRECT ANSWER	EXPLANATION ON PAGE
1.	(NA)	231
2.	C	236
3.	B	153
4.	B	149
5.	B	238
6.	C	239
7.	C	293
8.	B	295
9.	C	296
10.	B	49
11.	C	155
12.	B	43
13.	C	235
14.	A	47
15.	B	291
16.	C	49
17.	B	99
18.	A	156
19.	B	119
20.	A	121
21.	C	45
22.	C	151
23.	A	233
24.	B	49
25.	A	158

SECOND GRADE

In second grade, your child is steadily reading, doing math without counting on his fingers, and learning more about the world.

MATH

Your child learns how to "carry" over numbers in double digit addition by the end of second grade. She should understand the concept of multiplication, and be able to do some basic problems (this stems directly from grouping in first grade). Problems that involve more than one step emerge in second grade, as does the concept of place value and fractions. Don't forget to always reinforce earlier lessons as she progresses to more difficult things.

SOCIAL STUDIES

In social studies, skills from first grade are reinforced and expanded on. This is a good time to explore your own community. Children should learn a little more about the government—where the president lives, for example. They should have a basic understanding of geography and be able to differentiate between towns, cities, and states.

SCIENCE

Science is fun in second grade. Children love to observe weather patterns, explore nature, learn about animals. This is a great time to get a book of simple science experiments. Measurement is an important beginning skill for math and science.

ENGLISH

More structure is introduced in grammar—capitalization, combining sentences, and compound words. Children love to read and make up stories at this age, so encourage both. Check out the reading list for second graders.

HUMANITIES

Once your child has the hang of reading, let him at newspapers, magazines—anything! Comic books are really fun for second graders, and stereos aren't as intimidating, so let your kid at your record collection!

GENERAL

Card games are great for second graders. They can also start playing board games, a great way for them to do something with older friends. They love to know the rules of games they love like basketball, baseball, football.

SECOND GRADE QUIZ

1. **Which of the following animals is a mammal?**

   (A) A lizard
   (B) A hamster
   (C) A guppy

2. **What is the plural of "fox"?**

   (A) foxs
   (B) fockses
   (C) foxes

3. **How many pennies are in a dollar?**

   (A) 50
   (B) 100
   (C) 1,000

4. **Which of the following foods gives you the most vitamin C?**

   (A) Milk
   (B) Candy
   (C) Orange juice

5. **Why are Native Americans called Indians?**

   (A) Because they are from India.
   (B) Because they are from Indiana.
   (C) Because Columbus thought he had arrived in India when he first came to America.

6. **What is a colony?**

   (A) A baseball field
   (B) A type of religious ceremony
   (C) A land ruled by a country that is far away

7. **Which of the following covers most of the earth?**

   (A) Land
   (B) Water
   (C) Cereal

8. **March comes in like a lion and goes out like a _____.**

   (A) bear
   (B) lamb
   (C) hermit crab

9. **What is a calendar used for?**

   (A) To measure time
   (B) To measure distance
   (C) To measure detergent

10. **How often does a full moon appear?**

    (A) Every night
    (B) Once a week
    (C) Once a month

11. **Why do we celebrate Thanksgiving?**

    (A) To remember a feast held by Pilgrims and Indians
    (B) To remember a basketball game between Pilgrims and Indians
    (C) To remember a dance invented by Pilgrims and Indians

12. **Name two dairy products.**

    _____

    _____

13. **Which form of transportation won't get you from the United States to Europe?**

    (A) A boat
    (B) A train
    (C) An airplane

14. **Where do you play basketball?**

    (A) On a field
    (B) On a court
    (C) On a boat

15. **4 x 3 =**

    (A) 7
    (B) 12
    (C) 16

16. **Where would you look to find the definition of a word?**

    (A) A dictionary
    (B) An atlas
    (C) The closet

17. **Which of these figures is a triangle?**

    (A) ▢

    (B) ◯

    (C) △

18. Pick out the verb in the following sentence:

    The dog ran up the sidewalk and into the house.

    (A) up
    (B) dog
    (C) ran

19. What pronoun should be used to take the place of "duck"?

    (A) it
    (B) they
    (C) he

20. What do we call a group of animals that no longer exist?

    (A) Mammals
    (B) Extinct
    (C) Species

21. What is an antonym for the word "ugly"?

    (A) Pretty
    (B) Sad
    (C) Funny

22. When you play Monopoly, what happens when you pass go?

    (A) You land on stop
    (B) You go to jail
    (C) You collect $200

23. Which word listed below needs a capital letter to be spelled correctly?

    (A) spy
    (B) chicago
    (C) radio

24. The Big Dipper is a group of

    (A) stars
    (B) numbers
    (C) toys

25. How many inches are in a foot?

    (A) Sixteen
    (B) Five
    (C) Twelve

ANSWERS TO THE SECOND GRADE QUIZ

QUESTION NUMBER	CORRECT ANSWER	EXPLANATION ON PAGE
1.	B	241
2.	C	56
3.	B	161
4.	C	245
5.	C	302
6.	C	304
7.	B	248
8.	B	251
9.	A	299
10.	C	250
11.	A	301
12.	(NA)	247
13.	B	306
14.	B	105
15.	B	163
16.	A	50
17.	C	160
18.	C	53
19.	A	54
20.	B	240
21.	A	58
22.	C	101
23.	B	52
24.	A	242
25.	C	170

THIRD GRADE

Here's where the real work begins. There's a lot to learn in third grade, and a lot more homework and class work. Help your child by helping him keep organized. This will be one of the first times he'll have to plan out an assignment that may be due later.

MATH
Mastery of the times table is key. A really great thing to do is to test your child whenever you have free time. Just do a times table: 5 x 6? 5 x 8? If your child is completely comfortable with these numbers she'll be able to master later concepts much more easily. Kids need to know more about fractions and how they work. Estimation is still important and a very important concept, and rounding off is introduced.

SOCIAL STUDIES
Third graders are ready to learn more about the world around them—Native Americans in your area, early settlers, and life in colonial times. Third graders also often study other countries. Look in your library for books about different places around the world. They should also learn a little more about our government and how it works.

SCIENCE
Seasons, weather, and properties of things in nature are introduced. These are all good science lessons for third graders. They can look at a prism and watch it split light into bands of colors. Observation and exploration are key to all grade school science programs.

ENGLISH
Your child should understand more about how a sentence is put together. Different tenses are studied. More details about the parts of speech are introduced, including adverbs and adjectives. Homonyms are interesting to learn about. Vocabulary begins to expand through reading and conversation.

HUMANITIES
Your child should learn to find her way around a library in third grade—all by herself!

GENERAL
How do you read music? How do you play chess? These are new ideas for third graders.

THIRD GRADE QUIZ

1. **Which of the following gases pollutes the air?**

   (A) Oxygen
   (B) Nitrogen
   (C) Carbon monoxide

2. **Which word is correct in the sentence below?**

   I told them to get_____coats.

   (A) there
   (B) their
   (C) they're

3. **Which of these states borders the Pacific Ocean?**

   (A) California
   (B) Illinois
   (C) Florida

4. **Which of these sentences is a question?**

   (A) Rover ran away.
   (B) Rover got hit by a milk truck.
   (C) How's Rover?

5. **Where are the symbols on a map explained?**

   (A) A dictionary
   (B) A legend
   (C) A mountain

6. **Name three colors in the rainbow.**

   _____

   _____

   _____

7. **Who wrote the Declaration of Independence?**

   (A) George Washington
   (B) Thomas Jefferson
   (C) Bill Clinton

8. **Which is right?**

   Between my sister and me, I am the_____.

   (A) smarter
   (B) smartest
   (C) smart

9. David keeps his CDs on shelves that hold 12 CDs each. He has four shelves completely filled. How many CDs does David own?

(A) 48
(B) 24
(C) 16

10. Which word in the sentence below is the adjective?

The fun game moved quickly.

(A) Quickly
(B) Fun
(C) Moved

11. Round to the nearest thousand and add.

$$1,274$$
$$+ \ 2,648$$

(A) 3,000
(B) 4,000
(C) 5,000

12. What is the subject of the sentence below?

"Full House" is my favorite show.

(A) my favorite show
(B) "Full House"
(C) is

13. What is the present tense of the verb "hated."

(A) hate
(B) will hate
(C) hating

14. On Saturday, Jane had a party for 27 children. 18 had pizza, and the rest had hot dogs. How many had hot dogs?

(A) 9
(B) 10
(C) 2

15. Who is Calvin's sidekick in the comics?

(A) Hobbes
(B) Snoopy
(C) Tonto

16. Cat is to kitten as dog is to_____.

(A) puppy
(B) dog catcher
(C) golden retriever

17. What does it mean to be fortunate?

(A) Happy
(B) Lucky
(C) Silly

18. Circle the two regions of the United States that fought in the Civil War.

19. In chess, which piece can ONLY move diagonally?

(A) Bishop
(B) Knight
(C) Jester

20. Complete the following expression:

"Birds of a feather . . ."

(A) need a few more feathers.
(B) have a hard time flying.
(C) flock together.

21. What note does this represent?

(A) E
(B) A
(C) G

22. Which of the following is NOT a part of a plant?

(A) Roots
(B) Lungs
(C) Leaves

23. Which fraction is largest?

(A) 1/3
(B) 1/6
(C) 1/2

24. **How many strikes can you make in baseball before you are called "out"?**

   (A) Ten
   (B) One
   (C) Three

25. **Who gave the famous speech that began, "I have a dream . . ."?**

   (A) Ronald Reagan
   (B) Richard Nixon
   (C) Martin Luther King, Jr.

ANSWERS TO THE THIRD GRADE QUIZ

QUESTION NUMBER	CORRECT ANSWER	EXPLANATION ON PAGE
1.	C	255
2.	B	61
3.	A	257
4.	C	21
5.	B	309
6.	(NA)	256
7.	B	315
8.	B	60
9.	A	176
10.	B	62
11.	B	178
12.	B	67
13.	A	69
14.	A	172
15.	A	127
16.	A	72
17.	B	73
18.	(NA)	311
19.	A	108
20.	C	70
21.	A	128
22.	B	259
23.	C	175
24.	C	110
25.	A	313

FOURTH GRADE

Fourth grade is a turning point for a lot of students. Those who struggled (perhaps because they were younger) begin to catch up. Sometimes those who were so far ahead (often because they were older) start to fall into line with everyone else. You need to keep your child on track in this important year.

MATH

In math there is more multiplication. Division is introduced along with reducing fractions, graphs, and word problems. There's a big curriculum in math this year. Make sure your child gets each concept as it is introduced. Measurement and solid figures are important in fourth grade.

SOCIAL STUDIES

Studies from the previous years are expanded on—more about American History, governments, and other countries. Your child should recognize famous names from history and know about the Declaration of Independence.

SCIENCE

Kids love to study rocks in fourth grade. Encourage your child to start a collection, if she has not already done so. They also love to study bugs. They need to understand energy and sources of fuel. These are all things you can supplement at home just by looking in your backyard, or around your house. Use the lesson about the five senses to explain how we learn about the world around us.

ENGLISH

American folklore and myths are a great way to study English and Social Studies together. Read stories about historical figures and discuss how some are true and some are probably made up. Your child should learn how to use punctuation well, and how to identify the elements that make up a good story.

HUMANITIES

In fourth grade most kids are ready to write well-organized stories, especially if they read a lot of folklore. The history of music will also be of great interest to the musically inclined.

GENERAL

Learning difficult games like poker is well within the grasp of a fourth grader. So is cooking and reading recipes.

FOURTH GRADE QUIZ

1. **Name the five senses:**

   _____
   _____
   _____
   _____
   _____

2. **Which of the following is NOT an insect?**

   (A) A spider
   (B) A beetle
   (C) A butterfly

3. **Which of the following people was NOT a composer?**

   (A) Bach
   (B) Mozart
   (C) Picasso

4. **What type of government does the United States have?**

   (A) Monarchy
   (B) Democracy
   (C) Autocracy

5. **Which of the following is NOT an element of a story?**

   (A) Character
   (B) Plot
   (C) Book cover

6. **At what temperature would you most likely set your oven to bake cookies?**

   (A) 200 degrees
   (B) 350 degrees
   (C) 500 degrees

7. **Read the following paragraph and pick out the topic sentence:**

   (A) There are as many different types of clothing as there are types of people. (B) You wouldn't wear a bathing suit to the North Pole, and you wouldn't wear a fancy dress if you were working in a factory. (C) Sometimes people dress up for big events like weddings and graduations.

   (A) A
   (B) B
   (C) C

8. $\dfrac{4}{20} =$

   (A) $\dfrac{1}{4}$

   (B) $\dfrac{2}{5}$

   (C) $\dfrac{1}{5}$

9. In what season are days the shortest?

   (A) Summer
   (B) Fall
   (C) Winter

10. Which king ruled at Camelot?

    (A) King James
    (B) King Arthur
    (C) King Richard

11. Which of the following is a type of rock?

    (A) Aluminum
    (B) Sedimentary
    (C) Voluminous

12. Convert this number to a decimal

    $1\dfrac{3}{10} =$

    (A) 1.3
    (B) 0.13
    (C) 13.0

13. What was unusual about Paul Bunyan?

    (A) His great size
    (B) His great intelligence
    (C) His magic lantern

14. A fossil is

    (A) a living plant or animal
    (B) the remains of a dead animal or plant preserved in rock or ice
    (C) a very old stone

15. Who was the main enemy of the United States in World War I?

    (A) England
    (B) Canada
    (C) Germany

16. Which of the following was the rock and roll group famous for the songs "Let it Be," "Help," "Yellow Submarine," and "Back in the USSR"?

    (A) The Rolling Stones
    (B) Arrested Development
    (C) The Beatles

17. Which of the following is a type of cloud formation?

    (A) Cirrus
    (B) Styrofoam
    (C) Barometer

18. What is the answer to the division problem below?

    $8\overline{)976}$

    (A) 142
    (B) 976
    (C) 122

19. How many pints in a quart?

    (A) 2
    (B) 4
    (C) 8

20. Cat is to kitten as dog is to _____.

    (A) puppy
    (B) dog catcher
    (C) golden retriever

21. Which president left office in a scandal called Watergate?

    (A) Richard Nixon
    (B) Andrew Jackson
    (C) James Polk

22. What is the possessive form of the "plane" in this sentence:
    The _____ main engine is very powerful.

    (A) plane's
    (B) planes
    (C) planes'

23. **Which figure is a cylinder?**

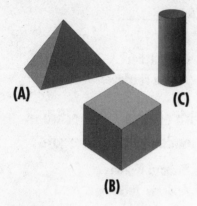

(A)

(B)

(C)

(A) A
(B) B
(C) C

24. **Which of the following was the chief immigration station of the United States in the early 1900s?**

(A) The Statue of Liberty
(B) Ellis Island
(C) The Empire State Building

25. **Which word should be used to begin this question?**

_____ I go to the movies with Jake?

(A) May
(B) Can
(C) Either May or Can

Answers to the Fourth Grade Quiz

Question Number	Correct Answer	Explanation on page
1.	(NA)	21
2.	A	263
3.	C	133
4.	B	16
5.	C	129
6.	B	269
7.	A	74
8.	C	186
9.	C	261
10.	B	130
11.	B	265
12.	A	189
13.	A	131
14.	B	266
15.	C	324
16.	C	136
17.	A	268
18.	C	183
19.	A	188
20.	A	72
21.	A	319
22.	A	76
23.	C	182
24.	B	321
25.	C	79

Fifth Grade

In fifth grade, your child learns a lot about how our country began and how it continues to grow. Lessons about history and knowledge of current events are both important. Encourage your child to start reading the newspaper and learning about what's happening in the world. Watch political debates together and discuss the issues. You'll be surprised at how much your kid knows.

Math
Fractions, decimals, geometry, and order of operations are all introduced. If your child starts to have trouble in math, don't wait long to bail him out. Each concept builds on the previous one, so make sure he gets it as it comes along.

Social Studies
More about American History—especially more current events and immigration. Your child needs more detailed information about how democracy and government work at this grade level. Your child may also study native cultures of other lands, South America, for example.

Science
The human body is a big focus in fifth grade. Knowing the different systems and how they all work together are both important in fifth grade. Fifth graders also learn more detailed information about the properties of nature.

English
Organizing thoughts into outlines is a great fifth grade skill. At this age, your child will probably be doing longer reports that require note taking and research skills. More advanced parts of speech and grammar are also emphasized. Don't forget to read!

Humanities
Encourage your child to study whichever fine art he is most interested in. Greek mythology and different kinds of dances appeal to a broad range of fifth graders.

General
Health is a big topic in fifth grade. We've put AIDS information here, and a more detailed human reproduction chapter in sixth grade, but many kids get that lesson in school in fifth grade. Games and sports terms are also covered.

FIFTH GRADE QUIZ

1. **Who is the leader of the United Nations?**

   (A) Bill Clinton
   (B) Boutros Boutros-Ghali
   (C) Frank Sinatra

2. **Which part of a computer do you type on?**

   (A) The monitor
   (B) The hard drive
   (C) The keyboard

3. **Which decimal has the greatest value?**

   (A) .1
   (B) .01
   (C) .0019

4. **How many lungs does the average person have?**

   (A) One
   (B) Two
   (C) Sixteen

5. **What is the name of the force that holds water molecules together?**

   (A) Surface tension
   (B) Magnetism
   (C) Electricity

6. **Who was the leader of Germany during World War II?**

   (A) Adolf Hitler
   (B) Harry Truman
   (C) Winston Churchill

7. **Which document begins "We, the People . . . "?**

   (A) The Constitution
   (B) The Gettysburg Address
   (C) The Declaration of Independence

8. **In which sport do competitors perform a triple lutz?**

   (A) Figure Skating
   (B) Jai Alai
   (C) Golf

9. **What is the name of the punctuation mark below?**

   :

   (A) Colon
   (B) Comma
   (C) Question Mark

10. **Maria needs to earn $30 to buy a new pair of jeans. On Monday she earned $8.00, and on Tuesday she earned $10. Which number sentence will help you figure out how much more money she needs?**

    (A) 30 x (8 + 10)
    (B) 30 - 8 + 10
    (C) 30 - (8 + 10)

11. **What was the Great Depression?**

    (A) A time of crisis and poverty for many Americans during the 1930s.
    (B) Part of the Grand Canyon formed in this century.
    (C) A psychological slump America experienced in the 1970s.

12. **Sally scores 83, 86, and 92 on three math tests. What is her average score?**

    (A) 87
    (B) 86
    (C) 83

13. **Which of the following is a way you can get AIDS?**

    (A) Sharing a drinking glass with an infected person
    (B) Going to school with someone who is infected
    (C) None of the above

14. **Before writing a report or a story you should**

    (A) make an outline
    (B) ask your older sister to write it for you
    (C) sit down and have a good cry

15.   5,000
        × __400__

    (A) 20,000
    (B) 2,000
    (C) 2,000,000

16. **How many events are there in a decathlon?**

    (A) Three
    (B) Ten
    (C) One hundred

17. **What is the perimeter of the rectangle?**

    5
    3

    (A) 16
    (B) 8
    (C) 15

18. **What type of book would you read to find out about a real person's life?**

    (A) Novel
    (B) Biography
    (C) Myth

19. **Which of the following words is misspelled?**

    (A) receive
    (B) formal
    (C) brougt

20. **Which of the following is equal to the Roman numeral DXLVII ?**

    (A) 5,480
    (B) 547
    (C) 567

21. **Our car ride takes 1 hour and 17 minutes. If we leave at 6:50, at what time will we arrive?**

    (A) 8:07
    (B) 8:15
    (C) 7:43

22. **What is the noun form of the word "intelligent"?**

    (A) intelligent
    (B) intellectual
    (C) intelligence

23. **In which country did the Aztec civilization flourish?**

    (A) Mexico
    (B) The United States
    (C) Cuba

24. Which is smaller,

$$\frac{3}{8} \text{ or } \frac{5}{7}?$$

   (A) $\frac{3}{8}$

   (B) $\frac{5}{7}$

   (C) Neither, they are the same

25. Which price is about right for a new paperback book?

   (A) 75 cents
   (B) $7.95
   (C) $27.95

Answers to the Fifth Grade Quiz

Question Number	Correct Answer	Explanation on page
1.	B	330
2.	C	272
3.	A	201
4.	B	273
5.	A	276
6.	A	327
7.	A	332
8.	A	113
9.	A	77
10.	C	199
11.	A	326
12.	A	213
13.	C	275
14.	A	85
15.	C	191
16.	B	115
17.	A	205
18.	B	137
19.	C	83
20.	C	193
21.	A	195
22.	C	88
23.	A	333
24.	A	206
25.	B	215

CULTURESCOPE

SIXTH GRADE

This is it! The last year of grade school. Your child seems so grown up, but she's still young.

MATH
Percentages, more decimals, some algebra, and more advanced geometry are covered. Kids are gearing up for high school in their sixth grade math class. If there's a lesson they don't get, don't hesitate to look back to fifth or even fourth grade for a more detailed explanation. Also, don't forget to reinforce old multiplication and division skills.

SOCIAL STUDIES
Ancient cultures—Egypt, Rome, and Greece—are studied in most sixth grades. Geography is also important. Don't forget about American history and current events in sixth grade.

SCIENCE
More advance biology facts are introduced. Some genetics are introduced. Human reproduction and puberty are covered either here or in fifth grade (if it was covered in fifth, it should certainly be reinforced in sixth). The earth and the universe are studied in detail in sixth grade as well.

ENGLISH
Grammar, vocabulary, and reading skills are expanded in sixth grade. Keeping writing good and clear is important. DON'T FORGET READING.

HUMANITIES
Your child is finally ready to spend more than fifteen minutes in an art museum! Congratulations.

GENERAL
Brain teasers, computer services, and religion are all covered in sixth grade.

SIXTH GRADE QUIZ

1. **How long does the average star live?**

   (A) A million years
   (B) A billion years
   (C) Ten billion years

2. **What is the area of this circle?**

   (A) 9 π
   (B) 9
   (C) 3.5 π

3. **Which of these three cities was a city-state of Ancient Greece?**

   (A) Rome
   (B) London
   (C) Athens

4. **Which of the following is not a computer on-line service?**

   (A) Prodigy
   (B) America On-Line
   (C) Windows

5. **Who was the messenger of the gods in Greek mythology?**

   (A) Hermes
   (B) Hera
   (C) Zeus

6. **What determines things like hair color and height?**

   (A) Blood type
   (B) Brain cells
   (C) Genes

7. **Which of the following is a stereotype?**

   (A) On the last biology test, boys scored higher than girls.
   (B) Boys are usually smarter than girls.
   (C) There are fewer girls than boys in my biology class.

8. **Hieroglyphics are**

   (A) a group of ancient Egyptian rulers
   (B) ancient burial tombs
   (C) an ancient form of writing

9. Choose the word that comes closest to the meaning of the prefix in the following words:

   *mis*understand   *mis*conduct

   (A) Bad
   (B) Under
   (C) Mean

10. Which of the following countries is the most populated?

    (A) China
    (B) United States
    (C) Russia

11. A man leaves home and makes three lefts and ends up back at home again. What's he wearing?

    (A) Huh?
    (B) A dress
    (C) A baseball uniform

12. What is the value of b?

    $$15b = 60$$

    (A) 4
    (B) 20
    (C) We need more information

13. Where did the U.S. fight a war during the 1960s and 1970s?

    (A) Bulgaria
    (B) Vietnam
    (C) Korea

14. What is 40% of 250?

    (A) 25
    (B) 1000
    (C) 100

15. "Crazy cats catch canaries" is an example of

    (A) alliteration
    (B) onomatopoeia
    (C) metaphor

16. Which of the following words has a root that comes from Latin?

    (A) Dictionary
    (B) Barbecue
    (C) Buckwheat

17. Dianne bought 12 pounds of nectarines at $.69 each. How much was the total bill?

    (A) $12.00
    (B) $6.90
    (C) $8.28

18. **What kind of letter might begin "Dear Sir or Madam?"**
    (A) A personal letter
    (B) A business letter
    (C) A thank-you letter

19. **Which of the following is an equilateral triangle?**

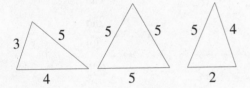

    (A) A
    (B) B
    (C) C

20. **When does a human female begin to menstruate?**
    (A) Before she is born
    (B) When she reaches puberty
    (C) Throughout her life

21. **In what type of dance do partners "do si do"?**
    (A) Square dance
    (B) Ballet
    (C) Break dance

22. **Who was the first woman appointed to the United States Supreme Court?**
    (A) Kathy Lee Gifford
    (B) Sandra Day O'Connor
    (C) Susan B. Anthony

23. **Which prophet founded the Muslim religion?**
    (A) Buddha
    (B) Jesus Christ
    (C) Mohammed

24. **Who painted the Mona Lisa?**
    (A) DaVinci
    (B) Picasso
    (C) Michelangelo

25. **What is the only country that forms a continent as well?**
    (A) Africa
    (B) Australia
    (C) America

CULTURESCOPE

Answers to the Sixth Grade Quiz

QUESTION NUMBER	CORRECT ANSWER	EXPLANATION ON PAGE
1.	C	278
2.	A	229
3.	C	337
4.	C	282
5.	A	138
6.	C	285
7.	B	89
8.	C	335
9.	A	81
10.	A	339
11.	C	118
12.	A	224
13.	B	344
14.	C	217
15.	A	90
16.	A	92
17.	C	221
18.	B	95
19.	B	227
20.	B	279
21.	A	140
22.	B	342
23.	C	146
24.	A	143
25.	B	340

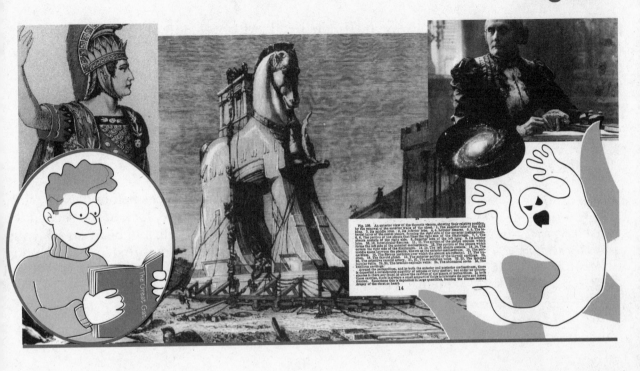

1. Put the following words in A-B-C order:

Hat

Ball

Orange

(A) hat, ball, orange

(B) ball, hat, orange

(C) orange, hat, ball

Putting words in **alphabetical** order is as easy as A-B-C. Take a look at the list of words that you want to alphabetize. Look at the first letter in each word, and then just start saying the alphabet to yourself. A? No words that begin with A. B? Yes, ball. Ball goes first in A-B-C order here. C? No. D? Nah. E? No way. F? Nope. G? Uh-uh. H? Yeah, there we go, Hat begins with the letter "h"—Hat

Dr Seuss' A B C, by Dr. Seuss. A fun beginning-to-read book with some great A-B-Cs.

Animalia, by Graham
Base. Who said the
alphabet was boring?
This book has beautiful pictures with
lots of hidden things to look at.

William Wegman ABC,
by William Wegman. If
you love dogs, you'll flip
for this funny ABC book.

comes second. I? No. J, K, L, M, or N? How about O? Yes, Orange—Orange comes third. Now, what do you do if more than one word starts with the same letter? Look at this list:

Banana

Broccoli

Apple

Bean

First, you can put Apple, because A comes before B. Now, since you have three words that all begin with B, look at the second letter in each word. You have Banana, Broccoli, and Bean, so ask yourself which comes first: a, r, or e. Since a comes first, e second, and r third, the three B words go in this order: Banana, Bean Broccoli and Here's the right A-B-C order for all the words:

Apple

Banana

Bean

Broccoli

Why bother alphabetizing? What's the big deal about putting words in alphabetical order? The main reason to put things in alphabetical order is so other people can find them easily. Take the phone book, for example. Imagine a long list of names, in no particular order. You'd have to read the whole book from cover to cover to find anybody's name and phone number. But, if the names are all in alphabetical order, and you're looking for someone named "Augustus Gloop" you can find his name in a second. Here's how: look under G. In the phone book, people are listed in alphabetical order by their last name.

Once you find the Gs, use your A-B-C order rules. Look for Gl, then Glo, then Gloo, then Gloop. After that, the first names will be in alphabetical order: Aaron Gloop will come before Augustus Gloop, because Aaron comes before Augustus.

Try it out! Look up your family name in the phone book.

Where else have you seen alphabetical order? Libraries, bookstores, school lists—lots of things are arranged alphabetically. See if you can find alphabetical order all around you. What could you arrange alphabetically to make it easier to look through? Your comic books or your bookcase would be good to alphabetize.

2. Put the following words into the best sentence order:

goes store to the Jill

A) Jill to the store goes.
B) To the store Jill goes.
C) Jill goes to the store.

Sentences are how we use language to tell each other things. When we want to say something, either out loud or in writing, we don't just put words together any old way. We make sentences. Look at the following two groups of words:

favorite potatoes food baked are my
Baked potatoes are my favorite food.

What are the differences between the first group and the second group of words? One is a **sentence**, one isn't.

Every language has its own rules for how to make sentences and put them together. This set of rules is called **grammar**. Let's go over some rules for making sentences.

Rule #1   A sentence begins with an uppercase letter.

Wrong   that store is great!
Right   That store is great!

Rule #2   A sentence must express a thought.

Wrong   Oranges like.
Right   I like oranges.

definition

grammar
(GRAM er) *noun*, the way in which words are used in a language.

"I ain't going to no birthday party!" screamed Sherry, using bad grammar.

Rule # 3   A sentence must end with a period (.) an exclamation point (!) or a question mark (?).

Right   I like that store.

Right   I like that store!

Right   I like that store?

Look at the three sentences above. How does the punctuation change the meaning of each sentence? Punctuation lets you know what the writer is thinking when she writes the sentence. In the first sentence, the writer is stating a fact. In the second, the exclamation point tells us that the sentence is saying something exciting. WOW! I like that store! In the third, the writer is asking a question—does she like that store?

CIRCLE THE REAL SENTENCES:

Marissa is going with Evan to the market.

Paul and David bananas

going out to the park with a bicycle

Harriet wrote in her journal.

Where are you going?

DID YOU CIRCLE THESE SENTENCES?

Marissa is going with Evan to the market.

Harriet wrote in her journal.

Where are you going?

All of these are sentences. They tell you something, they begin with uppercase letters, and they have punctuation. The other choices are all missing something that would make them sentences.

3. Put the following sentences in order:

(1) She bought some bread.

(2) She made a sandwich.

(3) Jenna went to the store.

(4) She brought it home.

(A) 3, 1, 4, 2

(B) 3, 4, 1, 2

(C) 1, 3, 1, 4

Once you've learned how to put together words to make sentences, you're ready to put sentences together to tell a story, or write a letter, or explain something that takes more than one sentence. When you put sentences together, the first thing to keep in mind is that the actions have to take place *in order*. In the above example, Jenna couldn't buy bread until she went to the store, and she couldn't make a sandwich until she brought it home.

Just like numbers, sentences go in a certain sequence. When you tell a story, the easiest way to tell other people what happened is to tell it in time order. That means you tell the story in the same order it happened. Telling a story in **time order** makes it easy for your listeners or readers to follow.

LOOK AT THE FOLLOWING PAIRS OF SENTENCES. WHICH COMES FIRST?

1. We loved the movie!
2. We went to see the new movie downtown.

1. I forgot my lunch money
2. Pierre lent me some.

1. I bought a new comic book.
2 I saved my money.

Do you see how important the sequence is when you are telling a story? Make your own story book. Think about something you did recently and write down the events in the time order that they happened. You can write them down like this:

1. We went to the store.
2. I saw my favorite book.
3. I bought the book.
4. My mom read it to me.
5. I loved that book!

WRITE YOUR OWN FIVE EVENTS:

1. _____
2. _____
3. _____
4. _____
5. _____

Put each line on a separate page and draw a picture to go with each line. Staple them together, make a cover, and you've written your own story book. Make sure to name yourself as **author** and **illustrator**.

4. What is the opposite of sad?

(A) Lazy

(B) Heavy

(C) Happy

Opposite means something that is completely different—as different as two things could be. So, the opposite of *dark* is *light*, the opposite of *up* is *down*, the opposite of *in* is *out*. One way to figure out the opposite of a word is to ask yourself what it means to be *not at all* that word. For example, *not at all* sad is happy. *Not at all* dark is light. *Not at all* up is down. *Not at all* in is out.

Can you think of the opposite of all the following words?

good

ugly

forward

cold

crooked

wet

on

Not all words have opposites. Can you think of an opposite for a word like "computer," or a word like "book"? You may be able to think of things that are not like those words. You could say that a book is not at all a television show, but those things are not completely opposite. Most **nouns**, or things, do not have real opposites.

5. Which word has a long "o" sound?

(A) Chicken

(B) Toe

(C) Clock

First, let's talk about **vowels**. Vowels are these letters of the alphabet:

a e i o u and sometimes **y**

All other letters are **consonants**. Vowels are different from consonants, because vowel sounds are made without closing your mouth or putting your tongue on the roof of your mouth.

Say all the letters of the alphabet. Notice that when you say a consonant, you have to either close your mouth or click your tongue somewhere. When you say a vowel, air goes through your mouth without stopping.

Unlike consonants, which always sound pretty much the same, each vowel can sound "long" or "short." We say a vowel sounds long when we hear its name. In the words above, "toe" and "crow" and "no" are all examples of words with the long "o" sound, because you can hear the letter "o" when you say the words. But "o" can also sound like "uh" or "ah" as in "some" or "clock." When a vowel doesn't sound like its name, we call it a short vowel sound.

When you look up a word in the dictionary, there is a funny-looking word in parentheses following the word. Inside the parentheses are letters and symbols that tell you how to pronounce the word. Here are the basic pronunciation symbols for long and short sounds:

a	=	short a, like "apple."
ā	=	long a, like "ape."
e	=	short e, like "head."
ē	=	long e, like "eel."
i	=	short i, like "mitt."
ī	=	long i, like "bike."
o	=	short o, like "hot."
ō	=	long o, like "roll."
u	=	short u, like "ugly."
yo͞o	=	long u, like "use."

definition

pronounce

(pro NOWNS) *verb*, to say the sound of a word or letter.

Ms. Flabbergast always pronounces Bridget's last name wrong.

LONG WORDS

The longest word in the English language is "pneumonoultramicroscopicsilicovolcanoconiosis," which has forty-five letters. It means "a lung disease caused by the inhalation of very fine silica dust."

6. Where would you look to find the definition of the word "cockroach"?

(A) A dictionary
(B) An atlas
(C) The closet

What do you do when you read or hear a word you don't know?

You can ask someone to explain it to you or you can look in a dictionary. How about if you want to know the last year the Yankees won the World Series, or what the tallest building in the world is? There are lots of books that are filled with facts and information you can look up. You may need information for a report, for your own projects, or just for fun. Here is a list of the main reference books available to kids. All are in your local library and bookstores.

The **dictionary** is where you can find out what a word means, how to spell it, and how to pronounce it. Often, the dictionary will tell you where the word came from. You can also look up a famous person's name in a dictionary and find out a little bit about that person, including his or her birthdate. How to find information: Words and names in the dictionary are in alphabetical order (p. 44). Some dictionaries have names and place names in separate sections. Look in the table of contents in the front.

An **encyclopedia** is a book, or a set of books, that gives information on a bunch of different topics. Some children's encyclopedias are one big book, but most encyclopedias are a set of books. How to find information: Like the dictionary, the encyclopedia has its entries arranged in alphabetical order. You may have to figure out what volume of the set the information is in. On the spine of the book, you will find the letter or letters that that volume covers. For example, if you are looking for "cockroaches," you would look in the volume of the encyclopedia marked "C."

What if you can't find something you are trying to look up? One thing you can do is think about another category that the thing might fit into. If "cockroach" is not listed, you can try looking under "insect."

An **almanac** is a book of facts. The first almanacs had information about the weather, crops, the phases of the moon, and things like that. Check out the Farmer's Almanac to see what old almanacs looked like. Now, most almanacs have information about who won the World Series, what special holidays are coming in that year, and

definition

table of contents (TAY bul of CON tents) *noun*, the page in a book that tells you what page each chapter starts on.

*Mr. Tangelo asked Tim to read the chapter on Frogs to the class, so Tim turned to the **table of contents** to find what page it started on.*

who are the presidents of different countries. Kids' almanacs have lots of fun facts. Almanacs are fun to read through and are great ways to settle arguments! How to find information: Almanacs are usually arranged according to topic. Information about cities, for example, would all be in one place. Look at the table of contents in the front of the book to see how things are laid out, and check the index in the rear of the book to find a specific topic. Let's say you want to know the population of India. The easiest way is to look up India in the index.

7. Which word listed below needs a capital letter to be spelled correctly?

(A) spy

(B) chicago

(C) radio

There are only five reasons to capitalize a word. These are:

1. **To begin a sentence**. All sentences begin with capital letters:

   Whenever you go to the movies, be sure to bring a sweater. Movie theaters are always so cold.

2. **To name a specific person or place.** These are called proper nouns:

   George Washington, the first president of the United States, never lived in Washington, D.C.

3. **To identify words that are the title of a book, a movie, or a song:**

   "A Whole New World," from the Disney movie *Aladdin*, was one of the most popular songs of 1993.

   The Secret Garden, by Frances Hodgeson Burnett, is one of my favorite books.

4. **To identify the title of an event, a person, or a group:**

   When I met President Clinton, he was going to the meeting of the National Organization of Women to make a speech.

   My brother wants to go to Lollapalooza, a big concert event that is touring the country.

5. **When you use the letter "I" to refer to yourself:**

   I've always thought that I have the prettiest eyes.

WHEN TO CAP

When you capitalize to show the title of someone, you only capitalize if the title comes directly before that person's name. For example, you could say:

President Bill Clinton
       or
Bill Clinton is our president.

You could say
Queen Elizabeth
of England
       or
In England, the queen's name is Elizabeth.

8. Pick out the verb in the following sentence:

The dog ran up the sidewalk and into the house.

(A) up
(B) dog
(C) ran

A complete sentence has a subject and a verb. A subject is the thing in the sentence that is performing the action. The verb is the action part. In other words, to make a sentence, something's got to happen and something (or someone) has to do it. Take a look at the following sentences. The subjects are in *italics* and the verbs are in **bold** letters.

Jacques **is** such a great dancer.

Linda and Ali **are going** to the new restaurant in town.

My best friend Boris **ran** in that race.

His neighbor, Natasha, **encouraged** Boris to run.

When **will** *the restaurant* **open**?

Diane, Emily, and Nina **planted** a vegetable garden in their yard.

Subjects are not always people. In the second to last example, the restaurant was the subject. Ask yourself: what was opening? *The restaurant* was opening.

Subjects are not always one word. Look at the fourth sentence. Who encouraged Boris to run? *His neighbor, Natasha.*

Subjects are not always one person. Who planted the vegetable garden? *Diane, Emily, and Nina.*

Rover **loves** to play with his leash.

9. What pronoun should be used to take the place of "duck"?

(A) It

(B) They

(C) He

definition

pronoun

(PRO nown) *noun*, a word used in the place of a noun to refer to a person, place, or thing.

"She," "he," and "it" are all pronouns.

You could have said "Marvin went to the store and Marvin bought some candy," but that would have sounded silly. You don't need to say "Marvin" twice because you can use a pronoun, "he," instead. **Pronouns** are words that stand in for nouns. Take a look at our list of pronouns and what type of nouns they stand for:

SHE, HER, HERS

Use *she* whenever you are referring to a girl or a woman or a female animal.

- My cat, Sheba, is the most wonderful animal. She always purrs when I pet her.

- My sister, Wanda, thinks she is so great!

- That book is hers.

HE, HIM, HIS

Use *he* to refer to a boy, a man or a male animal.

- Trevor says that he is never too full for chocolate chip cookies. Cookies are his favorite snack, so why don't you give them to him?

IT, ITS

Use *it* to refer to anything that is not a person or animal.

- The weather is so awful! I hope *it* will improve.

THEY, THEM, THEIRS

Use *they* to refer to more than one person or animal or thing.

- My friends are the best. They are all so nice and helpful. I want to go with them to their party.

I, ME, MY, MINE

Use *I* to refer to yourself.

- I'm the greatest! My favorite game is chess. Would you like to play with me?

YOU, YOURS

Use *you* to refer to the person you're talking to.

- *You* want to go to a movie? What's *your* favorite one?

Pronouns are great, but one of the big problems with pronouns is that they can get confusing. Take a look at this sentence:

Inga and Ida wanted to sing together at the recital but she got a sore throat.

Who got the sore throat? Inga or Ida? It's hard to tell. Make sure it is clear who or what the pronoun is standing in for when you use one. If you mention two girls and then say "she," your reader will be confused. You would have to say:

Inga and Ida wanted to sing together at the recital but Inga got a sore throat.

How about this one?

Inga and Steven wanted to sing together at the recital but she got a sore throat.

Well, since this sentence is about a girl (Inga) and a boy (Steven), the reader knows for sure that the "she" must refer to Inga, not Steven.

WHICH PRONOUN WOULD YOU USE TO REFER TO THE FOLLOWING?

1. Nicole
2. Graham
3. My friends
4. Rafael
5. A bicycle
6. Uncle Pedro

ANSWERS

1. She
2. He
3. They
4. He
5. It
6. He

10. What is the plural of "fox?"

    (A) Foxs

    (B) Fockses

    (C) Foxes

Say you're talking about a person, place, or thing. If there's *just one*, you use what's called the **singular** form of that noun. If there *are more than one*, you need to know the **plural** form.

There are some standard plural rules:

- Most nouns can be made plural by adding an "s"

    cat → cats

    cartoon → cartoons

- Nouns that end in the following letters will need an "es" on the end:

    -ch

    -s

    -sh

    -x

    -z

cat

cats

Here are some examples of nouns that get an -es:

box → boxes

church → churches

loss → losses

- If a noun ends with a consonant and then "y," the y gets changed into an "i" and the "es" is added to make a plural. For example: copy becomes copies, penny becomes pennies. But notice that day becomes days. You don't change the "y" to an "i" here because there's no consonant before the y.

- Sometimes a final "f" becomes "v" to make a word plural. For example loaf becomes loaves, leaf becomes leaves.

- Then, there are those weird words that change completely to become plural.

Goose → Geese

Mouse → Mice

Man → Men

Foot → Feet

definition

exception
(ecks SEP shun) *noun*, a person or something left out.

*Shawna hates all vegetables, with the **exception** of cauliflower, which she eats for breakfast every day.*

goose   geese

- And, just when you thought you might be getting pluralization straight, don't forget those words that stay the same whether they are plural or singular: one deer, two deer.

Remember, English is a language that has as many exceptions to the rules as it has rules!

11. What is an antonym for the word "ugly?"

(A) Pretty
(B) Sad
(C) Funny

Antonym is another word for opposite. The antonym of a word is the opposite of that word.

ANTONYMS

Up → Down   Hot → Cold

In → Out   Nice → Mean

The **synonym** for a word is simply another word that means the same thing, or almost the same thing. A synonym for "pardon" is "excuse." In other words, you could say "Excuse me," or "Pardon me," and you would mean the same thing. Not all synonyms are exact matches, but synonyms are important to keep in mind when you are writing. Let's say you are writing an essay about summer. You could say:

"In the summer here it is really **hot**. The **hot** weather makes us all feel **hot**. The only way to escape feeling so **hot** is to go someplace where it is not so **hot**, like a movie theater or a store."

Or you could say:

"In the summer here it is really **hot**. The **steamy** weather makes us all **swelter**. The only way to escape the summer's **heat** is to head someplace **cool**, like a movie theater or a store."

Synonyms help you avoid repeating the same words over and over again. Using synonyms helps make your writing more creative and interesting to read. You can find lots of synonyms in a

PHOBIAS

If you combine "phobia" with another word, you get just about all the things you can be afraid of. Here are some common phobias:

Zoophobia–fear of animals
Pyrophobia–fear of fire
Phasmophobia–fear of ghosts
Acrophobia–fear of heights
Scholionophobia–fear of school
Hydrophobia–fear of water
Xenophobia–fear of strangers

book called a thesaurus. These books give you lists of words that mean the same thing. Check out *A First Thesaurus* by Harriet Wittels and Joan Greisman, or ask your bookstore for a kid's thesaurus.

CLEVER COMPLIMENTS
....

<u>SMART</u>
INTELLIGENT, BRIGHT, ALERT, WISE, CLEVER, QUICK
<u>SINCERE</u>
HONEST, TRUTHFUL, GENUINE, UNAFFECTED
<u>NICE</u>
PLEASANT, AGREEABLE, GOOD, FINE

INTELLIGENT INSULTS
....

<u>IDIOT</u>
IMBECILE, MORON, HALF-WIT, FOOL, SIMPLETON
<u>MEAN</u>
INCONSIDERATE, THOUGHTLESS, UNKIND
<u>SILLY</u>
FOOLISH, SENSELESS, INANE

---

12. Which of these is a compound word?

   (A) Short-term

   (B) Witch

   (C) Simple

Compound words are made up of two or more parts that are words in themselves. In the above examples, "birth" and "day" combine to make "birthday," "home" and "work" combine to make "homework," "inch" and "worm" combine to make "inchworm." Can you find two separate words in baseball? New compound words are constantly being created in our language. As new things occur or are made, people often put together words that are already around to describe the new thing. For example, when airplanes started delivering mail quickly, people just started to call it *airmail*. Now, if you send letters by computer, you may be sending electronic mail, or e-mail. Compound words may be two separate words, like *"electronic mail,"* a hyphenated word, like "short-term," or one big word, like "birthday." Unfortunately, there's no hard and fast rule for whether a compound word stays as two separate words or becomes one. The only way to know is to look in the dictionary.

13. Which is right?
Between my sister and me, I am the ___.
(A) smarter
(B) smartest
(C) smart

When you are describing something, you use an adjective. "Anthony is **smart**." If you are comparing that thing to something else, you need what is called the comparative form of the adjective. "Anthony is **smarter** than John." To form the type of adjective you would use to compare two things, you need to either add "-er" to the end of a word or to put "more" in front of that word. "Mary Jo is **more interesting** than Paula." In general, you use the "-er" after short adjectives, like these:

smart → *smarter*

pretty → *prettier*

big → *bigger*

tall → *taller*

And, you add *"more"* in front of longer adjectives:

interesting → *more interesting*

expensive → *more expensive*

handsome → *more handsome*

thoughtful → *more thoughtful*

Now, if you are comparing more than two things, you need what is called the *superlative* form of the adjective. You do this by putting an "-est" at the end of a short adjective. "Katie is the **smartest** in the class." Or, by using "most" in front of a longer adjective:

definition

superlative
(soo PER luh tiv) *adj.*, the best, the most supreme; above everything else.

Mr. Potboiler said Clyde's essay on cockroaches was **superlative***, then he fainted when Clyde showed him his pet roach, Louie.*

"Mary Jo is the **most interesting** person I have ever met."
Add "-est" for short adjectives:

smart → *smarter* → *smartest*

pretty → *prettier* → *prettiest*

big → *bigger* → *biggest*

tall → *taller* → *tallest*

Add "most" for long adjectives:

interesting → *more interesting* → *most interesting*

expensive → *more expensive* → *most expensive*

handsome → *more handsome* → *most handsome*

thoughtful → *more thoughtful* → *most thoughtful*

14. Which word is correct in the sentence below?

I told them to get _____ coats.

(A) there
(B) their
(C) they're

THERE/THEIR/THEY'RE

There means "to a certain place." Put that chair over **there**. **Their** is the possessive form of **they**. When you want to show that a group of people have something, you use *their*. **They're** is a contraction of the words "they" and "are." **They're** so good at that game! (**They are** so good at that game.)

YOUR/YOU'RE

Your is the possessive form of you. If you want to say that someone has something you say your. Is that *your* pen? *You're* is the contraction of the words "you" and "are." If you want to say You are, you can also use you're. *You're* invited to our party. (*You are* invited to our party)

definition

contraction
(con TRAK shun) *noun*, a word formed by putting together two words and leaving out a letter or letters.

"There's" is a contraction for "there is."

PRINCIPAL/PRINCIPLE

The **principal** with an "a" is the head of your school. You can remember this one by thinking "your *principal* is your *pal*." **Principal** Green told us that she hoped we'd have a great summer. The **principle** with an "e" is a rule or a belief. The most important **principle** of our club is that everyone should be treated fairly.

OTHER NYMS

A *PSEUDONYM* IS A FALSE NAME. IF AN AUTHOR USES A PEN NAME, THAT IS CALLED A PSEUDONYM. MARK TWAIN IS A PSEUDONYM—SAMUEL CLEMENS WAS MARK TWAIN'S REAL NAME.

An *ACRONYM* IS A WORD MADE UP FROM THE FIRST LETTERS OF SEVERAL WORDS. NASA, FOR EXAMPLE, STANDS FOR NATIONAL AERONAUTICS AND SPACE ADMINISTRATION.

A *HOMONYM* IS A WORD THAT SOUNDS JUST LIKE ANOTHER WORD. *WEIGHT* AND *WAIT* ARE HOMONYMS. SO ARE *NONE* AND *NUN*.

15. Which word in the sentence below is the adjective?

The fun game moved quickly.

(A) quickly
(B) fun
(C) moved

Adverbs and adjectives are words that describe other words. An **adjective** describes a person, place, or thing (a noun). An **adverb** describes a verb (an action word), another adverb, or an adjective. Let's look at each.

ADJECTIVES

Adjectives describe nouns. Lets take a look at some nouns:

Janine	**house**	**cat**
teacher	**Mr. Smith**	**Dallas**

Okay. Now let's say we want to describe each of those things to you. What kind of words might describe each of those nouns?

We might say that Janine is:

smart   **nice**   **pretty**   **intelligent**

glamorous   **dark**   **mysterious**   **impatient**

We might say that a house is:

small   **blue**   **ugly**   **warm**

cozy   **dirty**   **shabby**   **historic**

We might say that a cat is:

lazy   **frisky**

furry   **mean**

white   **long-haired**

noisy   **cuddly**

This cat is lazy.

We might say that a teacher is:

interesting   **boring**

nice   **stupid**

helpful   **silly**

fun   **sharp**

We might say that Dallas is:

hot   **friendly**   **fun**   **exciting**

interesting   **confusing**   **familiar**   **huge**

Get the idea? All those describing words are adjectives. Adjectives make your writing interesting and imaginative. They help you make what you are saying specific and precise.

ADVERBS

Adverbs describe verbs. Look at these verbs:

run   **think**

You might say that you run:

fast   **quickly**   **slowly**   **awkwardly**

---

definition

modifier
(MOD i fye er) *noun*, a word that changes the meaning of another word slightly.

*"I feel a little guilty for burning down the school," said Monty. If Monty hadn't used the **modifier** "a little," they judge may have gone a little easier on him.*

You might say that you think:

quickly   intelligently   well

Adverbs also describe other adverbs and adjectives.

Look at these adverbs and adjectives:

fast   well   smart

You may want to say that you run *very* fast. You may want to say that you think *awfully* well. You may want to say that Michael is *really* smart. Those are adverbs too. The world would be a boring place without adverbs and adjectives to describe it.

3

16. Which of these sentences is a question?

(A) Rover ran away.
(B) Rover got hit by a milk truck.
(C) How's Rover?

You've known about questions since you were little. Children learn almost from the beginning of their lives to point at something and ask about it as a question."This?" "What?" Questions are how we get information. You may have been told by a parent or teacher, "If you don't know—ask!" It's true. Asking questions is the best way to find things out. But people ask questions for a lot of reasons. You may ask a question to find out information ("Where does cheese come from?"), to see if someone else knows something ("Do you know how to play chess?"), or just to be silly or bossy ("Oh yeah?"). There are a few different types of questions:

YES/NO QUESTIONS

These can be answered with a "yes" or a "no."

Question: *Are you going to the dance?*

Answer: *No.*

definition

anagram
(AN uh gram) *noun,*
word in which the
letters are mixed up
from another word.

*An **anagram** of
"BLUE" is "LUBE."*

INFORMATIONAL QUESTIONS

These are designed to get more information. They cannot be answered with a simple "yes" or "no."

Question: What *time did you get home last night?*

Answer: *I got home at 7:30.*

RHETORICAL QUESTIONS

These are questions that don't require an answer. People ask rhetorical questions to show off or to be silly.

Question: *Who died and made you king?*

Answer: *Nobody.*

When you ask a question out loud, you show that what you are saying is a question by letting your voice rise up at the end in a "questioning" way. In writing, you show people that the sentence you are writing is a question by putting a question mark at the end of it. Statements are sentences in which you tell something. You **state** it. Here are some examples of plain old statements:

I like roses.

School is a good place to learn things.

I wish I had a radio.

Statements end with periods. Listen to your voice when you state something. It doesn't rise up at the end as it does when you ask a question. It stays flat. Right? Right. An exclamation is exactly what it sounds like—you **exclaim** something. It's got that extra zing. IT'S SORT OF LIKE SPEAKING OR WRITING IN CAPITAL LETTERS! Here are some exclamations:

I can't believe you went to that party!

What a day I had!

Exclamations end with exclamation points. That's how the reader knows you're excited about what you're saying. When what you are saying is an exclamation, you might speak a little more loudly, or with a little more emphasis on each word.

Statements and exclamations are the same except for the punctuation. You can take almost any regular statement and zing it up with an exclamation point, or you can calm down an exclamation by replacing the exclamation point with a period.

I wanted that cd too!

I wanted that cd too.

What a beautiful day!

What a beautiful day.

HOW TO MAKE A FORTUNE TELLER

Get a regular piece of note paper or construction paper and fold down one corner to the other side. Cut off the bottom strip so you have a square.

Unfold and fold down the opposite side. Unfold. Now you have a square with a big X fold. Fold each corner to the center. Flip over and fold each corner to the center line. Under each flap write the answer to a yes/no question, like

Impossible   No way
Absolutely   The stars
                  say yes.

Write a number on each flap, as shown. Push the four corners together and hold from underneath. Have your friend ask the fortune teller a yes/no question, and pick a number on the outside. Open and close the fortune teller the number of times she called. Tell her to pick a number on the inside. The answer is under that flap.

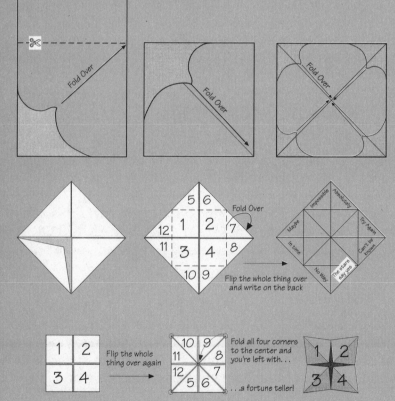

DON'T OVERUSE EXCLAMATION POINTS. IT'S LIKE READ-ING A BOOK ALL IN CAPITAL LETTERS. YOU BEGIN TO FEEL LIKE THE WRITER IS SHOUTING AT YOU. USE EXCLAMATION POINTS SPARINGLY!! RIGHT? RIGHT. RIGHT!!!

17. What is the subject of this sentence:

"Full House" is my favorite show.

(A) my favorite show
(B) "Full House"
(C) is

The subject of a sentence is usually a noun and the stuff that describes the noun. You know that a sentence needs a subject, the person or thing that perfoms the action in a sentence. The **predicate** of the sentence is the action, or verb part, and the description that goes with it. It usually follows the subject, but not always. Here are some examples with the subject **bold** and the predicate in *italics*.

Brandon and Sabrina *wanted to go to the movies.*

I *love to read the Encyclopedia Brown books.*

My favorite thing to do *is work on the computer.*

I *hate to do homework.*

My neighbors, Eileen and Dan, *are having a barbecue this weekend.*

Do you ever get bored while you're driving around in the car? Here are some fun word games to play.

GHOST

In this not-very-scary game, the leader says a letter. Each person adds a letter, trying **not** to complete a word. Words must be at least four letters to count. If, by adding a letter you make a word, you get a "G." The next time you make the same mistake, you get an "H." The first person to spell out GHOST, loses. Here's the trick: you must be thinking of a word that you intend spelling towards all the time (you can't just add a random letter).

For example:

The first person might say	"S"
Player #1	"T"
Player #2	"O"
Player #3	"P"

Oops, Player 3 made the word "Stop." He gets a "G" and starts the next round.

MIX-UP

Have someone in the car pick a really long word. If you are going somewhere, make your destination the word. Give everybody ten minutes to write down as many words as they can using the letters in your word. Words must be at least three letters long.

DISNEYWORLD

world   old   sold   wise

How many more words can you find in the word "Disneyworld"? Pick another long word and try again.

18. What is the present tense of the verb "hated"?

(A) hate

(B) will hate

(C) hating

Verbs show action. Tense is the form a verb takes to show when the action took place. There are three main tenses you need to worry about: past, present, and future. Most of the time when you are reading or telling a story, verbs will be in the past tense.

The **past tense** shows the reader that what is being told about happened already. For example, if you went on a visit to your uncle's house, you would tell your friends, "I *visited* my uncle yesterday." "Visited" is the past tense of the verb "visit."

Present tense is the verb tense you use to show someone that something is happening right now, today, or that it happens in a regular way every day. For example, if you were telling your friends that your visit is a daily thing, you might say, "I *visit* my uncle every day." We use another form of the present tense used if something is happening this very minute. If you were at your uncle's house right now, you would say, "I *am visiting* my uncle."

Future tense is what you use to talk about something that is going to happen. If you were telling everybody about a visit to your uncle's that you're planning for next week, you might say, "I *will visit* my uncle next week." Take a look at a few common verbs in their past, present and future tenses:

PAST	PRESENT	FUTURE
I helped	I help or I am helping	I will help
I danced	I dance or I am dancing	I will dance
I sang	I sing or I am singing	I will sing

You don't need to keep a story or report all in one tense. Your story could say, "I *went* to the deli. I *am eating* the sandwich I bought. I *will* go outside when I finish eating." Your report could say, "Michael Jordan *is* my favorite basketball player. He *scored* an average of 32.2 points per game in his career. I hope that someday I *will play* as well as he did." Just make sure that when you shift from tense to tense your meaning is clear to your reader.

19. Complete the following:

Birds of a feather _____.

(A) need a few more feathers.
(B) have a hard time flying.
(C) flock together.

Sayings are phrases that, over the years, have come to have particular meanings beyond their "real meanings." For example, your grandmother might see you and all your friends playing soccer and say, "Birds of a feather flock together." She wouldn't be talking about birds at all. This expression

means "similar people like to hang out with each other." Here are some other common expressions.

BEAUTY IS ONLY SKIN DEEP.

This saying means that just because someone is beautiful on the outside, that doesn't mean they're "beautiful," or nice and thoughtful, on the inside.

BURY THE HATCHET.

Where do you think this expression comes from? If you said "Native Americans," you'd be right. When a war was over, Native Americans would sometimes actually bury their weapons to show that they had made up. Anyone who wants to "bury the hatchet" wants to make peace.

DON'T COUNT YOUR CHICKENS BEFORE THEY ARE HATCHED.

Any farmer will tell you that this is not a good idea. Not all eggs hatch into chicks. Some never hatch at all. You will certainly be disappointed if you see twelve eggs and assume you'll have twelve chickens. This expression means you can't always be sure that everything you plan for will go perfectly. If you're planning a party and expect everyone you've invited to show up, your dad may say, "Don't count your chickens before they hatch." He just means don't get too excited, because you may be disappointed.

A CLOSE SHAVE.

In days gone by, men would go to the barber shop to get a shave. When a barber shaved too closely, the poor guy in the chair often got a bad cut, or barely avoided some gruesome injury. If someone tells you that "I just had a close shave!" it means they were almost in a disaster.

---

definition

idiom

(ID ee um) *noun*, any group of words that have a special meaning different from the exact meaning of the words.

*" I can't put my finger on it," said Libby, using an **idiom** to explain that she couldn't remember when she stopped loving strained carrots.*

A STITCH IN TIME SAVES NINE.

Have you ever gotten a small tear in your pants or skirt? You might have learned that sewing it up right away can prevent the tear from getting bigger and needing even more stitches. In other words, don't put off solving your problems—they usually just get bigger and bigger. Take care of things as they come up.

HAVE A CHIP ON YOUR SHOULDER.

Imagine some big bully from the wild west putting a piece of wood (or wood chip) on his shoulder and saying, "Go ahead—I dare you to knock it off." Anyone today who always seems ready for a fight or who gets all in a huff easily is said to have a chip on his shoulder.

Can you think of other expressions like this? If you hear one that you don't understand, ask someone what it means. As you can see, all expressions have one thing in common—they don't mean *exactly* what they seem to mean, so you might need an explanation. Figuring out expressions can be tricky.

20. Cat is to kitten as dog is to _____.

(A) puppy
(B) dog catcher
(C) golden retriever

An **analogy** is used to compare things. When I say your breath smells like garbage, or your hair is like silk, I am comparing your breath and your hair to other things.

Why make analogies? Analogies help to describe. If you pick the right analogy, it brings a picture sharply into focus. If you didn't know what a puppy was, but you knew what a kitten was, I could explain puppies to you by using the analogy above—a puppy is like a dog as a kitten is like a cat.

It's important to use analogies when you write. Two common types of analogies are **metaphors** and **similes.** A simile compares two things by using the words "like" or "as," while a metaphor does not use "like" or "as." For example:

Simile:

> Her description was so vivid, it was like she'd painted a picture of her vacation cottage.

Metaphor:

> Her words painted a picture of where she'd been.

Metaphors and similes add spice to your writing, but don't use too many. When you are describing something, it's good to compare it to one thing, but it's overkill to compare it to ten. Otherwise, just writing about two people meeting each other can end up sounding like this: "When Eloise walked into the room, Xavier felt a mighty flood of emotion explode in him like a rocket. Her eyes were like two diamonds in a bed of blue satin. Her voice was a Beethoven concerto, like maple syrup on his pancakes. He looked into the ocean of her velvet irises and said, 'hello'."

21. What does "fortunate" mean?

(A) Happy

(B) Lucky

(C) Silly

A good **vocabulary** helps you express yourself in creative and original ways. It also helps you understand what you're reading better. So how do you improve your vocabulary? It seems like some people have really great vocabularies and others just use the same tired old words over and over again. Here are some tips for building your vocabulary.

The best way to improve your vocabulary is to read. Even the smartest adult sometimes comes across words he's never heard before in books, newspapers, or magazines. What do you do if you're reading and come across a word you don't

> **definition**
>
> **metaphor**
> (MET uh fohr) *noun,* a figure of speech that describes something by presenting it as something else.
>
> *Sigmund used the* **metaphor** *"we're two peas in a pod" to describe how close he felt to Anna.*

4

LANGUAGE FACTS

The languages spoken by the most people in the world are (in order)

Mandarin Chinese.
 Over 885 million people speak Mandarin.

Hindustani
 Over 460 million people speak Hindustani.

English
 Over 450 million people speak English.

Spanish
 Over 350 million people speak Spanish.

definition

vocabulary
(voh KAB yoo layr ee)
noun, all the words
you use and
understand make up
your vocabulary.

*Mrs. Shadoobee has
such a great
vocabulary, her class
never knows what she's
talking about.*

Roget's Thesaurus. Or
any thesaurus, for that
matter. A thesaurus is
essential for writing research papers,
and good to have around in general.

know? Keep a card with you when you read (you can tuck it in a book) and write down any words you don't know on it. Write down the page number next to the word. You can look up the word later, and check back to see how the writer used it. Unless you're reading with a dictionary in your lap, you won't want to stop and look up every word while you're reading. You can often figure out what a word means by the way it is used in a sentence. Read the following sentences.

"John saw something shining in the dirt. He reached down and picked up a beautiful gold coin. He couldn't believe how *fortunate* he was!"

You may not have known what "fortunate" means, but you can get a pretty good idea by reading it in a sentence. "Fortunate" must be something good! Many difficult words have parts to them you might recognize. Sometimes, the parts of a word are like clues to the meaning of the word. "Fortunate," for example, has the word "fortune" in it. Think of "good fortune" and you may have a better chance at getting the meaning of the word.

Don't overlook magazines and newspapers when you're looking for something to read. They usually have really good vocabulary words. When you don't feel like getting into a book, you can probably find time to sit with a magazine. Grownups use lots of words that kids never use. When you hear a word you don't know—ask what it means!

22. Read the following paragraph and pick out the topic sentence:

(A) There are as many types of clothing as there are types of people. (B) You wouldn't wear a bathing suit to the North Pole, and you wouldn't wear a fancy dress if you were working in a factory. (C) Sometimes people dress up for big events like weddings and graduations.

(A) A
(B) B
(C) C

A **topic sentence** is the sentence in a paragraph or essay that tells what it is all about. The topic sentence may also be referred to as the main idea. One way to find a topic sentence is called the **headline technique.** The headline is that group of five or ten words in bold print above the story in a newspaper. The headline tells you very quickly what the story is about. For example:

SIXTEEN STUDENTS BREAK TEETH ON STALE CAFETERIA BREAD

Sixteen students today broke assorted teeth while biting into what appeared to be totally harmless peanut buter and jelly sandwiches. "It felt as if I had bitten into a piece of rock," eight-year-old Kelly Stone told our reporter. The cafeteria lunch lady, Ms. I. Cannacook, claimed that she was not to blame. "I've only had that bread for two weeks! It wasn't moldy! What do you kids want! Gourmet food?"

The school principal could not be reached for comment.

The headline lets you know the main idea of the story right away. You go on to read about the details: how it happened, when it happened, who did it, etc. Of course, outside of newspapers, the things we read and write don't always have headlines. To spot the main idea in any paragraph, pretend you are a newspaper editor and have to come up with a headline for the paragraph.

Read the paragraph. Using no more than six or seven words, think up a good headline for that paragraph or story. The main idea won't have a lot of details in it. It will just tell you straight out what the whole paragraph is about. Now that you have your headline, look through the paragraph at the different sentences and see which sentence is the closest to your headline in meaning. There are two things to remember: topic sentences often come either first or last in a paragraph, and they tell the general idea of the paragraph. The sentences around the topic sentence tell more about the main idea.

definition

topic
(TOP ik) *noun,* the subject of a paper, essay, discussion, movie, book, etc.

*The **topic** of discussion today is "How to Fly Like an Eagle."*

HERE'S AN EASY WAY TO ORGANIZE YOUR PARAGRAPHS

1. Write your topic sentence
2. Write three or four more sentences to explain your idea and give more details.

23. What is the possessive form of the noun "plane" in this sentence:

The _____ main engine is very powerful.

(A) plane's
(B) planes
(C) planes'

A **possessive** shows who owns or is connected with something. In the example, the main engine is connected with the plane, so we call it "the plane's main engine." Don't get confused between the "s" that's added at the end of a word to make it plural and the "s" that is added to a word to show possession. A possessive "s" will have an apostrophe before it ('). "*Heather's* coat has six different colors in it." "The *plane's* engine had too many parts for Sam to remember all of them." What if the noun is plural? The preferred way is to put the apostrophe after the "s," like this: The Smiths' house is very cool. "The Smiths" is plural, and the apostrophe shows that it is their house you are referring to.

CALVIN AND HOBBES copyright Watterson. Dist. by UNIVERSAL PRESS SYNDICATE. Reprinted with permission of UNIVERSAL PRESS SYNDICATE. All rights reserved.

Pronouns can be made possessive as well.

PRONOUN	POSSESSIVE FORM
Her	Her or Hers
Him	His
It	Its
They	Their or Theirs
Me	My or Mine
You	Your or Yours

Some examples:

Her house is lovely.

His new bicycle goes fast.

Their test scores were as good as *yours.*

Possessive pronouns do *not* have an apostrophe before the "s."

24. What is the name of the punctuation mark below?

:

(A) Colon

(B) Comma

(C) Question mark

You can end a sentence with a period (.), an exclamation mark (!), or a question mark (?), depending on the kind of sentence you are writing. Since they all show that the sentence has ended, they are called "full stops." In the old days, when people sent telegrams (before E-mail (p. 283) and faxes, telegrams were the only way to send a message quickly), they would use the word "stop" between sentences, like this: Dear Maureen stop Ship is sinking stop Hope I make it home stop All my clothes are wet stop Miss you stop Love Peter stop.

punctuation

(punk choo AY shun)
noun, the system of
using periods,
commas, colons, semi-
colons, etc. to make
writing more clear.

Felix never uses
punctuation *in his*
letters to Oscar, so
they're really hard to
read.

"Stop" in this telegram could represent a period, a question mark, or an exclamation point. It told the reader to come to a full stop before continuing. The punctuation inside of a sentence is different. It slows you down instead of stopping you. Commas, semi-colons, and colons work just like pauses in sentences when you are speaking. When you are writing you can tell your reader to pause briefly by using punctuation inside the sentence. These punctuation marks help writers emphasize and clarify their meanings. Let's look at the main types of punctuation inside of sentences:

THE COMMA (,)

A comma can do a number of things. It may set words apart in a list:

My mother loves to play tennis, ski, and run marathons.

It may set aside a thought in the sentence:

If you want to go to Israel, whose capital is Jerusalem, you should go this year.

It separates a phrase:

Unlike his cousin, Myles was a real go-getter.

If you combine two or more ideas in one sentence, it sets off the parts:

We went to the shore, and what a lovely day we had!

THE SEMI-COLON (;)

The semi-colon gives you more of a break than a comma does, but not as much as a period. Whenever you use a semi-colon, you should be able to break the two parts of the sentence into two complete sentences. In other words, both parts of the sentence must have a complete thought—a subject and a predicate. You can use semi-colons when you want to tell your reader that the two parts of the sentence are closely connected. When you combine ideas that are complete sentences and don't use "and" or some connecting words, you use a semi-colon. For example:

Sarah looked at the adorable little monkey; it was the cutest monkey she had ever seen.

instead of

Sarah looked at the adorable little monkey, and it was the cutest monkey she had ever seen.

The day was long; it went on forever.

instead of

The day was long, and it seemed to go on forever.

THE COLON (:)

A colon calls attention to a list of things that follow. Whenever you see a colon, you can expect an example or list of what was just mentioned to come right after it. For example:

They wanted to do three things on their vacation: water-ski, canoe, and hike.

She heard someone in the room, a scream in the night: it was Marie!

25. Which word should be used to begin this question?

_____I go to the movies with Jake?

(A) May

(B) Can

(C) Both are right

"Can" shows that you are able to do something. If you ask, "Can I go to the movies with Jake?" you are asking if it is within your ability to go to the movies with Jake. "No, you have a fever of 106°" is an answer to that question. "May" is the word to use when you are asking permission. "May I?" "Yes you may." In other words, "Yes, I give you permission."

What are some other words like this? Between and among are two confusing words. "Between" is the word to use when you are talking about two people:

Between you and me, that's the best ice cream I've ever had.

Among is used whenever there are three or more people involved:

> Among the members of the jury, Amy was the only one who believed in Terry's innocence.

BUST AND BURST

A balloon bursts. A complete failure is a bust.

> My bubble was burst, and after that the day was a complete bust.

FEWER/LESS

Use fewer to refer to things you can count; use less to refer to things you cannot count.

> I would like fewer french fries, and less mashed potatoes.

> I would like fewer egg rolls, and less soup.

MANY/MUCH

Same as fewer and less. Many refers to things that you can count; much refers to things that cannot be counted.

> How many fries do you want? How much mashed potatoes?

> How many egg rolls for you? How much soup do you want?

GOT/HAVE

Do not use "got" when you mean "have."

> I *have* my favorite stuffed animal.

SHOULD HAVE/COULD HAVE/WOULD HAVE

Should of, could of, and would of are all wrong. What you mean to say is:

> "I would have come if you called."

> "I should have studied for this test."

> "I could have won the race."

The problem is that the contractions "should've," would've," and "could've," sound like "should of," "would of," and "could of." Just be careful when you're writing these words not to go by how they sound.

AFFECT/EFFECT

To affect (a verb) means "to influence." After you have affected something, the result is the effect (noun). Here again, we have words that sound alike but have to be written differently.

These are just some of the words that people misuse all the time. Using the wrong word can ruin a perfectly good sentence. Be a word detective—keep on the lookout for misused words.

"The difference between the right word and the nearly right word is the same as that between lightning and the lightning bug."

—*Mark Twain*

26. Choose the word that comes closest to the meaning of the prefix in the following words:

   *mis*understanding   *mis*conduct

   (A) Bad
   (B) Under
   (C) Mean

Prefixes and suffixes are parts that can be tacked onto words to change their meanings. If you know what certain prefixes and suffixes mean, you can often figure out the meaning of a word you may not be sure about. **Prefixes** go at the beginning of a word. Look at the prefix "mis-." It means bad or wrong. So tack it onto understanding, and you have a word that means a "bad understanding." Place it before "conduct," and you have a word that means "bad conduct."

definition

root

(RUTE) *noun,* in grammar, the basic word to which a prefix or suffix (or both) is attached.

*The **root** of "motionless" is motion. The **root** of "predate" is date.*

Here are some other common prefixes, and their meanings:

PREFIX	MEANING	ROOT WORD	NEW WORD
un-	not	known	**un**known (not known)
		able	**un**able (not able)
non	not	sense	**non**sense (no sense)
pre	before	view	**pre**view (to see before)
		school	**pre**school (before regular school)

Suffixes are stuck onto the end of a word to change it around. Some suffixes change the parts of speech of a word:

FROM A NOUN	TO AN ADJECTIVE
Beauty	Beautiful
Oil	Oily
Rain	Rainy

rain
(noun)

rainy
(adjective)

FROM AN ADJECTIVE	TO AN ADVERB
Slow	Slowly
Quick	Quickly
Strange	Strangely

Other suffixes have a specific meaning: -ite or -ian added to the end of a place name often changes it to mean someone who lives in that place.

Manhattan	Manhattanite (one who lives in Manhattan)
California	Californian (one who lives in California)

Some other common suffixes:

SUFFIX	MEANING	ROOT WORD	NEW WORD
-less	without	clue	clueless (without a clue)
		fear	fearless (without fear)
-er	more	silly	sillier (more silly)
-est	most	silly	silliest (the most silly)

27. Which of the following words is misspelled?

(A) receive

(B) formal

(C) brougt

Most computers these days have something called a **spell check**, a program that finds all the misspellings in a document and suggests corrections. Even if you do not have a computer at home, you probably figure that you will have one someday, as you get older and need to do more difficult work. Almost everybody these days has access to a computer, even if he doesn't own one. So, why bother learning how to spell? Well, computers can certainly help you if you don't spell perfectly, but there are a few problems with relying on a spell check.

• Spell checks work by picking out words that are not in the dictionary. Therefore, if you spell "brought" as "brougt," the computer would pick up that word, because "brought" is not a word in the dictionary. But, if you misspelled "brougt" as "bought," the spell check wouldn't help you because "bought" is in fact a word.

• If you misspell a word *completely,* the computer cannot help you to spell it correctly. If you had spelled "brought" as "brot," the spell check would have no idea what you meant to say. You would have to look it up yourself.

• You won't always have a computer handy! You may need to write a note to someone, or you may have to write on a board in front of people. You need to know how to spell the words you want to write.

You don't need to have perfect spelling (no one does) and you don't need to have beautiful, neat handwriting. But the bottom line is: If people can't read or understand what you write, they cannot appreciate it. Everyone misspells occasionally, but if you have ten misspellings in a single paragraph, the reader will suspect that you don't know what you're doing.

definition

phonetic

(foh NET ick) *adj.,* the way you would spell something to indicate the way it was pronounced.

Throughout this book, we include phonetic spellings of words so you can better pronounce them.

EVEN AUTHORS MAKE MISTAKES

If you find a misspelled word in this book, write it down, with the page number, and send it to The Princeton Review, c/o Culturescope, 2315 Broadway, New York, NY 10024. We all make spelling mistakes, even people who write books!

CAN YOU SPOT THE MISPELLINGS?

COUNTY TEEN WINS NASHUNAL SPELLING BE!

Marietta Wilcox of 123 Spring Drive, is the furst winner of the Pillsbox Nashunal Spelling Be. Ms. Wilcox, who gos to County Junior High School, sez "I owe all my sucess to my sister: she wuz the one who quized me all the time." Congradulations Marietta!

Did you find them?

Nashunal = National, Be = Bee, furst = first, gos = goes, sez = says, sucess = success, wuz = was, quized = quizzed, Congradulations = Congratulations!

Spelling correctly is a habit. Some kids pick up the habit, some don't. Your first step to spelling correctly is to recognize when a word is incorrectly spelled. Reading and paying attention to words when you read is the best way to get that skill. Whenever you are not sure how to spell a word, look it up. This can be a real pain, but that's exactly the point. Bothering to thumb through the dictionary

THE DICTIONARY GAME

You need at least 4 people to play a really good game of dictionary.

The oldest person is the "reader"—this person looks through a big dictionary for the weirdest words he or she can find.

*The reader reads the word to the group

*Everyone makes up their own definitions for the word and writes it down on a piece of paper. The reader writes the real definition down.

*Pass all the slips to the reader. He reads all the slips and everyone votes on what they believe to be the real definition. You score a point if you guess the right definition and you score a point for every person who votes for your definition. First person to reach a certain point level—say 20 points--wins.

o look up a word may help you remember how to spell it—if only
o that you won't have to look it up ever again!

Get in the habit of proofreading your work. That means reading
t over and looking for misspellings—without a spell check. Use the
pell check AFTER you check your work yourself. Write carefully.
Many misspellings are just careless errors.

28. Before writing a report or a story you should

(A) make an outline

(B) ask your older sister to write it for you

(C) sit down and have a good cry

When you write anything longer than two or three paragraphs, you
an use an outline to organize your thoughts. Outlines are every
reat report writer's best tool. Here's a good way to write a report
r story:

• Get started on all your research, if you need to do any.

• After you have read through your information, or thought up your story, write down a list of the topics you want to cover in your paper. For example, Harold Goodguy is writing a paper on his life story. Here are his topics:

HAROLD'S TOPICS

The day I started school

When and where I was born

The day I broke my arm when I was three

The other people in my family

My favorite things

- Decide the order in which you want to tell your story. The easiest and clearest way to tell a story is in time order, or chronologically. But Harold also has a couple of topics that are just general information ("My favorite things" and "The other people in my family"). He can put those sections anywhere, but it makes sense to put "The other people in my Family" early on, since he will be discussing his family in other chapters as well. "My favorite things" he might decide to put last. Once he's decided on the order of the main topics, it's time to start putting together the outline. Each main topic gets a separate Roman numeral:

I. Where and when I was born

II. The other people in my family

III. The day I broke my arm when I was three

IV. The day I started school

V. My favorite things

- Harold may want to remind himself of things in each main topic that he wants to be sure to discuss. Add some of the most important details about each topic to your outline by listing them under each Roman numeral with an uppercase letter. For example:

I. Where and when I was born

A. April 1st—April Fool's Day!

B. Newbaby Hospital

C. 2:17 a.m.

---

definition

chronological
(kron oh LOJ i kul)
adj., in time order.

*In **chronological** order, Mr. Blister gets up, makes some coffee, takes a shower, gets dressed, drinks his coffee, then watches TV all day.*

II. The other people in my family

    A. Parents

    B. Sisters

    C. Grandparents

III. The day I broke my arm when I was three

    A. How it happened

    B. The hospital—I cried!

    C. My cool cast

IV. The day I started school

    A. I was scared

    B. Mrs. Klein

V. My favorite things

    A. Baseball

    B. Chocolate chip cookies

    C. Music

BOOK REPORT OUTLINE

I. Background information about the book

    A. Title

    B. Author

    C. When it was written

II. Characters

III. Setting
(Where and when the story takes place)

IV. Plot summary
(What happens in the story. Keep it short!)

V. Your opinion about the book

    A. Was it good or bad?

    B. Why was it good or bad?

    C. Would you recommend it? To whom?

- Now, Harold has a pretty good idea of exactly what to write. From here on, Harold can go topic by topic, writing a paragraph or two on each topic (the I, II, III part), and a sentence or two on each detail (the A, B, C) part. There is no rule about how many topics a paper should have—it depends on how long the paper is.

You should always make an outline before you write. It will keep your thoughts organized, make your paper much clearer and better to read, and will help you remember all the things you want to discuss.

29. What is the noun form of the word "intelligent"?

(A) intelligent
(B) intellectual
(C) intelligence

We've covered bits and pieces of the parts of speech, but now let's put them all together:

NOUN   A NOUN IS A PERSON, PLACE OR THING.

              Examples: cat, dog, David, car, house

VERB   A WORD THAT DESCRIBES AN ACTION OR A STATE OF BEING

              Action Examples: run, sit, jump, skate

              Being Examples: is, are, were

ADJECTIVE   A WORD THAT DESCRIBES A NOUN

              Examples: beautiful, nice, pretty, thoughtful

ADVERB   A WORD THAT DESCRIBES A VERB, ANOTHER ADVERB OR AN
              ADJECTIVE

              Examples: beautifully, very, slowly, well, quickly

PRONOUN   A WORD THAT REPLACES A NOUN

              Examples: he, she, it, they, I, we

CONJUNCTION A WORD THAT JOINS PARTS OF A SENTENCE

              Examples: but, and, or

ARTICLE   A WORD THAT GOES BEFORE A NOUN

              Examples: a, an, the

PREPOSITION   **A WORD THAT IS USED TO SHOW THE POSITION OF A NOUN**

Examples: below, in, around, of, under

INTERJECTION   **AN EXCLAMATION**

Examples: Yikes! Oh! Rats!

Can words be changed from one part of speech to another? Sure, it happens all the time. You can, for example, change an adjective to an adverb, often by adding -ly:

Jessica is **patient**. (**Patient** describes Jessica—it is an adjective)

Jessica works **patiently**. (**Patiently** describes how she works—it is an adverb)

David is so **responsible**. (**Responsible** describes David—it is an adjective)

David behaves so **responsibly**. (**Responsibly** describes how he behaves—it is an adverb)

30. Which of the following is a stereotype?

(A) On the last biology test, Klaus scored higher than Laurice.

(B) Boys are usually smarter than girls.

(C) There are fewer girls than boys in my biology class.

A **stereotype** is an idea that is fixed in people's minds about a certain type of person. Stereotypes are based on prejudices rather than facts. You hear and see stereotypes all the time: pretty girls are dumb, boys who are smart are geeks and not athletic, all black people are great athletes and musicians, Asian people are brilliant at math and science, fathers can't cook or run a washing machine. These are stereotypes. In literature (p. 129), stereotypes are often used to create "stock characters"—just take a beautiful blonde woman and make her stupid and ditzy, and everyone will laugh. Using stereotypes is a crutch for lazy writers who don't want to challenge themselves or their audience. Stereotypes are often not true. Not all Asians are human calculators. Not all Blacks are great dancers. Mothers are not natural cooks and fathers don't drive better. Stereotypes are just ideas people have: they may be true about

stereotype
(STER ee oh tyep)
noun, a fixed idea held
by a number of people
about a group or type
of person.

*Mr. Cramden told Jackie
not to believe the
stereotype that the kids
at Flannel Middle School
are all really smart.
"Some are dumb as
rocks," he explained.*

some people in a given group, but not about all people who happen to be part of that group. The problem is that people grow to believe the stereotypes about others and even about themselves. A pretty girl may act dumb because she thinks that's what people expect of her. It insults people to assume they fit into some category. You wouldn't like it if people decided what you were like before meeting you, would you? Let's take another look at the statements above:

(A) On the last biology test, Klaus scored higher than Laurice.

(B) Boys are usually smarter than girls.

(C) There are fewer girls than boys in my biology class.

Now, we can check to see if (A) is true because we can look at test scores. The same with (C) since we can compare the number of girls and boys in the class. (B) is a stereotype—boys are smarter. There is no way to prove that statement. When you are writing and you create a character, avoid stereotypes. As a writer, you always want to be fresh and different. When you pull a character ready-made from the stereotype vat, your reader will be bored right away. It doesn't take imagination to write a story about a dumb blonde, a geeky nerd with thick glasses, a dumb jock and a mean teacher. Try to make your characters surprising. Stereotypes are never surprising. In life, try not to put people into stock categories. When you meet someone, keep an open mind about what they will be like. Stereotypes lead you to judge people by the way they look or dress or talk. Listen to what people have to say; watch what people do. Judge them by their acts and their ideas—not by someone else's notion of who they are.

31. "Crazy cats catch canaries" is an example of

(A) alliteration

(B) onomatopoeia

(C) metaphor

Alliteration is the use of the same sound at the beginning of a series of words. Alliteration is used for many reasons. In poetry it is used to emphasize the rhythm of a line. It may be used to make something sound funny. Tongue twisters are a common use of alliteration:

She sells sea-shells by the sea shore.

Peter Piper picked a peck of pickled peppers.

Sometimes alliteration sets a mood. Read the following description from one of the *Just-So Stories* by Rudyard Kipling:

"the great grey-green greasy Limpopo River"

Doesn't that sound more interesting than "the big dark green oily Limpopo River"?

The repeated "g" sounds give a sense of heaviness. Alliteration can make a phrase "catchy." That's why you see it so much in advertisements and commercials.

Foot-loose and fancy free

Look before you leap.

"Mex to the Max"

Likewise, many alliterative nicknames tend to stick:

Buffalo Bill

Krazy Kat

Tiny Tim

Keep on the lookout for alliteration all around you on signs, posters, menus, or whatever. You might also try using it yourself the next time you are writing a poem or a paper.

Onomatopoeia is a figure of speech in which words are made to copy sounds. Sometimes onomatopoeia uses words that sound like real sounds, like "whooosh" or "crunch" or "ding-dong." Sometimes it means writing a word so that it looks sort of like the sound it makes: "CRAASSSHHH." Onomatopoeia is a cool thing to use in writing. It's often used to convey animal sounds:

THE FOURTH

Oh
CRASH!
my
BASH!
it's
BANG!
the
ZANG!
Fourth
WHOOSH!
of
BAROOM!
July
WHEW!
—*Shel Silverstein*

definition

alliteration
(uh LIT er AY shun)
noun, the use of the
same sound at the
beginning of a series
of words.

*Alliteration always
acts as an admirable ally.*

"I heard the buzzzz of the bees and I know it was time to hightail it out of there."

"The cow mooed its way down to the pasture."

In comic books or funny stories, it's used to depict the action:

KER PLOOIE

WHAM

You can use onomatopoeia to describe sounds that don't have other words for them.

The whirring buzzing clicking of the machine.

"Tapocketa, Tapocketa"

32. Which of the following words has a root that comes from Latin?

(A) Dictionary
(B) Barbecue
(C) Buckwheat

Many English words originally come from **Latin,** the language that was spoken in ancient Rome. Although it is now a "dead" language—which means it's no longer spoken in conversation—Latin is important because it is the "parent" language of five other languages: French, Italian, Spanish, Portuguese, and Romanian. Below are some Latin roots that are used to form many English words. Knowing these roots can help you to remember the meanings of words. But be careful: sometimes, a word may seem to have a Latin root (p. 81), yet actually not come from Latin at all but from a similar-sounding word in another language.

LATIN WORD	ENGLISH MEANING	ENGLISH WORDS FROM THIS ROOT
pax	peace	**pact**: an agreement
		pacify: to make peaceful or calm
malus	bad	**dismal**: depressing; causing sadness
		malice: desire to harm another; ill will
		malady: a disease or illness

LATIN WORD	ENGLISH MEANING	ENGLISH WORDS FROM THIS ROOT
manus	hand	**manual**: made or worked by hand
		manufacture: the making of something
factum/fictum	that which is made	**factory**: the building where things are done are manufactured
		facsimile: a reproduction or copy
		fiction: a made-up or imaginary story
		efficient: making something with mininum effort
equus	equal, even	**adequate**: good enough
		equivalent: equal in quantity, value, force, meaning, etc.
donare	to give a gift	**donate**: to give or contribute
		donor: a person who gives
		pardon: to release from punishment
culpa	blame, fault	**culprit**: a person accused of a crime
		culpable: deserving blame
circum	around, on all sides	**circumference**: the line which marks a circle
		circumnavigate: to sail or fly around
		circuit: the line forming the boundaries of an area

33. What is the error in the following sentence?

Wendy liked swimming, running, and to go to school.

(A) We all know that Wendy can't swim, hates running, and always skips school.

(B) A comma should be inserted between "liked" and "swimming."

(C) The phrase "to go" should be "going."

You've already learned many of the basic building blocks of grammar, such as the parts of speech and the basic structure of a sentence. Now let's look at some of the finer points of grammar. Good grammar makes things clear and smooth. Using good grammar saves your readers time and effort—they don't have to get bogged down with figuring out what you're trying to say, so they can give all their attention to appreciating your ideas. The mistake in the sentence above was that the elements of the sentence did not match each other; they were not "parallel." When should you worry about parallel structure in sentences? Whenever you are writing a list of things or activities. For example:

WRONG: That play was interesting, funny, and beauty. (Interesting and funny are adjectives; beauty is a noun)

Instead you should say:

RIGHT: That play was interesting, funny, and *beautiful.* (All are now adjectives)

Remember parallel structure when you are listing activities:

WRONG: The kids at the Halloween party enjoyed playing games, bobbing for apples, and to put costumes on.

RIGHT: The kids at the Halloween party enjoyed playing games, bobbing for apples, and *putting costumes on.*

How about this sentence?

Whenever Matt and Derrick go to the movies, he likes to get popcorn.

What's the problem? Pronoun trouble. Who is getting the popcorn? Derrick? Matt? They're both "he's," so that pronoun could refer to either one of them. You would have to say, "Whenever Matt and Derrick go to the movies, Derrick likes to get popcorn." It sounds a little strange, but it is much more clear. Remember to check pronoun reference whenever you use a pronoun. What is it referring to? Is the reference clear?

WRONG: We brought home a new kitten to play with the cat and she didn't do well at all.

Who didn't do well? The kitten or the cat?

RIGHT: We brought home a new kitten to play with the cat and the cat didn't do well at all.

When you replace a noun with a pronoun, be sure to use the pronoun that goes with that noun.

WRONG: *Each of the women* fought for *their* rights.

RIGHT: *Each of the women* fought for *her* rights.

The same principle of agreement holds true when you have another noun in the sentence that refers to the first noun:

WRONG: These different *vitamins* all come in a different *jar.*

RIGHT: These different *vitamins* all come in different *jars.*

HELLO, COUNTY LIBRARY? YES, DO YOU HAVE ANY BOOKS ON WHY GIRLS ARE SO WEIRD?

THAT'S WHAT I SAID. OR YOU MIGHT ALSO TRY LOOKING UNDER "OBNOXIOUS."

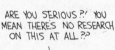

ARE YOU SERIOUS?! YOU MEAN THERE'S NO RESEARCH ON THIS AT ALL??

I'LL BET THE LIBRARY JUST DOESN'T WANT ANYONE TO KNOW.

34. What kind of letter might begin "Dear Sir or Madam"?

(A) A personal letter

(B) A business letter

(C) A thank-you letter

6

Letter writing is an art, although it's one that is definitely on the

salutation

(sal yoo TAY shun)
noun, the "Dear --------"
part at the beginning
of a letter.

*"Dear love of my life,"
was the **salutation**
Twiggy used when writing her boyfriend, Lester.*

Free Stuff for Kids. Now that you are writing letters, why not write away for some free stuff? This book tells you how.

decline these days. But even in our modern world of telephones and electronic mail, well-written letters impress the people you write to. It's worth making an effort to write letters and to do a good job of it.

Business letters are sent to businesses (duh!) whenever you want to find out about something, request something, or apply for a job. It's best to find someone at the business to address your letter to. If you know the person well, use his or her first name (Dear Jennifer:), if you've never met the person, you must use Mr. or Ms. (Dear Ms. Jordan:). Frequently, however, you'll find yourself writing a letter to someone whose name you don't know. In that case, use the "Dear Sir or Madam:" opening. Here's a sample business letter:

Your Name
Your Address
Your Phone Number
The Date

The title of the person you're writing to (i.e., Director of Public Relations)
Company Name
Company Address

Dear Sir or Madam:

I am writing to ask you for more information about your summer tour schedules. I wil be visiting your town this summer, and I was hoping to tour your factory. I have been studying your company and would love to see where everything happens. My trip will be from August 15–22. If you have any information, I would appreciate your sending it my way.

Thank you so much for any help you may be able to give me.

Yours Truly,

Your Name

Keep business letters brief and to the point. Tell the person you are writing to why you are writing and what you would like. End with a brief thank you. Appropriate ways to end are "Yours truly," "Sincerely," or "Sincerely yours." Don't use a more casual closing. Sign your full name, unless you are friendly with the person. Remember to be polite and to ask for information, not demand it.

Personal letters are way more fun to write. These are the letters you might send to a pen pal, a friend, or a relative. Here are a few tips to keep personal letters in good form:

- Put the date in the top right hand corner of the letter.
- It's a much better idea to write a personal letter by hand. Typed letters look impersonal.
- Think more about content than structure. Try to sound like yourself—don't worry if it is not perfectly written.
- There's no strict rule about length—a personal letter can be just a few lines or can go on for a few pages.

Thank-you notes are sent to the hosts if you stay at someone's house overnight, or for a present that you did not thank someone for personally (in other words, you don't need to send your grandmother a thank-you note if she gives you a birthday present in person and you say "thank you," but you do need to write one if she sends the birthday present to you.) You may also send thank-you notes to someone who has done you a special favor. People love to get thank-you notes. Don't get those preprinted ones that have corny sayings already written inside of them. Write your own—it's really no big deal, and usually you'll only need about two paragraphs. Tell why you liked the gift/overnight stay/favor. Tell what it means to you/ how you will use it, or whatever. Say thank you. That's it.

If someone you know dies, and you are not able to go to the family and tell them how sorry you are, you may want to write a condolence note. These notes do not need to be long. The best ones relate some memory you have of the person who died (if you have one, or maybe your parents have told you something about the person). Offer your support to the family or friends of the dead person by telling them that you know how badly they must be feeling or by offering your help with anything they need. Don't worry about saying something stupid. People appreciate any effort you make when someone close to them dies.

R.S.V.P means "Respondez-vous s'il vous plait." or "please respond" in French. Often when an invitation comes in the mail you will need to tell the host if you are coming or not. If you see R.S.V.P. with a phone number in the corner of an invitation, you're off the hook. That means that you only have to call the person who's invited you to tell him whether you are coming or not. But a really formal invitation, like to a wedding, will need a written response. Almost all formal invitations these days have "response cards" inside. You only need to check whether you are coming or not and send it back. They even put the stamp on for you! Just don't forget to mail that card.

ANSWERS

1. B	2. C	3. A	4. C	5. B	6. A	7. B	8. C	9. A	10. C
11. A	12. A	13. A	14. B	15. B	16. C	17. B	18. A	19. C	20. A
21. B	22. A	23. A	24. A	25. C	26. A	27. C	28. A	29. C	30. B
31. A	32. A	33. C	34. B						

1. Juan and Peter are playing tag, Juan is "it" and he tags Peter. What happens to Peter?

(A) Peter develops a taste for pumpkins

(B) Peter is "it"

(C) Peter must go home

1

Hide and Seek is a great game. Just in case you don't already know how to play, here are the basics.

First you pick someone to be "it." Then you pick a home base—trees, front steps, and street lights all work well. "It" counts to 100—if "it" can't count that high, fifty is okay. While "it" counts, the rest of the group runs off and hides. When "it" is finished counting, he yells "Ready or not, here I come!"

One, two, three...

"It" starts looking for everyone. If "it" spots someone, "it" races that person to home yelling, "1,2,3 on (the kid's name) in the (hiding place)." For example, if "it" finds Karen in the treehouse, "it" yells "1,2,3 on Karen in the treehouse!" If "it" tags home first, the other kid becomes "it." If the other kid tags home first, "it" keeps looking for the other players until he gets someone else to be it. If someone cannot be found "it" may yell "All outs in free." And start again!

Of course, lots of kids make up their own variations on the game. One cool variation is called "sardines." It's like backwards hide and seek! Only one person hides. The rest of the group heads out to look for the one who's hidden. As each person finds the hider, he piles on top. The last person to find the hider is "it" for the next round and hides.

Tag is another really basic game that you can add variations to. In tag, you mark off an area to play in. One person is "it," and everyone runs around trying not to be tagged by "it." Whoever gets tagged becomes "it." One great variation on tag is freeze tag. In freeze tag the person tagged must freeze in the position she was caught in. Anyone not frozen may unfreeze someone by tagging them again. The game is over when everyone is frozen. The person frozen the longest becomes "it" for the next round.

Think ya' gotta quick hand? Then how 'bout a game of **jacks**? You need a set of ten jacks for this game. You can get them at most toy or stationery stores. There are lots of different games of jacks, but the one most people know is called "Plainsies." This is how it's played.

definition

opponent

(uh POH nent) *noun,* a person who is on the opposite side in a contest or a game.

*Frieda shook her **opponent's** hand and said, "Good game."*

You start on onesies. Toss your jacks on the floor. Pick up the ball and toss it up. While it bounces, you must pick up one jack and catch the ball in the same hand. The ball can only bounce once, and while you're picking up one jack you can't move any others. Pick up the jacks one by one until you get all ten.

Once you finish onesies, you move on to twosies. For this next round you do the same thing, except you have to pick up two at time. Then you move on to threesies. Threesies are a little different, because there's going to be one jack left over after you pick up all the threes. Advanced players only pick up the extra jack at the end. Work your way up to tensies, always picking up the extra jacks last. That means that for sevens, for example, you pick up seven and then three. When you miss, either by missing the ball or "moving" jacks you are not picking up, it's the next player's turn. On your next turn you start at the level you missed on. One more rule: After the game starts, you can't change where you're sitting to get a better position.

2. When you play Monopoly, what happens when you pass go?

(A) You land on stop

(B) You go to jail

(C) You collect $200

Board games have been around for thousands of years, and they're still one of the most popular ways for people to have fun. Created in 1933 by Charles Darrow, **Monopoly** is one of the most popular games of all time, with over 85 million copies sold in nineteen languages. In Monopoly, you pretend to be a real estate investor and try to buy, sell, and build on property. Did you know that the street names in the game of Monopoly come from the streets of Atlantic City, New Jersey? People like Monopoly because it can take a long time to play. The longest Monopoly game on record lasted for 660 hours—that's over twenty-seven days!

Scrabble was invented in 1931 by Alfred M. Butts. The idea of Scrabble is to build on your opponent's words to make words of your own, like you're making a big crossword puzzle. You start

CAZIQUES
....

The highest score ever earned for one word in Scrabble is 392 points for the word "caziques."

HOW TO PLAY BATTLESHIP WITH ONLY TWO PADS AND TWO PENCILS

Make a grid on your paper with ten lines going across and ten lines going down. Number 1-10 across the top, and A - J down the side. Put 5 A's to represent an aircraft carrier, 4 B's to represent a battleship, 3 C's to represent a cruiser, 3 S's to represent a submarine and 2 D's to represent the destroyer. Don't let your opponent see your grid. Now draw an empty grid below.

You and your opponent take turns calling out locations, like this: "A-3." If there's something in the spot that your opponent calls out, you say "hit"; if not, you say "miss." Once your opponent hits all the spots on one of your ships, that ship is sunk. You then say, "You sunk my _____" (battleship, cruiser, whatever). Keep track of where your hits and misses are on the empty grid and where your opponent's hits and misses are on the grid with all your ships on it. The winner is the first to sink all the other player's ships.

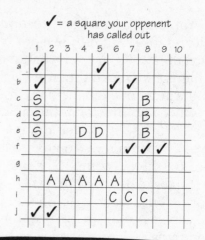

✓ = a square your opponent has called out

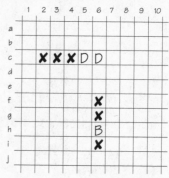

✗ = a square you have called out

with seven tiles, each with a letter on it. You must attach the word you form to the rest of the puzzle by adding to a word already on the board or using a letter in that word to make your new word. Your score depends on how many letters you use and how many points the ones you use are worth. A "q" is worth ten points because it's a harder letter to use than an "a," which is only worth one point. You also get extra points for putting letters on certain squares of the board.

The game of **Life** is exactly that—a game about real life. You make decisions about things like going to school or work, getting married, getting a job, having a family, or buying insurance. The winner is the one who's not broke at the end. Is that what life's about?

Who killed Mr. Boddy? In **Clue**, you play detective and figure out who did it, where, and how. Gather together your clues and be the first to figure it out. There's a cast of weird characters to choose from.

3. Name the two missing suits of cards:
   Spades, clubs, _____ , _____

   (A) hearts, diamonds
   (B) diamonds, golds
   (C) football, baseball

You've probably already played something easy like "go fish," but there are tons of more challenging card games out there. The best thing about card games is that you can take a deck of cards with you just about anywhere, and any number of people can play.

I **Doubt It** is a fun game, as long as you have at least three people. If you have more than eight people, you can use two decks of cards. Deal out all the cards. The person to the left of the dealer goes first and puts, face down in the center of the circle all her Aces. Now, no one else can see what she really puts down. She can put down just Aces, or she can "bluff" and put down something else and say they are aces. If she doesn't have any aces, for example, she'll have to pretend. When she puts down her cards, she must say out loud what she is doing. Like this: "Three Aces!" The next person puts out twos (or pretends to put down twos!) saying, for example, "Two twos!" Play continues around

the circle, with the next person putting down threes, then the next person fours. If, at any time, someone suspects that the person putting down cards is bluffing, he or she says, "I doubt it!" The player turns over just the cards she played. If she was bluffing and the cards she put down are what she said they were, the doubter has to take all the cards in the pile. If they were not what she said they were, she has to take all the cards in the pile. The first person to get rid of all his or her cards wins the round. Remember, if you are using one deck, there are only four of each type of card in the deck (there are only four twos, four threes, etc.) Remember that fact when you bluff—it will make your bluffs more believable. You wouldn't want to say "four threes" if you didn't have four threes, because anyone holding a three will know you are bluffing!

Pyramid is a version of **solitaire**—a card game you play by yourself. Shuffle your cards and lay out seven rows of cards, face up, like a pyramid, with seven in the first row, six in the second, five in the third, and so on.

It will look like the picture on the left. By doing this you lay out twenty-eight cards altogether. Put the rest of the deck face down in front of you. Turn over the top card on the deck. If you can add that card to any one card in the bottom row to get 13, you pick up that card and put the two in a discard pile. For example, if you turn over a 7, and there's a 6 in the bottom row, take the 7 and 6 and discard them. In this game, a Jack is 11 points, a Queen is 12, a King is 13, and an Ace is 1. If you can't make 13, put the card you just drew in a pile next to your discard pile. Turn up your next card. After you take a card from the first row, you can move to the card above it on the next row. You may only take cards that are not covered by any cards below. Since they are worth 13, Kings may be picked up and discarded right away.

The game is over when you either:

A. Clear away the pyramid—you win!

B. Go through the face-down deck you started with. Sorry, you lose!

There are lots of great card games out there. For more cool games, look for *Card Games for Kids*, by Gail MacColl (it comes with a deck), or any of the pocket rule books of card games.

4. Where do you play basketball?

(A) On a field

(B) On a court

(C) On a boat

When the weather is nice, nothing's better than playing games outdoors. Although basketball is played on a court, and baseball is played on a diamond, you don't have to have those things in your backyard in order to have fun. In fact, you don't even have to have a backyard!

For **Four Square** you need a rubber "gym" ball or some other type of bouncy ball. A basketball will not work as well. The game has to be played on a concrete surface, like a schoolyard, sidewalk, or driveway. Draw a giant square. Your square should be big enough for four people to stand in with a few feet around each person.

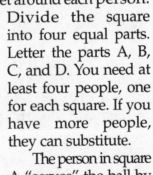

Divide the square into four equal parts. Letter the parts A, B, C, and D. You need at least four people, one for each square. If you have more people, they can substitute.

The person in square A "serves" the ball by bouncing it once and slapping it with his open hand to a person in another square. That person lets the ball bounce and then slaps it to another

definition

court

(kort) *noun*, a space set up for a certain game or sport, such as a basketball or tennis

Martina showed up at the tennis court an hour early to watch her friend Sven play.

square. If you hit the ball outside the lines of the square, you miss the ball, you hit someone else with the ball, or, you hit the ball with a fist, you are fouled out and move to square D (if the person in D fouls out he is replaced by one of the waiting people). Everyone then moves up one letter. The object is to get to A and stay there for as long as possible.

Jumping rope is great exercise, and you can do it alone or with a couple of friends. Nothing could be easier, but here are a few tips. If you are alone, just get a length of rope. Make sure to get a nice heavy rope or it won't twirl well. To figure out how long the rope should be for jumping alone, take a rope, hold it in one hand, drop it down to your foot (put your foot on top to hold it in place) and pull it up to your other hand. Hold both hands a little above your waist.

If you have two friends, you'll need a rope about twice that long. Two people turn the rope by holding either end, and the other person jumps in without messing up the turn of the rope. The rope should slap the ground each time it makes a turn and pass easily above your head in the middle. To jump in easily:

- WATCH IT TURN A FEW TIMES; GET THE RHYTHM.
- STAND ABOUT HALFWAY BETWEEN THE HIGHEST POINT OF THE ROPE AND ONE OF THE TURNERS.
- WAIT FOR THE ROPE TO HIT ITS HIGHEST POINT AND GO.

Don't worry if you can't get in on the first try. It takes practice.

Now that you're in, try skipping and jumping while turning around, hopping on one foot, or touching the ground. There are lots of fun jump rope rhymes to keep the game going.

JUMP ROPE RHYME

....

Try to do all the things this rhyme asks you to do.
I'm a little Dutch girl
Dressed in blue.
Here are the things
I like to do:
Salute the captain,
Bow to the queen
Turn my back
On the submarine.
I can do the tap dance.
I can do the split.
I can do the holka
*   polka*
Just like this.

HOPSCOTCH

Find a nice-sized stone or piece of wood. You don't want anything too light or too large. About the size of your palm is probably about right, but experiment with different sizes. The youngest player goes first, tossing his stone onto the number 1. If he misses, his turn is up and the next player goes. If he gets it, he must hop and jump onto the other squares (hop on one foot where there is only one square in the row, jump on two feet if there are two squares in the row), avoiding the one with the stone (in this case, square 1). When he gets to the end, he jumps around and heads back, picking up the stone on the way by stopping on the square next to the one the stone is on and scooping up the stone with one hand. When he gets back, he tosses his stone to square 2 and repeats the whole thing. This player's turn continues until he misses a square or misses his stone when he goes to pick it up. Then the next person goes . The first player can go back to where he missed on his next turn (if he missed square 6, he starts again at 6). The winner is the first to get to the last square.

BUTTERFINGERS!

If you fumble as you throw your stone, you can call "butterfingers" before it lands and get a second chance.

5. In chess, which piece can ONLY move diagonally?

(A) Bishop
(B) Knight
(C) Jester

Chess is a great game to start playing when you're a kid. It is a complicated game that takes a lifetime to master. You may not be able to win right away, but losing is part of learning any difficult game.

Kids Book of Chess, by Harvey Kidder. The title says it all.

To play chess you'll need a chess board (it's the same as a checker board) and chess pieces. Set your board up like this:

Here's a quick guide to the way each piece moves. In chess, each piece has its own role to play.

The **pawn** moves one space forward only, with two exceptions—on its first move, it can move two spaces forward. When it captures (or takes) another piece, it can only capture a piece that is diagonally one space away.

PAWN

definition

diagonal
(dye AG nul) *adj,.*
slanted.

Ellen moved her bishop along a **diagonal** *line and took Bea's last pawn.*

The **castle** can move any amount of spaces but in a straight line, horizontally or vertically, only.

ROOK OR CASTLE

The **bishop** moves diagonally as many spaces as you like. It will always stay on the same colored square.

BISHOP

The **knight** moves in the most fun way. It's an "L"-shaped move—three squares across and two up, or three squares up and two across like this:

KNIGHT

Searching for Bobby Fischer, starring Joe Mantegna. A great story about a young chess champ.

The **king** can move one square in any direction—across, diagonally, up, or down.

KING

The **queen** may move any number of squares in any direction—across, diagonally, up, or down.

To start the game white moves first. Your goal is to "corner" your opponent's king. This is called "checkmate." You both move around the board, capturing each other's pieces, trying to get to each other's kings. There's a lot of planning involved in getting at the other king while protecting your own. If you get your opponent in a spot where, on your next move, you could capture the king, you must tell him "check." He gets an opportunity to try to move his king and get out of "check." If he cannot get his king out of "check," then that is what's called "checkmate." You win the game!

QUEEN

Try to play with players who are better than you—that's the best way to learn and improve at chess. Ask your opponent to explain why she is moving in a certain way. Chess is a very complicated game, but it can be very rewarding if you stick with it.

3

6. How many strikes can you make in baseball before you are called "out"?

(A) Ten
(B) One
(C) Three

definition

diamond

(DYE mund) *noun*, in baseball, the area formed by the four bases.

After Helen hit the home run, she jogged around the diamond as her friends cheered.

The Fish That Saved Pittsburgh, starring Julius Erving, Stockard Channing, and Flip Wilson. A madcap, zany film about a down 'n out basketball team whose luck turns around with the help of a whacky psychic and a cute, sports-lovin' kid.

Baseball has been considered "the great American pastime" for many years and is still one of the most popular sports around Each team has nine players. The team takes its place on the field and the other team is at bat. While players wait to bat, they sit in the dug-out on the sidelines. The manager of each team decides the order in which the players will bat. One of three things will happen to each batter:

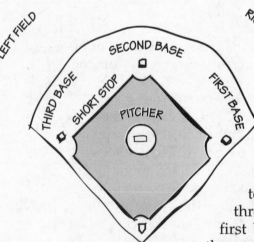

CENTER FIELD
LEFT FIELD
RIGHT FIELD
SECOND BASE
THIRD BASE
SHORT STOP
FIRST BASE
PITCHER
CATCHER

1. **He strikes out.** The pitcher pitches three good balls that the batter cannot hit. Remember? Three strikes and you're out!

2. **The batter hits the ball but he's out anyway.** He is out because either the ball is caught before it hits the ground (a fly out) or a member of the opposing team picks up the ball and throws or runs with the ball to first base before the batter gets there.

3. He advances to one of the bases. That happens if he hits the ball and runs to a base and gets there before someone on the other team can get the ball there, or if the pitcher throws four bad pitches (called balls) that the batter does not even swing at. If that happens, the batter "walks," and gets to go to first base.

The team at bat keeps hitting, each person batting in turn until the team gets three outs (like three strikes). Then, the teams switch and the other team gets a turn to bat. The batters move around the bases and score one "run" each time a batter gets all the way to home base. A typical baseball game lasts nine innings, though many **little league** teams play for six or seven innings.

A League of Their Own, starring Tom Hanks and Geena Davis. A funny movie about the first professional women's baseball league.

7. Which of the following beats a full house in poker?

(A) Four of a kind

(B) Flush

(C) Straight

4

Poker is a really cool card game that you can play with a group of friends or with your family. There are some rules to poker you need to know, but you will learn lots of variations on the game if you play with different people. One of the basic things, though, is understanding what's a good hand and what's a stinker. These are poker hands in winning order, that is, as you go down the list, each **successive** hand beats all of the hands above it:

Worst

HIGH CARD (IF NO ONE HAS ANY OF THE FOLLOWING HANDS, THE PERSON WITH THE HIGHEST CARD WINS)

A PAIR

TWO PAIRS

THREE OF A KIND

FLUSH (ANY FIVE CARDS OF THE SAME SUIT——ALL HEARTS FOR EXAMPLE)

STRAIGHT (ANY FIVE CARDS OF ANY SUIT IN ORDER——FOR EXAMPLE A 5,6,7,8,9)

FULL HOUSE (A PAIR AND THREE OF A KIND)

STRAIGHT FLUSH (A STRAIGHT, WITH ALL THE CARDS IN THE SAME SUIT)

FOUR OF A KIND

ROYAL STRAIGHT FLUSH (10, J, Q, K AND ACE——ALL OF THE SAME SUIT)

Best

definition

default
(dee FALT) *verb*, to fail to fulfill a contract, agreement, or duty.

*When Tommy **defaulted** on his payments to his sister, she told their parents he had borrowed the money to pay for the neighbor's broken window.*

You need to use some sort of markers, or chips, to bet with. Some people bet with money, but it is probably a better idea when you are learning to use chips and start everybody off with the same amount. If you do want to use money, use pennies. Whatever you bet, just remember, one of the keys to poker is not letting anyone else know how good or bad your hand is. You must keep a **poker face**. That way, if you have a good hand, people don't know it, they bet more chips or money, and you win more! Also, if you have a bad hand, you can bluff them into thinking you have a good hand, and they will drop out of the betting and you will win by **default**, even if your hand is terrible!

Now to the good stuff. Before dealing, the dealer asks everybody to "ante up." That means that each person has to contribute to the **pot** in the middle of the table, usually one chip each (the dealer decides how much everyone antes).

One person is designated the **dealer** for each round. Usually the dealer changes from hand to hand, moving around the table. The dealer shuffles the cards and decides which type of poker he would like to play. The most common form is called **Five Card Draw**. The dealer shuffles the cards, asks the person to his right to cut the cards (which means to split the deck in half, putting the bottom half on the top), and starts to deal out one card at a time to each person, going around the table, until each person has five cards.

At this point each person looks at his or her cards. The person to the dealer's left starts the betting. In **Five Card Draw**, you can only start betting if you have a pair of jacks or better in your hand. You can bet whatever you like within the limits set by the people playing the game.

You have a choice after the first person bets to **call** (put the amount of the bet into the pot), **raise** (increase the bet), or **fold** (put down your cards and go out of the game). If you "fold" you lose only what you put up for the ante. You always have these three choices when anybody makes a bet.

The dealer now asks each player if he would like to trade in one to four of his cards and get new ones. After you get your new cards, another round of betting goes on. The dealer puts your old cards on the bottom of the deck. Betting continues as long as people want to keep adding to the pot. The person left in the game with the highest hand wins the whole pot.

When you bet, you must try to trick your opponents. Sometimes, by pretending to have a better hand than you do, you can make your opponents fold. Remember, only those who remain in the game until the end can win the pot. If someone with a better hand than you folds, you can still win. When you "call someone's bluff," that means that you won't fall for their bluff and you want to see what they really have, so you match their bet.

There is an endless number of variations in poker—here's a couple.

Five Card Stud is the easiest poker game. The first card is dealt face down (only the person to whom it is dealt can see that card) and the rest are dealt face up, so that the whole table can see everybody's cards except for the first one. A round of betting occurs after each face up card is dealt, and the person with the best showing cards gets to lead the betting.

Seven Card Stud is exactly the same except for the deal. The first two cards are dealt down, the next four cards are dealt face up and the last card is dealt face down. The betting begins as each face up card is played, with the best cards leading the betting.

8. In which sport do competitors perform a triple lutz?

(A) Figure Skating

(B) Jai Alai

(C) Golf

There are many different types of sports, but all sports can be broken into one of two categories: team and individual. Are you a team player or an individual athlete?

definition
successive
(suck SESS iv) *adj.*, following in order without interuption.
Tommy made ***successive*** *attempts to convince his sister not to tell their parents about the neighbor's broken window.*

Many people love being part of a team. In a team sport, cooperation is the name of the game. Even if a team has certain players who are better than others, the team cannot win unless everyone plays well together. That's the lesson in playing on a team—working together, every team is stronger than its individual pieces.

Uniforms are important in team sports. They help distinguish one team from another, especially in games like football and basketball where different team members get all jumbled up on a field or a court. The proper clothes are important to insure that players do their best and avoid injuries. The right kind of shoes—rubber-soled sneakers for indoor games, and cleats (spiked shoes) for outdoor games—are usually recommended. Some uniforms keep a player cool. A basketball uniform, for example, is loose fitting and sleeveless. Other uniforms are protective. Field hockey players need shin guards, since hockey sticks frequently swing into players' legs. Football players wear helmets and padding to protect against tackling injuries. Baseball players need long pants to protect their legs if they slide into a base.

Every sport is played on a field or a court of a particular size and shape. Usually there are certain limits as to how large or small a court or field must

definition

referee

(REF er ee) *noun* an official in charge of watching the game to make sure all the rules are followed.

*With a furious crunch and a feeble tweet the Molachi brothers took out the quarterback and the **referee** on the same play!*

e for a regulation game. If a game is played by both adults and children, there may be a difference in the size of the field.

Some popular team sports are soccer, football, basketball, hockey (field and ice), baseball, and volleyball.

Some athletes prefer individual sports. In an individual sport, you don't have to worry about your other team members, and you can concentrate on your own performance. Sometimes individual athletes compete head to head against each other. In a running race, for example, you race against a field of competitors. In other sports, like gymnastics or figure skating, judges score each performance. In sports like archery or downhill skiing, competitors go one by one, trying to beat each other's scores or times.

Some other popular individual sports are tennis, golf, wrestling, weightlifting, rollerskating, swimming, and bowling.

definition

expeditious
(ecks pe DI shus) *adj.*
in a speedy and
efficient way.

*"YEEEHAW!" whooped
Constantine, the most
expeditious of all the
young wranglers, as the
roped-up cow was
downed in record time.*

9. How many events are there in a decathalon?

(A) Three
(B) Ten
(C) One hundred

5

Every two years, athletes from all over the world gather together to compete in the **Olympic Games**. Athletes represent their countries, and compete to earn gold, silver and bronze medals. A different city hosts the Games each time they are given, so it is truly an event for all the world.

The five interlocking rings on this flag are the official Olympic Symbol. The International Olympic Committee (IOC) governs the rules of the Games. Winter Olympic Games and Summer Olympic Games used to be held in the same year, every four years. But in 1992, the IOC decided to hold the Summer and Winter Olympics in alternating years, every two years. So, the 1992 Summer Olympics were held in Barcelona, Spain, the most recent Winter Olympics were in Lillehammer, Norway, in 1994, and the next Summer Olympics will be in Atlanta, Georgia, in **1996**.

Katarina Witt in motion

The Olympic Games were inspired by the competition held in Ancient Greece (p. 337) more than 2000 years ago. In fact, the Olympics get their name from the city of Olympia, Greece. The games originally consisted only of running races. Eventually, ancient Greeks competed in events like wrestling, running, and chariot racing. To commemorate the original Olympics, a torch is lit from a flame in Olympia and carried by a series of runners (and an airplane or two) to the site of the Olympic Games. In a dramatic moment, the final carrier of the flame runs with it into the Olympic Arena

👁 *Chariots of Fire.* A touching movie about two men who run, for very different reasons, in the 1924 Olympics.

and lights a torch that will burn for the duration of the games. The flame is extinguished on the last night.

Some of the most popular sports of the Summer Olympics are the **marathon**, the shorter running races, called sprints, the long jump, the high jump, swimming, diving, gymnastics and the decathalon. The **decathalon** is a series of ten track and field events. Because the winner of the decathlon must be good at running and jumping and throwing, among other things, the gold medal decathalon winner is often thought of as the world's best athlete.

Some of the Winter Olympic Games which people enjoy are ski jumping and racing, figure skating, speed skating, cross-country skiing, hockey, and bobsled racing.

Heptathlete Jackie Joyner-Kersey

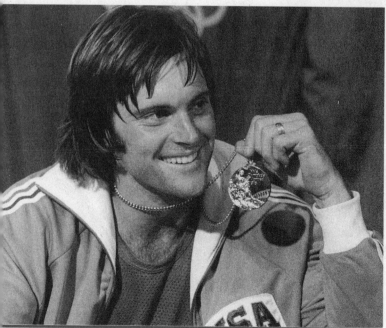
Bruce Jenner displaying his gold medal for winning the decathlon.

10. A man leaves home and makes three lefts and ends up back at home again. What's he wearing?

(A) Huh?

(B) A dress

(C) A baseball uniform

The Games' Magazine Kids' Giant Book of Games, edited by Karen C. Anderson. Tons of puzzles and games for kids of all ages.

The Eleventh Hour, by Graham Base. An engrossing mystery full of clues. The answer is sealed in the back.

Brain teasers are word or picture puzzles that make you think. Some are pictures that you have to look at to solve a question; some are **riddles**, like the one above. There are lots of famous brain teasers to try out on your friends.

The trick with a riddle or brain teaser is to try to think in a different way than you ordinarily would. These puzzles almost always work by setting you up to think one obvious thing. Right away, you have to cross out that obvious thing as a possible answer. For example, the brain teaser above was a classic set-up, and we'd bet anything you fell for it. It sets you up to imagine a man leaving his house. So, you can cross off that first image that jumps into your head. Now, think. Are there any words in the question that can be thought of in more ways than one? In this brain teaser, the trick depends on the word "home." In case you're still not getting it, it's home base in baseball, not the home you live in.

THIS GAME IS REALLY HARD

You and a friend each write a four-digit number on a sheet of paper. Don't tell your number!

• *Take turns guessing each other's numbers. If someone guesses a correct digit give him a dot. If he guesses the correct digit in the correct spot, he gets a star. For example, if my number is 3567 and you guess 5068, I would tell you that you have a dot (for guessing 5 --the correct digit, just in the wrong place) and a star (for guessing 6--the correct digit in the correct place) Go back and forth until one of you guesses the other's four-digit number.*

To make it more difficult:

• *Make your numbers five or six digits*

• *Repeat digits. Usually the rule is that you must use four different digits. If you don't require them to be different from each other, the game will be harder to solve.*

ANSWERS

1. B   2. C   3. A   4. B   5. A   6. C   7. A   8. A   9. B   10. C

HUMANITIES

1. What word rhymes with house?

(A) book

(B) mouse

(C) glass

1

A **rhyme** is a word that has the same ending sound as another word. Rhymes are often used in songs and poems. Although not all poems have rhymes, many do. Here are two very different poems that both use lots of rhymes. Can you hear the rhymes? They are the sounds that repeat.

definition

rhythm

(rithm) *noun* a regular repeating of sounds or movements in a pattern, as in poetry, dance and music; any kind of pattern in the way something happens.

*The **rhythm** of my heart goes BOOM BOOM BOOM, let's get up and dance and jump around the room.*

MY SHADOW

By Robert Louis Stevenson

I have a little shadow that goes in and out with me,
And what can be the use of him is more than I can see.
He is very, very like me from the heels up to the head;
And I see him jump before me, when I jump into my bed.

The funniest thing about him is the way he likes to grow —
Not at all like proper children, which is always very slow;
For he sometimes shoots up taller like an india-rubber ball,
And he sometimes gets so little that there's none of him at all.

He hasn't got a notion of how children ought to play,
And can only make a fool of me in every sort of way.
He stays so close beside me, he's a coward you can see;
I'd think shame to stick to nursie as that shadow sticks to me!

One morning, very early, before the sun was up,
I rose and found the shining dew on every buttercup;
But my lazy little shadow, like an arrant sleepy-head,
Had stayed at home behind me and was fast asleep in bed.

RUDY FELSH

By Shel Silverstein
Rudy Felsh
Knows how to belch
Better than anyone ever did.
Margo says that Rudy Felsh
Is a nasty vulgar kid.
Someday he will go to hell
Or jail or Canada, but now
Every night I pray that first
Rudy Felsh will show me how.

CAN YOU WRITE YOUR OWN POEM? LISTEN TO THE SOUND AND THE RHYTHM OF EACH WORD.

2. Where's the best place to see paintings and sculptures?

(A) Art museum

(B) Video arcade

(C) Library

The Museum of Natural History in New York City

Have you ever been to a **museum** before? A museum is a place where all sorts of things are kept, not just paintings and sculptures. A museum of natural history may have a display of dinosaur bones or Native American furs and tools. There are museums for art, museums for cars, games, even museums for things that have to do with television shows.

definition

museum

(myoo ZEE um) *noun* a building used to display and keep works of art or things of interest, such as history, science, technology, or animal and plant life.

The museum has an exhibit that includes the ruby slippers from The Wizard of Oz.

GAMES

The Game Preserve
110 Spring Rd.
Peterborough, New
Hampshire 03458
Here you'll find over a
thousand old board and
card games to view.
Early pinball games and
a parcheesi game from
India are here.

BUTTONS

The Cooper-
Hewitt Museum
2 E. 91st St.
New York City
10028
Over 1,000
buttons from
around the world are
here. There are buttons
made from stones, wood,
and even animal horns.

DOLLHOUSES

Washington
Dolls' Houses
and Toy Museum
5236 44th St., N.W.,
Washington, D.C. 20015.
You'll see a replica of a
1903 New Jersey seaside
hotel as well as
hundreds of dolls in
their original clothing
in this fascinating
collection.

The **Smithsonian Institution** in Washington D.C., which is made up of fifteen separate museums, is the world's largest collection. It houses over 139 million items and has over 6,000 employees to take care of them.

The **American Museum of Natural History** in New York City, founded in 1869, includes a planetarium. The museum has over 1.2 million square feet of space and houses over 30 million items and specimens. More than 3 million people visit it each year.

The Smithsonian Institution in Washington, D.C.

WHAT CAN YOU DO IN A MUSEUM?

- TAKE YOUR TIME LOOKING AT THINGS. THERE'S NO LIMIT TO HOW LONG YOU ARE ALLOWED TO STAND IN FRONT OF EACH EXHIBIT.
- TAKE A SKETCHBOOK AND DRAW WHAT YOU SEE. IT'S A GREAT WAY TO REMEMBER WHAT YOU SAW, AND ALSO A GREAT WAY TO PRACTICE YOUR OWN ART.
- DON'T TOUCH ANY OF THE ITEMS ON DISPLAY IN A MUSEUM UNLESS YOU ARE TOLD THAT YOU MAY. CHILDREN'S MUSEUMS AND SOME SPECIAL REGULAR MUSEUMS HAVE DISPLAYS THAT ARE MEANT TO BE TOUCHED. ASK A GUARD IF YOU'RE NOT SURE.
- SPEAK SOFTLY. MOST MUSEUMS ARE PLACES WHERE PEOPLE ENJOY JUST LOOKING AT THINGS, SO RUNNING AND SHOUTING ARE NOT GOOD THINGS TO DO.
- EAT ONLY IN THE SPECIAL AREAS SET ASIDE FOR EATING (LIKE A CAFETERIA OR COURTYARD).

CARS

William F. Harrah Automobile Museum
401 Dermody Way, Sparks, Nevada 89431
You can trace the history of automobiles here, from antique cars to electric cars.

3. Where's the best place to look for the score of last night's football game?

(A) An encyclopedia
(B) A newspaper
(C) A dictionary

You may see the **newspaper** sitting on your kitchen table, or in the library, or on a newsstand, and think that there's nothing in there but a lot of news stories. But a newspaper is good for much more than finding out what is happening in the news. Although all newspapers have different sorts of things in them, there are some things that most newspapers carry. Look near the front of the paper for an index—a listing of all the features in your paper.

First and most important, a newspaper is where you can read to find out about what is happening around you—from the big fire that may have happened in your area to what the president (p. 296) is doing to run the country. These articles are difficult to read, but you can always ask a grownup to read a story to you if it looks  interesting. Look for things you may be studying in school. Many stories also have to do with how schools are run, such as what new school lunches are being served. How can you find out which stories may interest you? Each story has a **headline** above it—that's the big, bold sentence above the story that gives you a quick idea of what the story is about. You can also look at any pictures that go along with the story to see what the story is about. Not all the articles may interest you, but looking at the paper is a good way to learn about what's going on in the world.

CULTURESCOPE

WHAT'S IN YOUR PAPER?

Get your newspaper and find the following sections.

Weather
Sports
Comics
Classified Ads
TV Listings
Dear Abby or
   Ann Landers
Movie Listings
Recipes
Crossword Puzzle
Advertisements
Kids Page

definition

headline
(HED lyne) *noun* the title above an article that tells you what the article is about.

When Brandon read the **headline** *"Big Snowstorm Tomorrow," he put away his homework and started playing video games.*

Newspapers all carry some information about the weather. Look for this section. Some may have a big map of the United States and show what the weather is doing all over the country. Others may just tell you what the local weather is. Newspapers will usually tell you how the weather was yesterday, how it is probably going to be today and give you the forecast for tomorrow. You can check to see if your newpaper has information about the weather in other parts of the world. If you are going on a trip, you will definitely want to know what kind of weather to expect when you get to your destination.

Want to know what's on T.V. tonight at 8? Interested in seeing if your favorite movie is playing at the local movie house? Want to know what you can listen to on the radio? Newspapers give you all this information. Find the television, movie and radio listings. They are usually grouped together in the same part of the paper. The newspaper lets you find out when and where things are playing, and also sometimes gives you the reviews of those shows. Did the reviewer like or dislike that new movie? You can use reviews to help you decide what to see.

If you want to buy or sell something, the **classified ads** are the place to do it. People place their own ads for cars, boats, houses, furniture, jobs, garage sales, pets—almost anything. It's fun to look through the ads and see what people are selling and how much money they are asking for.

Your local stores also place ads in the newspaper. Here's where you can check to see if your favorite toy store is having a sale, or what time the local comic book store opens. Not all stores advertise everyday, but you can find a lot of store advertisements scattered throughout the paper.

We saved the best for last. Although not all newspapers have these fun features, most do. Check your paper to see if you can find the comics pages. Does your paper carry Peanuts, Calvin and Hobbes, Garfield, or For Better or Worse? Your paper may also have some kids' pages occasionally, with crafts you can do, recipes, book reviews for kids, interviews with famous people. Does your paper carry Ann Landers or Dear Abby? Those are two famous advice columns. People write to Ann Landers and Abby to tell them about their problems and get advice.

There's something for everyone in the newspaper, and as you get older you'll find more and more that interests you.

4. Where in the library is the following book located?

> F   Bradley, Jasper
> B   <u>The funniest book ever written</u>/ Jasper
>   Bradley, with photographs by Marjorie
>   Morningstar.
>   356 pages.
>   With photographs
>   Summary: a really, really funny book.
>   ISBN 0-376-54398-5
>   I. Bradley, Jasper. II. Title

(A) ISBN 0-376-54398-5
(B) page 356
(C) fiction section under Bradley, Jasper

definition

classify
(KLAS i fye) *verb* to
place in a category or
a group.

*For her science
assignment, Beatrice had
to **classify** all of the
objects in her desk as
either animal, vegetable,
or mineral.*

Libraries are arranged by what is called a classification system. Some libraries use the Dewey Decimal system, other use the Library of Congress system. Most public libraries and grade school libraries arrange the books on the shelves according to the Dewey Decimal system. This system groups books by category. Fiction books are with all other fiction books, sports books are found together, animal books are found together, and so on. So, if you are just browsing for a book to read and don't have one in mind, you may want to head to the fiction section and just look around. But if you know the book you want to find, or an exact subject that you need a book on, check out the card catalog first.

THERE ARE THREE TYPES OF CARDS IN A CARD CATALOG
Subject cards are arranged alphabetically (p. 44) by the subject of the book. If a book is about Koala bears, for example, it would have a card in the K drawer, with the line KOALA BEARS in big capital

ASK THE LIBRARIAN
....
*Librarians are there to
help you find the books
you want. If you have
trouble—ask for help.
Some libraries now have
computers in which you
can enter the title or
author or subject of the
book you are looking for.
The computer will search
for you and give you a
list of possible books and
where they are located.*

Library Do's and Dont's

letters along the top of the card. Once you find your subject and pick out a book from the cards under the subject of the book, write down the number (and/or letter). You'll find the number in the upper left hand corner of the card.

Title cards are arranged by the title of the book. If you know the title of the book you want, but you don't know the author, look here. The author's name will be on the first line of the card. Again, write down the letters and/ or number you'll find in the upper left hand corner.

Author cards are arranged by the author's name, last name first, first name last. Remember, an author can have more than one card here, depending on how many books he's written. Once you find the card of the book you want, again, write down those letters and/ or numbers in the corner of the card.

The numbers in the corner of the card are called **call numbers** and they tell you where in the library the book is located. If you see a number like this, 323.7F, that means to go to the three hundreds and then find 323.7. First you find the number (they go in order), and then you find the letter after (it goes in A, B, C order).

5. Who is Calvin's sidekick in the comics?

(A) Hobbes

(B) Snoopy

(C) Tonto

Everyone loves reading the comics in the newspaper, but it's mostly kids (and cool grownups!) who buy comics to collect or books of comics. There are two basic types of comics: funny and serious.

"Peanuts" has been around forever, it seems. "Peanuts" books, and many papers carry the "Peanuts" comic strips every day. The main characters are Snoopy, Charlie Brown, his sister Sally, Lucy, her brother Linus, Woodstock, Peppermint Patty, Schroeder, and Pigpen. You'll never see a grownup face in a "Peanuts" comic strip. Maybe that's what makes them so great.

Lots of people go crazy for **"Calvin and Hobbes."** Hobbes is Calvin's stuffed tiger, who comes to life only for Calvin. Calvin's always getting into trouble with his parents and his teacher and loves to torture Suzy, his girl friend.

MAKE YOUR OWN COMIC STRIP BOOK

Cut out your favorite comic from the paper every day and glue a week's worth of them onto one page of a loose-leaf binder. After a while, you'll have your own comic book.

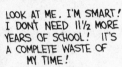

CALVIN AND HOBBES copyright Watterson. Dist. by UNIVERSAL PRESS SYNDICATE. Reprinted with permission of UNIVERSAL PRESS SYNDICATE. All rights reserved.

Garfield's funniness is all in his coolness—or maybe it's just laziness. Nothing seems to bother him—except the thought of going on a diet.

Kids also love to collect superhero comics, like "X-Men," "Spiderman," and "Superman." If you keep your collection in good shape, and make sure to get all the issues in a series, one day you may find you have something very valuable.

SPECIAL COMICS TO COLLECT

- THE FIRST COMIC BOOK IN A SERIES
- THE FIRST TIME A NEW CHARACTER APPEARS IN A COMIC BOOK
- A SPECIAL EVENT IN THE STORY (FOR EXAMPLE, THE DEATH OF SUPERMAN)
- A SPECIAL ISSUE (ONE WITH A NEAT COVER, OR AN ANNIVERSARY EDITION)

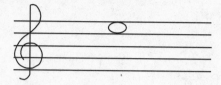

6. What note does this represent?

definition

pitch

(pitch) *noun* exactly how high or low a sound or note is.

Christine has perfect pitch—she can sing middle "C" on cue.

(A) E
(B) A
(C) G

When you look at a sheet of music, you might think it looks like a chicken dipped its feet in ink and strutted across the page. Musical notation is different from the writing we do with letters. All the millions of different songs in the world can be written with musical notation.

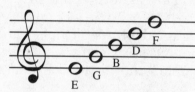

The **clef** indicates how high or low a note is played. This is the **treble** clef. Notes written in the treble clef are played higher than notes written in the bass clef.

The notes are written on or between the lines. On the treble clef the first lined notes are E - G - B - D - F, which you can remember by thinking: "Every Good Boy Deserves Fudge."

The notes in the spaces are F - A - C - E, which you can remember because they spell FACE. There are seven notes—C, D, E, F, G, A, B—that repeat over and over at higher and lower pitches. Musicians group eight notes together, forming what's called an **octave**. To go "up" or "down" one octave means going to the note eight notes away.

MUSICAL LINGO

Gig *A job playing music*

Pipes *A singer's voice.*

Bones *Trombone.*

Harp *Harmonica.*

Jamming *Improvising music, playing for fun.*

Skins *Drums*

Axe *Guitar*

7. Which of the following is NOT an element of a story?

(A) Character

(B) Plot

(C) Book cover

There are three important parts to any story: characters, plot, and setting.

The **characters** of a story are the people (or animals) in the story. In Little House on the Prairie, for example, Laura is the main character. She is also the narrator, the person who is telling the story.

The **plot**, or action, is the story itself. What happens? Something has to happen in a story to make it a story.

The **setting** is where and when the story takes place. The setting may refer to the state, country, or planet, where a story takes place, or it may refer to something more specific, like a house or a barnyard. The setting also includes the time period of the story. Examples could be a poem set during the Civil War or a short story about space travel whose setting is the future.

Two types of stories are **fiction** and **nonfiction**. The story of your family's trip to Florida last year would be a nonfiction story. When all the three elements—characters, plot, setting—are completely true, a story is nonfiction.

If you decided to change even ONE element of the facts, your story would become fiction. You could change the names of the members of your family around, make up some new family members, or get rid of a few. You might change the setting by changing the names of the places you went and making up new details about the hotel you stayed at or the beach you went to. You might even change the plot. Maybe your vacation was actually boring, and you want to jazz the story up by throwing in an adventure, like meeting a spy named Fabrice who takes you for a midnight spin in his convertible and teaches you the secret to success in all video games.

A really good story often has a combination of true and made up elements. You may want to imagine people you know (yourself and your friends or family) in places you are familiar with (your own backyard, even) doing things that come straight from your imagination. Or you may want to imagine a made-up character (an

definition

narrator

(NAYR ay tohr) *noun* the person who tells the story or speaks along with the story in a book, movie, or play.

I love a good story-- especially when I'm the narrator!

POINT OF VIEW

A story should always be told from a certain point of view. If the story has a narrator, the reader get the narrator's point of view. In The True Story of the Three Little Pigs, Jon Scieszka tells the familiar story of the three little pigs from the point of view of the wolf--of course the whole thing was the fault of those ridiculous little pigs!

alien, or a famous person from history) doing something you have done in a setting that's familiar to you. The possibilities are endless!

> **TRY TO REWRITE:**
> ....
> **CINDERELLA** FROM THE POINT OF VIEW OF THE UGLY SISTERS.
> **HANSEL & GRETEL** FROM THE POINT OF VIEW OF THE WITCH.
> **THE THREE BEARS** FROM THE POINT OF VIEW OF THE BEARS.
> **CAN YOU IMAGINE HOW THEY FELT?**

4

8. Which king ruled at Camelot?

(A) King James
(B) King Arthur
(C) King Richard

definition

quest

(kwest) *noun* a search for something.

The explorers were on a ***quest*** *to find the Lost City of Badminton when they stumbled upon the ruins of an ancient tennis court.*

Camelot was a castle, home of the legendary **King Arthur**. Historians believe that King Arthur lived in the early 500s, and that he was a popular leader in Great Britain. He is called legendary because most of what we hear about him is probably made up.

According to the stories told about him, Arthur was born to King Uther Pendragon and Duchess Igraine of Cornwall. They sent him to be raised by Sir Ector, without telling young Arthur that he was the son of the king. Arthur's real identity was finally revealed when he pulled a sword from a stone. The sword, called Excalibur, could only be removed from the stone by the true King of England.

Guided by **Merlin**, a great wizard, King Arthur formed the Round Table—a group of the bravest and most respected knights in the land. Some of the fabled Knights of the Round Table were Sir Lancelot, Sir Bors, Sir Percivale, Sir Tristram, Sir Gawain, Sir Kay, and Sir Galahad. Many stories about the Round Table have been passed down to us, including the famous story of the quest for the Holy Grail. The **Holy Grail** was supposedly the cup used by Jesus (p.146) at the Last Supper on the night before he died, and it was said to have special powers. According to the story, only Sir Bors, Sir Galahad and Sir Percivale were noble enough to search for the Holy Grail. Their dangerous journey makes for an exciting story and has been handed down from generation to generation for over a thousand years.

It was also said that some day King Arthur would return. For that reason, he is sometimes referred to as "The Once and Future King."

There are a lot of books about King Arthur. A really good one is *The Sword in the Stone*, by T.H. White. You can also rent the movie *The Sword in the Stone*, a Disney cartoon in which the young King Arthur pulls the sword Excalibur from the stone.

9. What was unusual about Paul Bunyan?

A) His great size
B) His great intelligence
C) His magic lantern

4

Before there were books, there were storytellers. People would gather around and listen to stories that had been passed down from generation to generation. You may have heard these stories called

definition

legend

(LEJ end) *noun* an often exaggerated story that has been passed down about a person or event.

*The **legend** of Principal Steelpants was known throughout Lintville. For fifty years he had ruled Lintville Prep with an iron fist.*

Pecos Bill, adapted by Brian Gleeson, illustrated by Tim Raglin.

Paul Bunyan, adapted and illustrated by Steven Kellogg.

by many names: fairy tales, folk tales, myths, legends, folklore, tall tales. All of these types of stories have one thing in common: they can tell you things about the culture they come from. Often folk tales help you to learn what the people of a country believed in and how they saw themselves. American folk tales are often about people who were big and strong and could accomplish great physical feats—that's why they are called tall tales. Many of them come from the cowboys and loggers and adventurers of our early days; they must have liked to imagine heroes who were big and strong.

Paul Bunyan was a legendary giant, who had a giant blue ox named Babe. He was a lumberjack and became famous for amazing feats of strength. One legend has it that the ten thousand lakes in Minnesota were formed by the huge footprints of Paul Bunyan and Babe. Another legend holds that Paul Bunyan carved out the Grand Canyon with his pickaxe.

Pecos Bill, one of the legendary figures of the Wild West, fell off a wagon when he was a baby and was raised by howling coyotes. He invented the lariat and tamed the meanest horses. Pecos Bill was so wild he battled a cyclone—in fact, legend has him carving out the Grand Canyon while trying to tame a twister. Bill also was said to have created Great Salt Lake and Death Valley.

Some folk tales are about real people. As a little boy,

Paul Bunyan and his big blue ox, Babe.

George Washington (p. 347) was supposed to have chopped down his father's best cherry tree with a hatchet. When his father angrily confronted him, George looked him in the eye and said "I cannot tell a lie." This story was told to show how honest and upright Washington was. Although it never happened, the story has been repeated so often that many people believe that it is true.

10. Which of the following people was not a composer?

(A) Bach

(B) Mozart

(C) Picasso

Composers are artists who create music. Music may be written for any instrument—piano, violin, cello, guitar, even drums. The voice is an instrument as well, and some of the most beautiful music is written to be sung.

J.S. Bach

Johann Sebastian Bach (1685-1750) was a German composer who wrote music in the style called "Baroque." Baroque architecture created complicated, ornate buildings. Baroque music is like that as well: complicated, but organized music. Bach's most famous work is The Brandenburg Concertos, and he wrote many other works for piano and violin. Bach also wrote chamber music, music designed to be played not by a big orchestra but by just a few musicians. Since there are fewer musicians, chamber music must be heard in a small room or "chamber." In chamber music, each musician plays a different instrument.

definition

prodigy
(PROD i jee) *noun* a person who displays an incredible talent or brilliance at a very young age.

*Ellen is definitely a belching **prodigy**, but I'm not sure being able to burp "Happy Birthday to You" is a talent many people appreciate.*

Wolfgang Amadeus Mozart

Wolfgang Amadeus Mozart (1756-1791) was a child prodigy—a kid with an unusual talent. He wrote his *Sonata in C* when he was just five years old, and went on to compose many brilliant symphonies and concertos. Mozart also wrote operas. An opera is a play that is set to music. Characters in opera sing rather than speak their lines, and music is played throughout by an orchestra. Mozart's most famous operas are *The Magic Flute*, *The Marriage of Figaro*, and *Don Giovanni*. Among Mozart's other famous works are *Eine kleine Nachtmusik*, a string quartet (written for four string instruments). It's hard to believe how much Mozart was able to accomplish when you consider that he died at the age of 35.

Another well-known composer is **Ludwig Van Beethoven** (1770-1827).

Beethoven Lives Upstairs. A movie about a ten-year-old boy who lives downstairs from Beethoven.

Although he was completely deaf by the end of his life, he composed some of the most beloved symphonies and concertos of all time. He is most famous for his symphonies, especially the *Fifth Symphony* and the *Ninth Symphony*. He was the first composer to write a symphony that used a choir.

Johann Strauss (1825-1899) was an Austrian composer famous for his waltzes. A waltz is the music used for the ballroom dance (the dance is also called the waltz) that was popular in the

Ludwig Van Beethoven

1800s. Waltzes are written and danced with a pattern of three beats, like this: 123-123-123. You put an extra stress on the 1s. The best-known waltz by Strauss is called *The Blue Danube*.

Peter Ilyich Tchaikovsky (1840-1893) was a Russian composer who wrote many famous ballets and symphonies including *Peter and the Wolf* and the *1812 Overture*. Tchaikovsky wrote music in the romantic style. Romantic music has a lot of emtion in it, and often tries to tell stories about common people. You can also recognize romantic music by its beautiful melodies. One Tchaikovsky work that you may know is the music for the ballet *The Nutcracker*, which is usually performed around Christmas (p. 299) time each year.

Duke Ellington (1899-1974) was a great musician and composer of **jazz music.** Jazz music was invented in the U.S. in the twentieth century by African American musicians. The movement grew in cities like New Orleans, Chicago, New York, and San Francisco. Because it is composed in a relatively unstructured form, jazz was a totally new type of music. Jazz musicians have lots of freedom to improvise while still sticking to one basic theme. Eventually, jazz music grew to include several forms: big band, be-bop, and swing are some of them.

Peter Ilyich Tchaikovsky

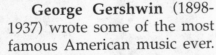

Duke Ellington

George Gershwin (1898-1937) wrote some of the most famous American music ever. He used influences from American jazz to create a completely unique style. He wrote "serious" music such as the opera *Porgy and Bess* and the symphonies *An American in Paris* and *Rhapsody in Blue*, as well as many popular songs, such as "The Man I Love," and "I Got Rhythm."

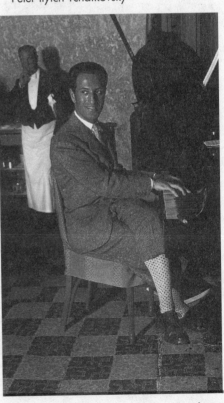

George Gershwin

Chuck Berry

The Everly Brothers

James Brown

Buddy Holly

Ray Charles

Jerry Lee Lewis

Sam Cooke

Elvis Presley

Fats Domino

Little Richard

11. Which of the following was the rock and roll group famous for the songs, "Let it Be," "Help," "Yellow Submarine," and "Back in the U.S.S.R."?

(A) The Rolling Stones

(B) Arrested Development

(C) The Beatles

In 1964, something called **Beatlemania** swept across the United States. **The Beatles**, a British band that was strongly influenced by American music, were so popular that they were mobbed by huge groups of screaming teenagers everywhere they went. A Beatles song called "I Want to Hold Your Hand," was a big hit. The four Beatles were a perfect mix of styles and personalities—Paul McCartney, John Lennon, George Harrison, and Ringo Starr.

The Beatles became so famous, in fact, that they eventually decided to no longer give live performances. Performing for huge, noisy, crazy crowds was taking too much time and energy from their songwriting. They recorded all their later albums in the studio and never performed any of them live. In 1967, they released what many rock critics consider to be the greatest rock and roll album ever made—*Sgt. Pepper's Lonely Hearts Club Band.*

"A Day In the Life," "She's Leaving Home," and "Sgt. Pepper's Lonely Hearts Club Band" are some of the most famous songs from that album (remember, those were the days before CDs. Today, of course, all the Beatles' albums have been put onto CD). They went on to become probably the last great rock and roll group to be listened to by everyone: grade school

The Beatles

children, teenagers, college students, teachers, even famous conductors. Their music was at once hugely popular and innovative. That unusual combination is probably what made them most remarkable. They also starred in two movies—*Help* and *A Hard Day's Night*. The Beatles were so famous, in fact, that after a while they couldn't take the strain of being the Beatles. In 1970 they released their last album, *Let It Be*, and then the four Beatles parted ways.

12. What type of book would you read to find out about a real person's life?

(A) Novel

(B) Biography

(C) Myth

You know that fiction books (p. 129) are made up stories, and non-fiction books (p. 129) are about real-life things. When you look through the library, however, you'll find there are some weird exceptions to this rule. Fairy tales, for example, are shelved in the library non-fiction area even though the stories they tell hardly come from real life. Do you have any idea why? Take a look at some other non-fiction categories.

A **biography** is simply a person's life story. If your best friend wrote the story of your life he would be writing a biography of you. The important thing is that a biography must be true and factual. When an author tells her own life story, it is called an autobiography. If you wrote the story of your own life, you would be writing your **autobiography.**

A **fable** tells a story, usually with animals as the main characters, that teaches as a lesson. The most famous fables were written down by **Aesop**, who lived in Ancient Greece about 600 B.C. You may be familiar with some of Aesop's fables. In the story of the tortoise and the hare, for example, the hare is so confident he can win a race with the tortoise that he takes a nap under a tree during the race. The tortoise plods along and wins the race. The moral is that "slow and steady wins the race." The story makes the point that having speed or great talent does not mean you will always win—often steady hard work and determination are more important.

Folk tales were originally told from person to person—by mouth or "orally." People believe that folk tales were probably the

definition

moral

(MOHR ul) *noun* a lesson about what is right and wrong.

*The **moral** of the story is never lie to anyone bigger than you are.*

earliest tales known to man. Many folk tales have different versions in different lands. For example, there are stories just like the Cinderella story that come from all over the world. How could you explain that?

A **myth** is a story from long ago that was made up to explain why things in the world are the way they are. The collection of myths that were told in a particular culture is called **mythology**. Two cultures especially famous for their mythology were the ancient Greeks and the ancient Romans.

5

13. Who was the messenger of the Gods in Greek mythology?

(A) Hermes

(B) Hera

(C) Zeus

Like any culture, the ancient **Greeks** used stories to explain the mysteries of life and to help them understand history and human behavior. The stories of Greek mythology explain how the world came to be. They tell about the origins of the planets and the stars, how the sun travelled through the sky, why there are earthquakes and tides, and things like that. Greek mythology is full of wild, entertaining stories that are fun just in themselves.

Most of the stories in Greek mythology have gods and goddess as well as human characters in them. Greeks believed that the gods ruled their everyday life. Ancient Greeks did not believe in one god, but rather a whole group of gods—each with a different role.

There were twelve in the top rank, six gods and six goddessess, called Olympians because they lived on Mount Olympus. They were:

1. ZEUS — THE RULER OF THE GODS.
2. HERA — THE SISTER AND WIFE OF ZEUS.
3. APOLLO — THE SUN GOD AND THE GOD OF MUSIC, POETRY AND PURITY. HE RODE A CHARIOT ACROSS THE SKY THAT PULLED THE SUN ALONG ITS PATH.
4. ARTEMIS — THE TWIN SISTER OF APOLLO AND THE GODDESS OF HUNTING.
5. ATHENA — THE GODDESS OF WISDOM AND WAR.
6. ARES — THE GOD OF WAR.
7. HEPHAESTUS — THE BLACKSMITH OF THE GODS.
8. DEMETER — THE GODDESS OF AGRICULTURE.
9. HERMES — THE MESSENGER OF THE GODS, SAID TO HAVE WINGS ON HIS FEET.
10. POSEIDON — GOD OF EARTHQUAKES AND THE OCEAN.
11. DIONYSUS — THE GOD OF WINE.
12. APHRODITE — THE GODDESS OF LOVE.

Zeus

These gods were always tempting humans, to test them or just to see what would happen.

One of the most famous Greek myths is the story of the **Trojan horse.** In this story, the Greeks built a giant wooden horse. They made it large enough that their soldiers could fit inside of it, and then they rolled it up to the gates of the city of Troy and hid inside. The Trojans believed that it was a gift, so they brought it inside the city gates. That night, while everyone was sleeping, the Greek soldiers snuck out of the giant horse and opened up the city gates for the entire Greek army to come in to conquer Troy. From this myth comes the famous saying "Beware of Greeks bearing gifts." In other words—watch out if your enemy comes to your door with a present. It may be a trick!

definition

blacksmith
(BLAK smith) *noun* a person who heats iron over a large stove, then bends into shape.

*Bonnie the **blacksmith** burned her hand while making a horseshoe for Mrs. Fussbudget's prize stallion, Blue Beauty.*

THE ANCIENT ROMANS HAD GODS TOO

Their names were different than the Greek gods' names, but they filled basically the same roles.

GREEK	ROMAN
Zeus	Jupiter
Hera	Juno
Apollo	Apollo
Artemis	Diana
Athena	Minerva
Ares	Mars
Hermes	Mercury
Hephaestus	Vulcan
Poseidon	Neptune
Demeter	Ceres
Hestia	Vesta
Aphrodite	Venus
Dionysis	Bacchus

The Trojan Horse

14. In what type of dance do partners "do si do"?

(A) Square dance
(B) Ballet
(C) Break dance

Dance is an important part of most societies. Some dances are rituals thought to bring good luck, or rain, or a good harvest. Some dances have specific steps called **choreography**. Sometimes dancing is just catching the beat on your own and moving however you feel like moving.

Folk dance is a dance that is part of the popular tradition of a particular country. The square dance is a traditional American folk dance. Some other famous folk dances are the **Irish jig** and the **Polka**.

One of the most popular of folk dances, the twelfth-century chain dance had participants move from left to right, grabbing alternate hands as they moved down the chain. This style of dance were started by peasants and soon became popular with the nobility.

The **waltz** was the most fashionable dance of the 1800s. It started in Austria and Germany, but soon spread around the world. The waltz is performed to a special kind of music (also called a waltz).

In traditional African cultures, dance is an important part of life. Birth, death, harvesting, and festivals are all celebrated with dances. Some dances celebrate the passing of children into adulthood. Although there are many different tribes in Africa, most of their dances share certain characteristics. African dances generally

An Irish jig

definition

choreograph
(KOHR ee oh graf)
verb to design or plan the movements of a dance.

*Uma was having trouble **choreographing** a dance to her favorite Metallica tune, "Enter Sandman."*

The waltz

Disco dancing

Ballet dancing

Tribal dancing

DANCES FROM AROUND THE WORLD

Argentina	*Tango*
Caribbean	*Cha-Cha*
England	*Hornpipe*
Germany	*Waltz*
Ireland	*Jig*
Israel	*Hora*
Middle Europe	*Polka*
Scotland	*Highland Fling*

take place in a line, or a circle. Rarely do people dance alone or with a partner. Sometimes the dancers wear masks or special clothes.

Ballet began in Italy in the 1600s. Many ballets tell stories through choreographed movement. All ballet movements begin and end with one of the five basic positions (picture of the five positions), created to provide balance and look elegant. Some of the world's most famous ballet dancers have been Margot Fonteyn, Rudolf Nureyev, Mikhail Barishnikov, Anna Pavlova, and Isadora Duncan. Swan Lake, Coppelia, and Giselle are among the most famous ballets.

Many dances have come and gone through the years. **The Lindy** and the **Jitterbug** were popular dances of the 1940s, designed to be danced by couples to the music of the time. More recent dances are designed for you to go at it alone. The Twist, the Hustle, the Jerk, and break dancing, for example, don't require partners.

15. Who painted the Mona Lisa?

(A) DaVinci
(B) Picasso
(C) Michelangelo

From the earliest times, people have tried to represent and interpret the world around them. Paintings, sculptures, and even photographs communicate emotions and ideas and help us see the world in new ways. Art is one of the best ways to show a friend how you feel, capture a mood of celebration or sadness, or imagine how you'd like the world to be. The great artists of history have created art that continues to "speak" to people even today. Here are some of the artists who have made their mark.

Italy was an exciting place in the fifteenth and sixteenth centuries, the period known as the **Renaissance**. Many of the great inventions and art of the time happened there. The aim of the great thinkers of the Renaissance was to make people who were "complete human beings"—good at many different things, from art to science. **Leonardo DaVinci** (1452-1519) was one of the best examples of "the Renaissance Man," someone very well-rounded. Not only did he paint beautifully, he also invented many cool things. His early sketches detailed the human body and nature, and even included plans for parachutes and flying machines. One of the most famous paintings of all time, the **Mona Lisa**, which today hangs in the **Louvre Museum** in France, was done by Leonardo DaVinci. Who was Mona Lisa? No one knows for sure, but her mysterious smile has intrigued people for years.

Mona Lisa, by Leonardo DaVinci

Getting to Know the World's Great Artists. This series of paperbacks published by Children's Press has great full-color pictures and stories about many famous artists including Picasso, Botticelli, and Van Gogh.

Michelangelo's *David*

Rembrandt's *Self-portrait*

Michelangelo (1475-1564) was another of the great painters and sculptors of the Renaissance. His statue of **David** was the first giant nude sculpture since ancient Greece. Michelangelo also painted the beautiful murals on the ceiling of the **Sistine Chapel** in Rome, depicting scenes from the bible. The most amazing thing about the Sistine Chapel ceiling is that Michelangelo painted most of it while lying on his back on complicated scaffolding—over the course of several years!

The portraits painted by **Rembrandt** (1606-1669) are also very famous. Rembrandt was a Dutch painter of the seventeenth century. His use of light and dark and his ability to capture wonderful facial expressions make his work unique.

In the late 1800s, an artist named **Claude Monet** (1840-1926) turned the art world upside down with a new style of painting called Impressionism. Rather than trying to paint a picture realistically, Monet painted with dabs and dots of color to create a soft, fuzzy look that conveyed the feeling of light playing off of objects. Impressionism soon became very popular; it is the style of many famous painters such as Renoir, Pissaro, and Cezanne, among others.

Vincent Van Gogh (1853-1890) painted wild, impressionist

Sunflowers, by Vincent Van Gogh

Picasso's *Les Dasmoiselles D'Avignon*

paintings that used vivid colors to express energy and emotion. His famous works include "Sunflowers" and "Starry Night." Although he was a great artist, the story of Van Gogh's life is a very sad one. After a fight, Van Gogh cut off his own ear. Eventually he was sent to an asylum, where he died after a year.

In the twentieth century, artists tried new things. The Spanish artist **Pablo Picasso** (1881-1973) was one of the most innovative artists of this century. He tried many different styles, but is probably best known for his odd, angular paintings in which people look distorted and out of proportion. He also invented the style called **Cubism**, which makes ordinary things look like lots of squares and rectangles put together.

Salvador Dali (1904-1989) was another Spanish painter. He is famous for his "surreal" art— things that turned real life on its edge.

Mary Cassatt (1845-1926) was an American artist and one of the first famous women painters. Her impressionistic paintings often depict mothers with their children. Cassatt was influence by Japanese art, and she spent of her life in Paris.

Dali's *Persistence of Memory*

The Boating Party, by Mary Cassatt

Jackson Pollock (1912-1956) was famous for his huge canvases that are covered with paint splatters. This style, which Pollock helped invent, is known as **Abstract Expressionism**. Abstract Expressionists rebelled against the "normal" way of painting. They dribbled, splattered, and blobbed paint on the canvas to create pat-

One, by Jackson Pollack

terns and wild designs. One of Pollock's most famous works is entitled "One." What do you think of it?

Everyone has his own taste in art. You don't have to like all art, but when you get the chance you should check out different types of artists and see what you think of them.

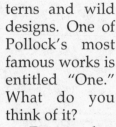

16. Which prophet founded the Muslim religion?

(A) Buddha

(B) Jesus Christ

(C) Mohammed

There are five major world **religions**. Let's go through each one in order, by number of followers.

There are 1.7 billion **Christians** in the world today. Christians are the followers of **Jesus Christ**, a Jew who lived in what is now Israel about 2,000 years ago. Throughout the years, Christians have divided into smaller churches, each with slightly different rules and traditions. The main churches within Christianity are the Protestant Church, the Roman Catholic Church and the Eastern Orthodox Church. The Christian Bible includes the Old and the New Testaments. The **New Testament** records the teachings of Jesus, while the **Old Testament** is just the Christian term for the Hebrew Bible—the holy book of Judaism. The holiest days of the Christian Calandar are Christmas (December 25, the celebration of the birth of Jesus) Palm Sunday (the Sunday before Easter, the day Jesus entered Jerusalem), Good Friday (the Friday before Easter, the day Jesus was crucified) and Easter Sunday (the day of Jesus's Resurrection from the dead).

The followers of the religion of **Islam** are called **Muslims**. There are 935 million Muslims in the world. Islam began in the seventh century when the prophet **Mohammed** founded the religion in Arabia. Mohammed was born in **Mecca**, Saudi Arabia, and every

Jesus Christ

Muslim tries to visit this holy city at least once in his or her lifetime. The Islamic religion is based upon a set of rules called the five pillars of Islam. Muslims worship one God, whom they call Allah. The holy book of Islam is the Koran, which Muslims believe to be the direct word of God as revealed to the prophet Mohammed. The Islamic festivals include the Day of Hijrah (the first day of the Islamic calendar), Ramadan (a month-long period of fasting), Eid ul-Fitr (the feast to mark the end of Ramadan), Lailat ul-Quadr (the Revelation of the Koran to Mohammed) Meelad ul-Nabi (Mohammed's birthday) and Lailut ul-Isra (the day of the death of Mohammed).

Hinduism is one of the world's oldest religions. It was founded more than 5,000 years ago in India. Today, there are 705 million Hindus in the world. There are many different sects of Hinduism, but all have in common the practice of worshipping not one god, but rather a group of gods. Although there are many Hindu gods, three of them are more important than the rest: **Vishnu**, **Brahma**, and **Shiva**. Vishnu comes to restore peace to the world. Brahma is the creator. He has four heads to show that he is all-knowing. Shiva is the destroyer, who rules over life and death. Hindus believe in reincarnation. Those who perform good deeds are reborn to a better life, while those who perform bad deeds may be reborn as animals or insects. The Hindu festivals include Holi (a two day spring festival), Janmashtami (a festival in honor of Krishna in August and September), Dussehra (10 days in September/October), and Diwali (a festival of lights).

Buddhism began in India as well, 2,500 years ago. Buddhists follow the teaching of **Buddha**. Buddha, born in 563 B.C., was originally named Siddhartha Gautama. He was a rich

Mohammed

A statue of the Hindu goddess, Shiva

prince who gave up his wealth and family after seeing the suffering in the world. He traveled and meditated and eventually achieved a state of complete understanding of the universe: Siddhartha became a monk and began teaching. Buddhist monks today give up all their possessions, keeping only a yellow robe, a needle, a razor, a water strainer and bowl. They beg for food and spend the rest of their day praying, teaching and meditating. Buddhists also believe in rebirth. They believe that a person's "karma"—a sort of tally of all the good and bad deeds in his life—will dictate how he is reborn. **Nirvana**, a state of absolute peace, may be achieved by following the Eightfold Path: rightness of views, intention, speech, action, livelihood, effort, mindfulness, and concentration. Some Buddhist festivals are Bodhi Day (the day Gautama became Buddha), Parinirvana (the passing of Buddha into Nirvana), Wesak or Vesakha Puja (a three day festival to celebrate Buddha's life), and Dharmacakra Day (when Buddha gave his first sermon).

Jews believe in one God who, 4,000 years ago, made a pact with **Abraham**. Jews believe that they are all descended from Abraham. Because of this pact, the Jews are the chosen people of God. They promise to obey God's laws and spread His word. Jews believe that a messiah, or messenger of God, will come to make the world a better place and restore the Jewish kingdom. There are many different sects in Judaism, which has seventeen million followers. Some follow stricter rules than others. Jewish people worship in a synagogue. They study two holy books: the **Torah** and the **Talmud**. The Torah, the most important, is the first five books of the Hebrew bible. The Talmud has the instructions for following a Jewish way of life and understanding Jewish laws. The holy days of the Jewish calendar include Rosh Hashanah (the Jewish New Year, in early autumn), Yom Kippur (the Day of Atonement, the holiest day, on the tenth day of the New Year), Passover (an eight-day spring festival), Sukkoth (the Feast of the Tabernacles, a nine-day autumn festival), Hanukkah (the festival of lights, an eight-day winter festival) and Purim (the feast of Lots, an early Spring festival).

ANSWERS

1. B	2. A	3. B	4. C	5. A	6. E	7. C	8. B	9. A	10. C
11. C	12. B	13. A	14. A	15. A	16. C				

Math

1. 3 + 4 =

   (A) 6

   (B) 7

   (C) 8

To handle addition problems with ease, you need to know these two things:

1. Think of the numbers you see as representing something in real life. . . think of the number "3" as 3 crayons for example, or 3 cats, or 3 fingers.

2. Now think of putting those things together. If your brother has 3 comics and you have 4 comics, you'll have 7 comics together (if you feel like sharing your comics); if you hold up 3 fingers on

definition

math

(math) *noun*, the study of numbers, amounts, and shapes and how these things are measured and related to one another.

*If you can learn **math**, you can learn anything.*

DON'T THINK, COUNT!

You could spend your whole life counting out whenever you have to add. Lots of people use their fingers and toes, but, as you can imagine, this can get messy and even rude if you have to take off your shoes in company. It's much easier in the long run to remember what numbers add up to. If you practice enough, you'll just know that 3 + 4 = 7 without having to count or think too hard.

one hand and 4 fingers on the other hand, you'll be holding up seven fingers altogether.

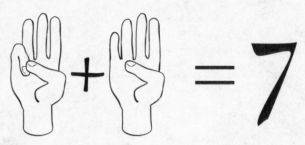

When you add, you can switch the order of the digits. The answer to any problem will be the same:

$$4 + 7 = 11 \quad 7 + 4 = 11$$
$$2 + 6 = 8 \quad 6 + 2 = 8$$

Here's a great way to practice addition. Have a grownup or older brother or sister make up a sheet with ten addition problems. Tell them to make sure all the problems are only single digit addition problems. Then ask that person to set a timer for sixty seconds (one minute) and see how many you can do in one minute. When you're starting out, you should do problems that use the same number, so you can get the hang of it. Like this:

$$1 + 1 =$$

$$1 + 2 =$$

$$1 + 3 =$$

$$1 + 4 =$$

$$1 + 5 =$$ **WHAT'S THE PATTERN?**

$$1 + 6 =$$

$$1 + 7 =$$

$$1 + 8 =$$

$$1 + 9 =$$

As you get better, have the person mix them up a little, like this:

3 + 2 =
4 + 1 =
5 + 3 =
7 + 2 =
5 + 5 =
4 + 7 =

When you get really good at this, try to do more than ten in one minute. Before you know it, addition will be easy.

2. What are the next two numbers in this pattern?

52, 54, 56, 58, 60, __, __
(A) 61, 62
(B) 65, 70
(C) 62, 64

How can you figure this one out? Maybe you knew it, because you noticed that the numbers were all even. Even numbers start with 2 and include every second number after that. Maybe you just thought about how these numbers could be counted out. Like this

52, 53, 54, 55, 56, 57, 58, 59, 60, 61, 62!

Whenever you do math, you should keep an eye out for patterns. Patterns are very important in math. You can find patterns all around you. Try to figure out the following patterns by filling in the missing shape:

definition

pattern
(PAH turn) *noun*, the way in which colors, shapes, or lines are arranged; a design.

*Filomena's dress had a neat flower **pattern** that made her look like a walking, talking, flower garden!*

No Numbers!

The Nambiquara Tribe of Brazil, South America, has no number system. They do have a word that means "they are alike," but, other than that, the Nambiquaras do not have a way of counting. Just try asking a Nambiquara how many fingers she has.

Where else can you find patterns? Look at flags on flagpoles. Do the colors on the flags have a pattern to them? Check out the petals on a flower, cars in a parking lot, or the squares in a game of "Candy Land" to see if you can spot the patterns.

THE PATTERN GAME

Ask a grownup to make up a number pattern and see if you can figure out what the next number will be.

Here are easy patterns:

2, 4, 6, 8, 10, 12, ___

5, 7, 9, 11, 13, 15, ___

Here are medium patterns:

5, 10, 15, 20, 25, 30, ___

10, 20, 30, 40, 50, ___

Here are difficult patterns:

3, 6, 9, 12, 15, ___

4, 8, 12, 16, 20, ___

3. What time is it?

(A) 6:00
(B) 6:30
(C) 7:30

A good way to start learning to tell time is to know hours and half hours. Let's take a clock and examine the pieces.

This is the beginning of every hour: whenever the minute hand (the long hand) points to the 12, a new hour has begun. To tell which hour has begun, take a look at the hour hand (the short hand). If the hour hand points to 6 and the minute hand points to 12, then you know that it is "six o'clock" or "6:00."

Now, look at the clock again. Notice that the 6 is straight down from the 12. If you made a line from 12 to 6, you'd cut the clock into two equal pieces. Whenever the minute hand is at the 6, the hour is half over. Since there are 60 minutes in an hour, and 30 is half of 60, that means that 30 minutes have passed. So, if you start at six o'clock, 30 minutes later it is "six thirty" or "6:30." What happened to the hour hand? It's halfway between the 6 and the 7, because we're half the way from 6 o'clock to 7 o'clock. Just remember to read the number that comes first (the 6) when you're reading the time. See how well you can do on the following clocks:

BIG TIME

The heaviest watch ever was on the Swiss Pavilion at Expo '86—a giant World's Fair. It weighed 38.5 tons— that's 77,000 pounds, more than six full-grown African elephants.

definition

digital clock
(DIJ i tel klok) *noun*, a clock that uses numbers only to show the time.

*Sammy got up at 7:00, when the alarm on his **digital clock** went off.*

I HATE TESTS!

Your teacher sometimes needs to see if everybody is understanding what he is teaching. One way to do this is to give a test. Nobody loves to take tests, but you can learn to like them. Here are some things to keep in mind:

1. Before you begin any test, make sure you completely understand what it is you're supposed to do. Don't guess—ask your teacher. Keep asking until you are completely sure of the instructions.

2. Go slowly. Kids often rush through tests and then end up making mistakes where they shouldn't. Go slowly and worry more about getting a question right than about getting to the end quickly.

3. Read each question carefully. Reading a simple problem like 4 + 3 as 4 - 3 will get you a wrong answer every time.

5. Don't worry about it. Your teacher just wants to see how you're doing. Relax and do your best. If you don't do your best, ask your teacher where you could do a little better next time.

FILL IN THE DIGITAL CLOCK TO MATCH THE READING ON THE ANALOG CLOCK

4. If Mary has 12 donuts and eats 3, how many will she have left?

    (A) 12

    (B) 15

    (C) 9

This is a subtraction problem. You could say "12 take away 3 is 9," or you could write 12 - 3 = 9, or you could write

$$\begin{array}{r} 12 \\ -\ 3 \\ \hline 9 \end{array}$$

definition

difference
(DIF ur ents) *noun,*
1. the amount left over when one number is subtracted from another number.

*The **difference** between 12 and 3 is 9.*

2. the way things are unlike each other.

*The **difference** between you and me is you are nice and I am mean.*

All three mean the same thing. Remember that subtraction means taking away. With addition, you get a **sum**; in subtraction, after you're finished taking one number away from another, what's left is called the **difference**. You can also say that the difference between 12 and 3 is 9.

$$12 - 3 = 9 \quad \text{and} \quad 9 + 3 = 12$$

See the pattern? Addition is the reverse of subtraction.

$$\begin{array}{cccc} 1 & 3 & 4 & 9 \\ +2 & -2 & +5 & -5 \\ \hline 3 & 1 & 9 & 4 \end{array}$$

Like addition, subtraction can be related to real things. If you've got 10 fingers, and you chop off 3 fingers, how many fingers will you have left?

And, just like in addition, with practice you'll be able to remember what the differences are between numbers, instead of counting out every time.

Now that you're an ace at addition, practice your subtraction. Just like before, start with ten problems, and have the person who helps you with them pick ones in which the numbers are kind of similar.

For example:

$9 - 1 =$ _____ $9 - 2 =$ _____ $9 - 3 =$ _____
$9 - 4 =$ _____ $9 - 5 =$ _____ $9 - 6 =$ _____
$9 - 7 =$ _____ $9 - 8 =$ _____ $9 - 9 =$ _____

Whenever you subtract a number from itself, the answer is zero. Listen to the sentence: "The difference between 9 and 9 is 0" or "9 take away 9 is zero."

CALVIN AND HOBBES copyright Watterson. Dist. by UNIVERSAL PRESS SYNDICATE. Reprinted with permission of UNIVERSAL PRESS SYNDICATE. All rights reserved.

5. How many crayons are there?

(A) 24
(B) 34
(C) 7

Let's say you've got a giant box of crayons. Your best friend wants to buy them from you (a good deal for you, since most of them are old and broken). Now, she tells you that she'll give you a quarter for every 100 crayons you have to sell. This could take all day--unless you think up a shortcut.

The quickest way to do this is to put your crayons in groups that are easy to count. A good group of crayons here would be 10. Why 10? Because 10 is not too big to count out, but not so small that it's a waste of time. Groups of 10 can be counted up to 100 easily. Grouping is a great "shortcut" for addition. For example, in the above question you do not need to count each crayon. You could notice that there are 3 groups of 10 and count them out, like this: 10, 20, 30. Then, all you need to do is count out the 4 single crayons and add them to the total of all your tens. Try it with any big bunch of stuff you have that you want to count out. Once you get it rolling, counting will not only be faster, but will probably be right more often. And if you lose count halfway through, it's a lot easier to catch up.

With this method of counting, you don't even have to count out each of the groups.

Once you lay out your first 10 crayons like this:

You really only have to line up the rest of the crayons like this:

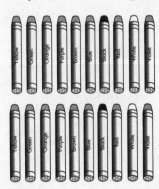

This works best for things that are about the same size. So, look around your house for collections of things you may want to count.

I'll Trade You This Gum Wrapper for That Comb

There are tons of cool things you can collect—autographs, books, cartoon strips, recipes. Some things are fun to collect when you travel all over the country and the world, like pennants and tee shirts. Some things are fun to collect just in your hometown, like models and trading cards. You can also collect things from nature, like butterflies, leaves, and rocks (p. 265)

Money is always the most fun. Just remember to sort by category, and then make your groups. Try different sized groups to see which count out quickest and easiest for you. You may prefer different sized groups for different things: groups of 20 for pennies, but groups of 10 for quarters. See if you can estimate how many you have in your collection before you start counting it out.

6. 24
     + 17

  (A) 41
  (B) 37
  (C) 31

Double-digit addition is very much the same as single-digit addition. Just take it step by step. Remember your digits? In a number with more than one digit, the "units" digit is the "ones" digit. In the number 24, 4 is the number of "ones" you have. The next digit over is called the "tens" digit. In other words, for the number 24, you have 2 "tens" plus 4 "ones." Where a digit is located in a number gives it a specific place value.

Look how the digit "4" changes value as we move it to different places:

    4
    40
    400

Now, to add together two-digit numbers, first you add together the units, or ones.

In the problem above, you have to add up:

    4
   +7
   11

Now, you have one "units" digit and one "tens" digit as a result. 4+7 is 11, which is one "ten" and one "one." Keep the ones digit in its

definition

place value
(place VAL yoo)
noun, the value given a number according to its place in the numeral.

The numeral 4 has a **place value** *of forty when it appears in the numeral 47.*

place and carry the "tens" digit up to
add together with the other tens digit
in step two of your problem.

1 (from the first step)

24

+17

41

Make sense? Just remember:

1. Add together the "ones" digits. If you end up with more than 9, write the "ones" digit in the "ones" place and carry over any "tens" to the "tens" place.

2. Add together the "tens" digits, including any carried over "tens" from the "ones" addition.

NUMBERS ABOVE A MILLION

Billion
1,000,000,000

Trillion
1,000,000,000,000

Quadrillion
1,000,000,000,000,000

Quintillion
1,000,000,000,000,000,000

Sextillion
1,000,000,000,000,000,000,000,000

Undecillion
1,000,000,000,000,000,000,000,000,000,000,000,000

---

7. Color in half of this circle.

So far, we've been talking about whole numbers. We talked about whole donuts and whole crayons. Now let's talk about parts of things--let's talk about fractions.

A fraction is simply a part of something. Here, you colored in half of the circle. We can also write that you colored in $\frac{1}{2}$ of the circle. The first fractions you need to know are these two: $\frac{1}{2}$ and $\frac{1}{4}$.

Any time you split something into two equal parts, you are dividing that thing into two halves. So if your sister wants to split an apple with you, she will take one half and you will take one half. The two halves put together make the whole apple.

definition

horizontal

(hohr a ZON tul)

adj., in line with the horizon, straight across, like the floor or the ground.

The carpenter held the level to the floor to make sure the floor was perfectly horizontal.

Halves ⟶

Whole ⟶

Now, if three friends come over, there are four of you, so when you split one apple into four exactly equal parts, you will be cutting that apple into quarters. Four equal parts of a whole make four separate quarters. You can say "one quarter" or you can write "$\frac{1}{4}$."

Quarter ⟶

Whole ⟶

Where have you heard this word before? Think about money: that's right—four quarters make up one dollar. A quarter is $\frac{1}{4}$ of one dollar.

2

8. Which of these figures is a triangle?

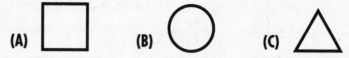

(A) (B) (C)

How many different shapes can you think of? The study of shapes is called geometry. Geometry is useful for all sorts of things. If you want to build something, for example, knowing the right shapes to use is very important.

Let's look at some shapes:

TRIANGLE   A TRIANGLE HAS THREE SIDES.

SQUARE   A SQUARE HAS FOUR SIDES OF EQUAL LENGTH.

RECTANGLE   A RECTANGLE HAS FOUR SIDES.

PENTAGON   A PENTAGON HAS FIVE SIDES.

HEXAGON   A HEXAGON HAS SIX SIDES.

OCTAGON   AN OCTAGON HAS EIGHT SIDES.

> ## definition
>
> **polygon**
> (PAHL ee gahn)
> *noun*, any figure that
> has three or more
> sides.
>
> *Triangles, squares,*
> *hexagons, etc, are all*
> *polygons.*

See how many shapes you can find around you. Which is the shape of a stop sign? Which is the shape of your favorite book?

9. How many pennies are in a dollar?

(A)   50
(B)   100
(C) 1,000

Open up your piggy bank. Chances are you'll see lots of different kind of coins and maybe even some bills.

Goooaal!
....

Sit across the table from your friend. Have your friend make a "goal" with his fingers. Take a quarter and start it at your end of the table. You get three taps on the quarter to get it to the other side and make a "goal." Be careful! If you knock the quarter off the table you lose your turn. After you get one try, pass the quarter to your friend and let her try. See who can get the most points.

A PENNY LOOKS LIKE THIS:

It is worth one cent. You would need 100 of these to be able to buy something that was worth one dollar. So, if you wanted a comic book that cost one dollar you could either hand over a dollar bill, or 100 pennies. How many pennies do you have ?

A NICKEL LOOKS LIKE THIS:

It is worth five cents. You need twenty of these to be able to buy something worth one dollar. How many pennies is a nickel equal to?

A DIME LOOKS LIKE THIS:

There are ten cents in each dime. Ten dimes are equal to a dollar. How many nickels in a dime?

A QUARTER LOOKS LIKE THIS:

There are twenty-five cents in each quarter. You need four quarters to equal a dollar. How many nickels are equal to a quarter?

A DOLLAR LOOKS LIKE THIS:

That's a one dollar bill. You can also get five dollar bills, ten dollar bills, twenty dollar bills, or if you are really lucky, 50 or 100 dollar bills. You'll have to save up those pennies for a long time to get a 100 dollar bill. Can you figure out how many? You'd need 10,000 pennies to trade for a 100 dollar bill. Can you even imagine how many pennies that is?

Just to make sure you understand how money works, try to answer this problem:

ALICE WANTS TO GO TO THE STORE TO BUY SOME REALLY GREAT FOOL'S GOLD AT ROCKS 'R US. SHE'S BEEN SAVING ALL HER MONEY IN HER PIGGY BANK AND THIS IS WHAT SHE HAS:

2 quarters

10 pennies

3 dimes

1 nickel

3 dollars

HER FAVORITE ROCK SPECIMEN HAS A PRICE TAG THAT SAYS $4.00. DOES SHE HAVE ENOUGH MONEY TO BUY IT?

ADD UP HER MONEY:

_____

Is that more than or less than $4.00? If Alice has more than $4.00, she'll be displaying her fool's gold at show and tell this week. If she has less than $4.00, she'll have to keep saving to get enough money to buy her rock!

10. 4 x 3 =
  (A) 7
  (B) 12
  (C) 16

You've already started grouping things together. When you have a bunch of groups that are all the same size, you can use multiplica-

tion to put them all together. Multiplication is just a shortcut for addition.

If you have a bunch of groups of pennies, like this,

and you want to know how many pennies you have all together, you can do a couple of things. You could count all the pennies, of course, but that would take a long time. You could make a number sentence, like this:

$$5 + 5 + 5 + 5 = \ ?$$

Or, you could multiply, and it would look like this:

$$5 \times 4 = ?$$

In other words, the second number sentence, 5×4, is the same thing as 5+5+5+5. 5×4 simply means "5, four times." Many people find that the easiest way to multiply is to memorize all the times tables. It's definitely a good idea to become acquainted with times tables.

TIMES TABLE

	2	3	4	5	6	7	8	9	10	11	12
2	4	6	8	10	12	14	16	18	20	22	24
3	6	9	12	15	18	21	24	27	30	33	36
4	8	12	16	20	24	28	32	36	40	44	48
5	10	15	20	25	30	35	40	45	50	55	60
6	12	18	24	30	36	42	48	54	60	66	72
7	14	21	28	35	42	49	56	63	70	77	84
8	16	24	32	40	48	56	64	72	80	88	96
9	18	27	36	45	54	63	72	81	90	99	108
10	20	30	40	50	60	70	80	90	100	110	120
11	22	33	44	55	66	77	88	99	110	121	132
12	24	36	48	60	72	84	96	108	120	132	144

To read the times table, just find the two numbers you want to multiply. Use our example, 4 and 5. Find the 4 on one side of the table and the 5 on the other. Run your finger along the line down from 4 and along the line across from 5. Where those two lines meet is the answer to 4 times 5. 4 × 5 = 20!!!

There are lots of ways to make times tables easier to understand. For example, when you multiply a number by ten, you just put a zero at the end of the number. 5 × 10 = 50, 2 × 10 = 20. If you think that was cool, run your finger along the 2 line. Isn't it just like counting by twos? Now run your finger along the 5 line. Isn't it like counting by fives? Look for patterns like these on the times table. It will make it easier to remember.

11. Which even number is greater than 14 but less than 17?

(A) 15

(B) 16

(C) 16 $\frac{1}{2}$

To solve this problem, you have to think about three different things. The first thing you need to find out is the group, or set, of numbers that is greater than 14. To do this, it is best to look at a number line.

| 0 1 2 3 4 5 6 7 8 9 10 11 12 13 14 15 16 17 18 19 20 |

All the numbers after 14 are the numbers that are greater than 14.

| 0 1 2 3 4 5 6 7 8 9 10 11 12 13 14 15 16 17 18 19 20 |

All the numbers before 17 are the numbers that are less than 17.

There are only two numbers that fall into both groups. Can you spot them? They are 15 and 16.

Now, let's talk about odd and even numbers. You can find all the even numbers by starting at two and counting every other one.

The following are even numbers:

2, 4, 6, 8, 10, 12, 14, 16, 18, 20, 22, 24, 26, and so on and so on.

Odd numbers are every other number.

1, 3, 5, 7, 9, 11, 13, 15, 17, 19, 21, 23, 25, 27, and so on and so on.

So, if you asked yourself which number is all three things—greater than 14, less than 17 and even—there'd only be one answer: 16.

Most kids have a hard time dealing with all the information in a word problem. Look at the way we solved the problem above. We broke the problem up into pieces to figure it out. This is the best way to approach word problems--especially if you are having trouble. In this problem you needed to know:

GREATER THAN
LESS THAN
EVEN NUMBERS

All the pages on this side of the book are even numbers

Breaking the problem into those pieces helps you sort it out more easily. Once you sort out the parts of a problem, you can take it step by step.

12. 4,237 =

   (A) 4 thousands + 2 hundreds + 3 tens + 7 ones

   (B) 4 ten-thousands + 2 thousands + 3 hundreds + 7 tens

   (C) 4 hundreds + 2 thousands + 3 tens + 7 ones

Once you start getting into double digits, it's time to learn about three-, four-, five-, and six-digit numbers—and even bigger ones, too. Take a look at the different place values, using a very, very large number:

2, 3 4 7, 6 9 0

0 IS THE UNITS DIGIT

9 IS THE TENS DIGIT

6 IS THE HUNDREDS DIGIT

7 IS THE THOUSANDS DIGIT

4 IS THE TEN THOUSANDS DIGIT

3 IS THE HUNDRED THOUSANDS DIGIT

2 IS THE MILLIONS DIGIT

You could also say this number like this: "2 million, 3 hundred and 47 thousand, 6 hundred and 90," or write out 2 millions, 3 hundred thousands, 4 ten thousands, 7 thousands, 6 hundreds, 9 tens and 0 ones. If you get a problem like this the tricky thing to remember is that teachers sometimes switch around the order, like this:

7 ONES

9 HUNDREDS

5 THOUSANDS

6 TENS

What does that equal?

WRITE THE FOLLOWING AS NUMBERS:

1. Fifty-six thousand, seven hundred and eighty-three.
2. Forty-nine thousand, seventy-one.
3. Five thousand, nine hundred and sixty-seven.
4. Forty-three
5. Ninety thousand, one hundred and seventy-six.

All the pages on this side of the book are odd numbers

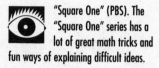

"Square One" (PBS). The "Square One" series has a lot of great math tricks and fun ways of explaining difficult ideas.

Watch out! It doesn't equal 7,956—it equals 5,967! Make sure to read place value questions very carefully. Always line the number up in order; the largest number starting on the left and the smallest number on the right. Here, the largest number was a thousands place and the smallest was a ones (or units) place.

What if there's a missing place? Just put in a zero to "hold" that place. For example, if you read that a number has:

4 THOUSANDS
3 ONES
6 HUNDREDS

You need to write 4,603. The zero is in the tens place because there are no tens. If you just leave out the tens place completely, you would have written 463, which would make your number too small. The 4 has to be in the thousands place, and the 6 has to be in the hundreds place. The only way to hold them to their right places is to put that zero in there.

13. Brian needs two cups of milk to make hot chocolate. He has 1 and $\frac{1}{4}$ cups already. How much more milk does he need?

(A) He needs $\frac{3}{4}$ cup of milk.

(B) He needs $\frac{1}{4}$ cup of milk.

(C) He needs $\frac{1}{2}$ cup of milk.

definition

estimate

(ES tim ayt) *verb*, to form a general idea about, to make a careful guess.

I estimate you'll need about two hours to finish that project.

When you see a word problem, you need to figure out what to do. First, read the problem all the way through. Don't start writing down any numbers until you've read the whole thing. When you see the line that asks the question you need to answer, underline it. It will help you to keep zeroed in on your goal.

To do question 13, you would do this:

Brian needs two cups of milk to make hot chocolate. He has 1 and $\frac{1}{4}$ cup already. How much more milk does he need?

Write down on a piece of scrap paper, or on the page, the numbers you are given.

Here, you are given the numbers 2 and $1\frac{1}{4}$

Look for key words in the question—"How much more," or "less," "difference," "sum," "all together." Those words help you understand what you need to do.

In this problem you need to know how much more 2 is than $1\frac{1}{4}$.

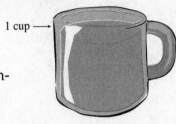

1 cup →

Look at what you have:
 What is the difference between the two? Write a number sentence to represent it:

$$2 - 1\frac{1}{4} = \frac{3}{4}$$

Now check your answer.

 Check a subtraction question by adding. If you know that:

$$2 - 1\frac{1}{4} = \frac{3}{4},$$

1/4 →
cup

then

$$\frac{3}{4} + 1\frac{1}{4} = 2$$

Just flip the problem around and see if it works with the opposite operation (adding instead of subtracting).
 When you have a question with fractions remember that to get a whole, you need the top of the fraction to be the same number as the bottom of the fraction. Like this:

$$\frac{4}{4} = 1 \qquad \frac{3}{3} = 1 \qquad \frac{7}{7} = 1 \qquad \frac{100}{100} = 1$$

So, if you have $\frac{1}{4}$, you need to get to $\frac{4}{4}$ to make a whole.

$$\frac{1}{4} + \frac{3}{4} = \frac{4}{4} = 1$$

Finally, have a rough idea in your head about what the answer should be before you start working it out. Here, for example, you had more than a cup of milk, and you need to have two cups altogether. If you had gotten an answer that was more than one, you would have been wrong. Coming up with a rough idea about the answer before you start is called **estimating**. Estimating will keep you from making careless errors.

14. How many inches are in a foot?

    (A) 16

    (B) 5 (or is that toes?)

    (C) 12

Once upon a time, years ago, old Farmer Monty wanted to go into town to sell his cow. He told people, "I have this really nice cow for sale—cheap." And what did they ask? (What would you ask?)

"Hey, Monty, how big is that cow? Maybe we could make a deal."

And Monty replied,

"Hey, my cow is big—as big as my wife, Bertha."

Now, none of these people knew Bertha, so they didn't know how big Bertha was. Monty was in trouble. No one bought the cow.

The End.

To solve this problem, thousands of years ago, in places like ancient Egypt, people started measuring things using body parts. For example, Monty could have said his cow was 15 hands tall. Of course, people don't all have hands the same size, so it still wasn't a perfect system, but it gave people a general idea.

Eventually people decided to make standard sizes for things. That means that when someone says, "That watermelon is a foot long," anyone can pick up a ruler and know exactly how big that watermelon is. There are scientists who have set all these sizes exactly, so a foot in Minnesota is the same as a foot in New York. There are two main "languages" of measurement: one is called the imperial system, and the other is the metric system. The imperial system uses feet, yards, and quarts. We use it in the U.S. The metric system, which is used in most other countries, measures in meters, kilometers, and liters. The United States has been trying to go metric, but we're pretty stuck on our inches and pounds. The only metric amount you probably hear regularly is the liter (for soda bottles), which is a little less than a quart.

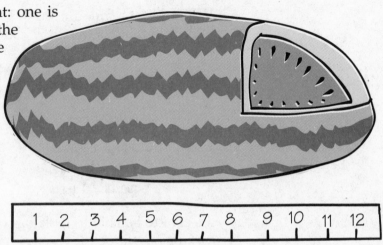

How do you measure the length of your pencil? How tall you are? What is the area of a soccer field? Generally, we use rulers and tape measures to get these measurements.

Some measurements of length are:

THE IMPERIAL SYSTEM	THE METRIC SYSTEM
12 inches = 1 foot	10 millimeters = 1 centimeter
3 feet = 1 yard	100 centimeters = 1 meter
1,760 yards = 1 mile	1,000 meters = 1 kilometer

How do you measure how much you weigh, or how much a sack of potatoes at the grocery store weighs? To measure weight, you'll need a scale

Units of weight are:

THE IMPERIAL SYSTEM	THE METRIC SYSTEM
16 ounces = 1 pound	1,000 grams = 1 kilogram
2,000 pounds = 1 ton	1,000 kilograms = 1 tonne

Volume is the amount of space something takes up. How much milk is in that container in your refrigerator? You need measuring cups to measure volume.

Some volume measurements are:

IMPERIAL	METRIC
2 cups = 1 pint	1 milliliter = 1 cubic centimeter
2 pints = 1 quart	1,000 millileters = 1 liter
4 quarts = 1 gallon	1,000 liters = 1 cubic meter

It's cool to be able to look at something and have an idea how big it is, or how much it weighs. You don't always have a measuring cup or a ruler or a scale on you. With practice you should be able to pick up a sack of potatoes and have a good idea what it weighs even if there's no scale around. How do you get this skill?

Whenever you have to measure something, take a guess first what you think it will be. Estimate the size of your foot, your weight, your height. Then, check it out—see how close your estimate is. After many years of doing this you will have an expert eye!

15. On Saturday, Jane had a party for 27 children. 18 had pizza, and the rest had hot dogs. How many had hot dogs?

(A) 9
(B) 10
(C) 2

We know that subtraction means taking away. But what do you do if you need to subtract two numbers whose units digits don't subtract so easily?

$$\begin{array}{r} 20 \\ -\ 7 \\ \hline \end{array}$$

You are not subtracting 7 from 0, you are subtracting 7 from 20. When you have 20 and subtract 7 you are left with 13. You can go grab a plate of 20 hot dogs or something, and take away 7, and see. The way you make this work in a subtraction problem is to borrow. You borrow whenever the digit you are subtracting is bigger than the digit you are subtracting from. In this problem, you borrow 1 from 2 which is in the tens place, to make the units digit of 0, bigger. You leave the leftover 1 in the tens column. Together the two ones make up the 2 that is in the tens place. Remember the 2 in the tens place really means 20.

$$\begin{array}{r} {}^{1}2\!\!\!/0 \\ -\ 7 \\ \hline \end{array}$$

You now have 10 minus 7, which gives you 3. You also have a 1 still left in the tens place because you started out with 2.

$$\begin{array}{r} {}^{1}2\!\!\!/0 \\ -\ 7 \\ \hline 3 \end{array}$$

Since there is no digit in the tens place of 7, you are subtracting nothing from 1. You are left with that same 1 in the tens place of your answer, which gives you 13.

$$\begin{array}{r} {}^{1}2\!\!\!/0 \\ -\ 7 \\ \hline 13 \end{array}$$

You can borrow just the same when there is a 0 in the tens or the hundreds place. Here's how it looks.

$$100 \atop \underline{-7}$$

To subtract the 7 from the 0, instead of borrowing a 1 from yet another annoying 0, you treat the hundreds and the tens digit as one number, the number 10.

$$100 \atop \underline{-7}$$

Grab a 1 for your units place 0 and get 10 - 7 = 3. and what do you have left after you take the 1 from the 10? 9, definitely.

$$\begin{array}{r} {}^{9}\cancel{100}{}^{1} \\ -7 \\ \hline 93 \end{array}$$

So, 100 - 7 = 93. If you are subtracting a number that involves carrying from more than one place, you will still be fine. Like:

$$\begin{array}{r} 1,030 \\ -35 \\ \hline \end{array}$$

Borrow a 1 from the 3 in the tens place for the units place 0, and you get 10 minus 5, which is 5.

$$\begin{array}{r} 1,0\overset{2}{\cancel{3}}\overset{1}{0} \\ -35 \\ \hline 5 \end{array}$$

Now you have a 2 in the tens place, because you borrowed a 1, and to subtract 3 from 2 you need to borrow another 1 from the 10 in the hundreds and the thousands place. You have 12.

$$9\overset{12\ 1}{\cancel{1,0\cancel{3}0}} \\ \underline{-\ \ 35} \\ 95$$

12 minus 3 is 9, and you still have the 9 left over from when you borrowed 1 from 10 in the hundreds and thousands place.

$$9\overset{12\ 1}{\cancel{1,0\cancel{3}0}} \\ \underline{-\ \ 35} \\ 995$$

16. Which fraction is largest?

(A) $\dfrac{1}{3}$

(B) $\dfrac{1}{6}$

(C) $\dfrac{1}{2}$

Think about it as getting a pie at the bakery and cutting it up. Or, if you're on a diet or something horrible like that, take a look at the handy illustrations.

If you cut the pie into 8 slices, you get smaller slices than if you cut the pie into 2 gigantic slices. So $\frac{1}{8}$ is smaller than $\frac{1}{2}$. Here's an even easier way to compare fractions so you don't have to draw pictures of pies at awkward moments. Call it the bow tie.

definition

denominator
(dee NAHM i nay tohr) *noun*, the number below the line in a fraction.

In the fraction 5/8, 8 is the denominator.

numerator
(NOOM er ay rohr)
noun, the number
above the line in a
fraction.

*In the fraction 5/8, 5 is
the numerator.*

Try multiplying the denominator (remember the number on the
bottom is the denominator) of the fraction on the right by the
numerator (the number on top) on the left and put the product
above the fraction on the left.

Now, multiply the denominator of the fraction on the left by the
numberator of the fraction on the right and put that product over
the fraction on the right.

Now which is bigger, 18 or 25? 25, so the fraction under the 25 is
the bigger fraction. If someone offers you $\frac{3}{5}$ or $\frac{5}{6}$ of a million dollars, take the $\frac{5}{6}$.

**17. David keeps his CDs on shelves that hold 12 CDs each. He
has four shelves completely filled. How many CDs does
David own?**

(A) 48
(B) 24
(C) 16

By now you should know your
multiplication tables backwards
and forwards. If you don't, this
is a good time to get someone to
quiz you on it so that at least
you know all the numbers from
1-10. Refer to the times table (p.
165) if you need help.

What if you want to multiply a number that's not on the times table? Something like this:

$$
\begin{array}{r}
35 \\
\times\ 26 \\
\hline
\end{array}
$$

You can't look that one up, and you'd never be able to memorize that many numbers. Luckily for you, you can break it up into all the pieces you do know, multiply those pieces, and then add the pieces together.

$$
\begin{array}{r}
{\scriptstyle 3} \\
35 \\
\times\ 6 \\
\hline
210
\end{array}
$$

What we did: First multiply 6 by the units place number, 5. 6×5 is 30. Leave the 0 in the units place and carry the 3 up to the tens place. 6×3 (the tens place) is 18. You have to add the 3 extra tens from the 30. $18 + 3 = 21$. So, $35 \times 6 = 210$.

$$
\begin{array}{r}
{\scriptstyle 1} \\
35 \\
\times\ 20 \\
\hline
700
\end{array}
$$

Now we multiply the tens digit, 20. Just put a 0 in the units place to hold it. Now, 2×5 is 10. Put the 0 down and carry up the 1 to the tens place. 2×3 is 6 and add the extra 1. So, $35 \times 20 = 700$.

Now, you just add 700 and 210 to get 910. Here's how it would look all together:

$$
\begin{array}{r}
{\scriptstyle 1\ 3} \\
35 \\
\times\ 26 \\
\hline
210 \\
+\ 700 \\
\hline
910
\end{array}
$$

definition

distribute
(di STRIB yoot) *verb*,
to deal out in share.

*He **distributed** the money among all the club members.*

Why does it work? Because of something called the distributive property. That means:

23 x 6 = (20 x 6) + (3 x 6)
20 x 6 = 120 and 3 x 6 = 18, so 23 x 6 = 120 + 18 or 138.

This is a good way to multiply big numbers in your head. Just break them up into pieces and add up all the pieces.

18. Round to the nearest thousand and add:

1,274
<u>2,648</u>

(A) 3,000
(B) 4,000
(C) 5,000

First of all, let's talk about how you round off a number. Take a small number, like 12, and round it to the nearest ten.

---

1 2 3 4 5 6 7 8 9 10 11 12 13 14 15 16 17 18 19 20

Look at the number line. When you round a number you take it to the nearest number of the group you are rounding to on the number line. Since you want to round to the nearest ten, you would round 12 to 10, not 20. 12 is closer to 10 than it is to 20.

Now, try rounding 325 to the nearest hundred. Again, think of a number line.

---

100 125 150 175 200 225 250 275 300 325 350 375 400

Now, which hundred is 325 nearer to—300 or 400?

Since 325 is nearer to 300, you would round 325 to 300 if you were rounding to the nearest hundred.

What if you were rounding 325 to the nearest ten? Let's go to the number line, one more time:

320 321 322 323 324 325 326 327 328 329 330

325 lies between 320 and 330. As a matter of fact, it lies exactly in the middle. If you are rounding and the number falls smack in the middle, the rule is to round up. 325 rounded to the nearest 10 is 330.

Why bother? That's the important question. Actually, rounding is a very important tool in mathematics. It has to do with estimating and making good guesses. You may not be able to add 36,795 and 22,126 fast in your head, but you can round off the numbers quickly to their nearest thousand, like this:

$$\begin{array}{r} 37,000 \\ +\ 22,000 \\ \hline 59,000 \end{array}$$

And now you can add them quickly in your head.

Look at the actual addition:

$$\begin{array}{r} 36,795 \\ +\ 22,176 \\ \hline 58,971 \end{array}$$

Rounding off got you pretty close to the right answer. You'll find there are many times that you need to do a rough calculation. You may have a grocery cart full of food and need to make sure you have enough money, or you may need to split the bill at a restau rant into 3 parts to get a rough idea of what each person owes.

Rounding off is an important skill. Practice it. When you go t the store, round off your purchases as you pick them up and se how close you are when it all gets added up at the cash register.

19. Refer to the following graph:

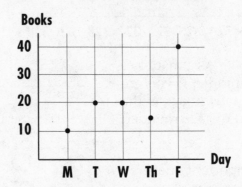

On which day were the most books sold?

(A) Friday

(B) Thursday

(C) Wednesday

A graph is made by taking two lines and making them intersect s that they look like a big plus sign, like this:

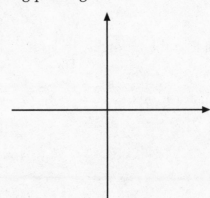

definition

intersect

(in ter SEKT) *verb,* to meet and cross.

Two straight, non-parallel lines **intersect** *at only one point.*

The line that moves horizontally is called the X axis, and the line that moves vertically is called the Y axis.

Graphs are a great way to organize information. For example, look at the following chart:

DAY	Temperature Outside	Number of Ice Cream Cones Sold
Mon	75	3
Tues	85	13
Wed	70	2
Thur	90	15
Fri	80	10

Now, if you put them on a graph, so that the X axis shows the temperature and the Y axis shows the number of cones sold, look what you can find out:

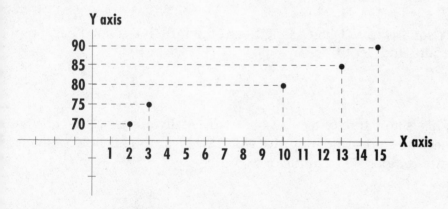

You can see clearly that the hotter the day is, the more ice cream cones are sold. Graphs show the relationship between two different things. If you want to know what the temperature was on the day the most ice cream cones were sold, look to the x that marks the spot farthest along the X axis (number of cones sold). That number is 15. Now follow the line along to the Y graph to see that the temperature was 90 degrees. Each spot on this graph represents two numbers—the number of cones sold and the temperature.

4

20. Which figure is a cylinder?

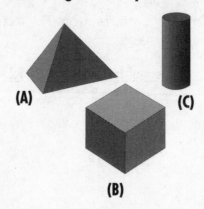

(A)

(C)

(B)

A **three-dimensional**, or solid, figure, is different from a two-dimensional, or plane, figure, because it has depth. For example:

A square ⬜ has a length and a width, but a cube has length, width and depth.

This is a picture of a cube . To really appreciate a cube, you need to find something that you can pick up and hold. A pair of dice is a perfect example of two cubes:

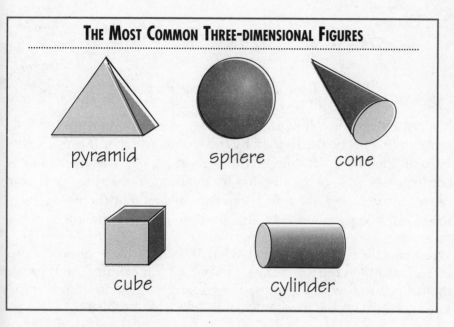

THE MOST COMMON THREE-DIMENSIONAL FIGURES

pyramid   sphere   cone

cube   cylinder

2 circles +
1 rectangle =
1 cylinder

1 triangle +
1 circle =
1 cone

Three-dimensional figures are made by taking a few two-dimensional figures and putting them together. For example, a cube is six squares put together. A cylinder is two circles (top and bottom) and a rectangle made into a tube. Can you see the different two-dimensional figures that make up each three-dimensional figure?

21. What is the answer to the division problem below?

8)976

(A) 142
(B) 976
(C) 122

You may see a division problem written in many different ways:

remainder
(ree MAYN der)
noun, the difference, the rest, what's left over.

*The **remainder** of the books were sold at a discount price.*

MULTIPLY IN REVERSE

Division is the opposite of multiplication. You can check all your division questions by multiplying the answer by the number you were dividing by. Go back to the division problem $8\overline{)976}$ *, and check this out:*

$$\begin{array}{r} 122 \\ \times\ 8 \\ \hline 976 \end{array}$$

That's a really good way to check yourself if you are unsure about an answer.

$$976 \div 8 \quad \text{or} \quad 8\overline{)976} \quad \text{or} \quad \frac{976}{8}$$

These all mean the same thing.

Just remember the following rules. If you see ÷, that means the first number (976) is being divided by the second number (8). You'd say "976 divided by 8." If you see this sign $\overline{)}$, that means the number inside (976) is being divided by the number outside (8). If you see a bar (yes, just like a fraction) that means that the number on top (976) is being divided by the number on the bottom (8).

What exactly is division? Just what it sounds like—dividing up. Here, I want to take 976 things, candy bars, for example, and break them up into 8 equal groups. How many will be in each group? Let's go through the mechanics of the division problem:

As in all math problems, we'll work step by step:

$$8\overline{)976}$$

First, ask yourself: How many 8s can go into 9? Only one. So, write a one right above the 9. If you multiply 1 (because 8 only goes into 9 one time) by 8, you get 8. That's what you put right underneath the 9. Like this:

$$\begin{array}{r} 1 \\ 8\overline{)976} \\ 8 \end{array}$$

Draw a line under that 8, just like we drew, and subtract 8 from 9. In other words, you want to see how many 8s go into 9 (just 1) and what's left over (1). Now we're going to drop down the next digit, 7, to look like this:

$$\begin{array}{r} 1 \\ 8\overline{)976} \\ -8 \\ \hline 17 \end{array}$$

Now, how many 8s go into 17?

Two. And 2 x 8 is 16. Here's what you get:

```
    12
  8)976
   -8
    17
   -16
     1
```

1 is left over again. Now drop down the last digit, 6. Now you have 16. How many times does 8 go into 16? 2 times, and that's it—nothing left over. Like this:

```
    122
  8)976
   -8
    17
   -16
     16
    -16
      0
```

The number at the top is your answer. Now, no matter how a division problem is written out, if there are more than two or three digits in either of the numbers, this is the easiest way to do it.

But here's another question: what would you have done if there were anything other than 0 left at the end? Just write that leftover number next to the answer as the remainder. Like this: 22 ÷ 5 = 4 r2. That means that you can divide 22 into 5 equal groups of 4 each, but you'll have 2 left over.

22. $\dfrac{4}{20}$ =

(A) $\dfrac{1}{4}$

(B) $\dfrac{2}{5}$

(C) $\dfrac{1}{5}$

Take a look at a pie, sliced up into little pieces (20 to be exact).

definition

reduce

(ree DOOS) *verb*, to make lesser or smaller in quantity or amount.

That store finally **reduced** *the price on my favorite CD.* **Reducing** *fractions makes the number in the numerator and denominator smaller, but the whole value of the fraction remains the same.*

Take a look at the same pie, cut into 5 pieces

Notice this: You can eat 4 pieces of the pie cut into 20 pieces and it would be EXACTLY the same as eating 1 piece of the pie cut into 5 pieces.

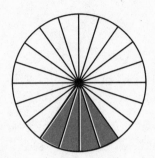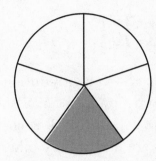

That's because $\frac{4}{20}$ is exactly the same thing as $\frac{1}{5}$.

Many times, you'll find that it's easier to use a fraction made up of smaller numbers, like $\frac{1}{5}$, in a problem, instead of one with bigger numbers like $\frac{4}{20}$. How can you turn a fraction like $\frac{4}{20}$ into one like $\frac{1}{5}$? By reducing.

To reduce a fraction, all you need to do is divide both the numerator and the denominator by the same number. Here you can divide both the top and the bottom by 4:

$$4 \div 4 = 1$$
$$20 \div 4 = 5$$

If a good number to use doesn't pop into your head, you can reduce bit by bit. An easy way to reduce fractions that have even numbers is to divide by 2. Say you just noticed that 4 and 20 were both even numbers. Divide them both by 2 and get:

$$4 \div 2 = 2$$
$$20 \div 2 = 10$$

$\frac{2}{10}$ is a reduced form of $\frac{4}{20}$. But not all the way, because you may notice that you can divide both 2 and 10 by 2 again:

÷ 2

A number is divisible by 2 if: It is even.
Examples: 4, 18, 22, 26, 104, are all divisible by 2.

÷ 3

A number is divisible by 3 if: It's digits add up to a number divisible by 3.
Examples: 123 is divisible by 3 because $1 + 2 + 3 = 6$, which is divisible by 3. 81 is divisible by 3 because $8 + 1 = 9$, which is divisible by 3. 27 is divisible by 3 because $2 + 7 = 9$ and 9 is divisible by 3.

÷ 5

A number is divisible by 5 if: It ends in a 5 or a 0.
Examples: 25, 85, 90, 10550, 1,765 are all divisible by 5.

÷ 10

A number is divisible by 10 if: It ends in a zero.
Examples: 10, 200, 450, 560 are all divisible by 10.
AND to divide by 10, just slash off that last 0 for Example:
$$\frac{450}{10} = 45$$

$$2 \div 2 = 1$$
$$10 \div 2 = 5$$

There you go—you've reduced $\frac{2}{10}$ further to become $\frac{1}{5}$. When you reduce a fraction, you can always start off by trying to reduce it by easy numbers like 2 or 3. Then, there are some tricks to check out if numbers are divisible by other numbers. Look at the sides of the page.

4

23. How many pints in a quart?
    (A) 2
    (B) 4
    (C) 8

You may remember that pints and quarts are measurements of volume. That means that they measure how things take up space. To fill a cup, a bowl, or a soda can, you need to know the volume of liquid or whatever will fill up that size.

definition

volume
(VAHL yoom) *noun*, the amount of space that something takes up.

*The **volume** of a basketball is more than the volume of a tennis ball.*

Volume is important. You may be cooking and have only a 4-ounce cup. You'd need to know how many of those 4-ounce cups to use to make 2 cups. Someday, you may want to know how many quarts of juice to buy to have enough for you and three of your friends. If you don't, someone may go thirsty, and that someone will most likely be you! To avoid such an embarrassing situation, read on.

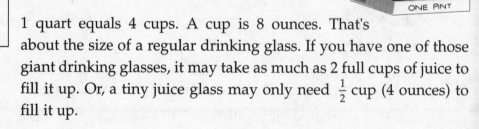

1 quart equals 4 cups. A cup is 8 ounces. That's about the size of a regular drinking glass. If you have one of those giant drinking glasses, it may take as much as 2 full cups of juice to fill it up. Or, a tiny juice glass may only need $\frac{1}{2}$ cup (4 ounces) to fill it up.

Here's another everyday situation that shows how important it is to understand volume. What if someone asks you to go to the store a buy a gallon of milk and you get there and you see the following sign:

Milk by the Quart on Sale!   **Milk by the Gallon**
$.50 today only!   **$2.50**

Well, because you are a whiz at math and measurement, you know that 4 quarts equal a gallon and that 4 x .50 = $2.00. $2.50 - $2.00 = $.50. You buy 4 quarts rather than 1 gallon and save $.50.

24. Convert this number to a decimal:

$$1\frac{3}{10} = \underline{\hspace{2cm}}$$

(A) 1.3
(B) 0.13
(C) 13.0

A decimal is just another type of fraction. Decimals can be a shortcut. Any fraction that has as its denominator a 10, 100, 1000 or any multiple of 10 can be converted into a decimal. Some examples:

$$\frac{3}{10} \quad = \quad .3$$

$$\frac{3}{100} \quad = \quad .03$$

$$\frac{23}{100} \quad = \quad .23$$

$$\frac{1}{10} \quad = \quad .1$$

definition

decimal point
(DES i mil poynt)
noun, the dot that separates the units digit from the decimal part of a number.

12.68
↑
decimal point

Here's how it works: That first space to the right of the decimal point is called the TENTHS digit. If a fraction is a tenth, like $\frac{2}{10}$, or $\frac{3}{10}$ or $\frac{4}{10}$, it will end right there.

$$\frac{2}{10} = 0.2$$

↑

tenths place

The second place to the right of the decimal point is the hundredths place. Any fraction written as over 100 will end there. For example: $\frac{2}{100}$, $\frac{24}{100}$, $\frac{34}{100}$. If you see more than one digit over one hundred, remember to write the number so that the last digit is in the hundredths place:

$$\frac{24}{100} = 0.24$$

↑

hundredths place

$$\frac{2}{100} = 0.02$$

↑

hundredths place

You've actually been working with decimals for a long time. You use decimals to write down dollar amounts. Why? Because dollars are broken up into 100 pieces—so all the parts of a dollar can be written as parts of 100. If I have 25 cents, for example, that's:

25 (pennies)
_____
100 (the number of pennies in a whole dollar)

Instead of writing $\frac{25}{100}$ for 25 cents, we write .25. How would you write 10 cents? .10 is 10 out of a possible 100 cents or $\frac{10}{100}$. So a good way to think about decimals right now is to think about money.

To add or subtract two decimals, you simply need to line up the decimal points and add or subtract, just like any other number. For example:

To add 2.35 and 12.8, you would write them out like this.

```
   12.8
 + 2.35
  15.15
```

Just remember to keep the decimal point in line and carry it down to the answer in the same spot and you can't go wrong.

25.   5,000
     x 400

   (A) 20,000
   (B) 2,000
   (C) 2,000,000

Really big numbers that are followed by lots of zeros are called multiples of 10. That means that the number 10 can be divided into that number perfectly (with no remainder). Any time you see a number that ends in a zero, that number is a multiple of 10. Another way of saying that is to say that 10 is a factor of that number. A factor is any number that divides perfectly into the number you are given.

definition

multiple
(MUL ti pul) *noun*, a number which is the product of a specific number and another number.

10 and 45 are multiples of 5, because 5 x 2 = 10 and 5 x 8 = 45.

Some multiples of 10 are:

100
500
5,000
26,000
247,970
60,000,000

As long as you see a zero at the end of a number, you can divide 10 into that number. But right now, let's focus on multiplying numbers with lots of zeros in them. First of all, you need to remember the zero rule:

Any number multiplied by zero is equal to zero.

Therefore:

1 x 0 = 0
10 x 0 = 0
5,000 x 0 = 0
26,597,457 x 0 = 0

No matter what the number, or how big or confusing it looks, if you multiply it by zero it will be zero. That makes sense, because multiplication just means times. If we give you $5,000 zero times, you'd have zero. We could also give you zero dollars 5,000 times and you'd still have zero dollars (although you'd be really annoyed.)

When you are multiplying big numbers with lots of zeros, you can do it the long way:

5,000	
x 400	
0000	(units place zero times 5,000)
0000	(tens place zero times 5,000)
20,000	(hundreds place 4 times 5,000)
2,000,000	(added together) now, insert your commas, and you get 2,000,000.

But a shorter way to multiply 5,000 and 400 is to multiply 5 x 4, which is:

20

and then add on to the end all the zeros combined in the two numbers. Between 5,000 and 400, there are 5 zeros. So, 20 with 5 zeros tacked onto the end looks like this:

2000000 or 2,000,000

Pretty cool.

Remember, any time you are unsure, all you need to do is multiply it all out. It may take a little longer, but don't worry about shortcuts if you are confused by them.

26. Which of the following is equal to the Roman numeral DXLVII ?

> **(A)** 5,480
> **(B)** 547
> **(C)** 567

Roman numerals are—you guessed it—the system of numbers used in ancient Rome. In the Roman system, letters were used instead of numbers. For some odd reason, people still have this thing for Roman numerals. You can see Roman numerals on many clocks. If you look closely at the credits at the end of a movie, you can see that the date the movie was made is often written in Roman numerals. Often, a big building has the date it was built written on it in Roman numerals. So, since these numbers are all around, it's a good idea to learn how to write and read them. Here are the basic numbers you need to know:

ROMAN NUMERAL		OUR NUMERAL
I	=	1
V	=	5
X	=	10
L	=	50
C	=	100
D	=	500
M	=	1,000

Now, to make just about any number, all you need to do is use these symbols in combination. Here's how it works: Notice that everything is either a 1 or a 5 (1 & 5, 10 & 50, 100 & 500). You can put up to three ones together; then, instead of four ones, four is represented by "one less than five." You do this by putting a 1 to the left of a five. For example:

1 = I, 2 = II, 3 = III, 4 = IV (one less than V), 5 = V

10 = X, 20 = XX, 30 = XXX, 40 = XL (ten less than L), 50 = L

100 = C, 200 = CC, 300 = CCC, 400 = CD (one hundred less than D), 500 = D

To go from 5 to 9, you add on to the five:

5 = V, 6 = VI, 7 = VII, 8 = VIII, 9 = IX (one less than X), 10 = X

15 = XV, 16 = XVI, 17 = XVII, 18 = XVIII, 19 = IXX,

20 = XX

ROMAN NUMERALS	OUR NUMERALS
XXIV	24
MCMXCV	1995
XIV	14
MMI	2001

To translate a Roman numeral into our own type of numeral (called an Arabic numeral), remember this: Look for the largest number represented. Numerals before that number are subtracted from it; numerals after that number are added to it. For example:

C M X L V I I I

Largest number, M, 1,000

C, 100 is subtracted from 1,000   =   900

L, 50, comes after (added)

X, 10, comes before, so it is subtracted from 50   =   40

V, 5 added to larger numbers   =   5

III, 3, added to larger numbers   =   __3__

C M X L V I I I   =   948

27. Our car ride takes 1 hour and 17 minutes. If we leave at 6:50, at what time will we arrive?

    (A) 8:07

    (B) 8:15

    (C) 7:43

When you're trying to calculate numbers quickly in your head, you can break them up into smaller pieces, or you can round them off. If you were trying to add together 39 and 47, you might round 39 to the nearest 10, 40, and round 47 to its nearest 10, 50. Now add 40 and 50 (90) and just subtract 1 (39 is one less than 40) and then 3 (47 is 3 less than 50). 39 + 47 = 86 (4 less than 90).

The same thing is true with time. When you are rounding in time, though, you probably want to round off to the nearest hour and work from there. Remember that:

- **1 hour = 60 minutes**

- $\frac{1}{2}$ **hour = 30 minutes**

- $\frac{1}{4}$ **hour = 15 minutes**

- **From one number to the next on the clock face is 5 minutes**

Let's look at the problem above and break it up into pieces. We leave at 6:50 and the car ride is 1 hour and 17 minutes. We can add this together in pieces.

1 hour added to 6:50

$$
\begin{array}{r}
6{:}50 \\
+\ \underline{1{:}00} \\
7{:}50
\end{array}
$$

Now, we have 17 minutes left to add to 7:50. How many minutes until you reach 8:00? Remember, 60 minutes in an hour, and 7:50 means 7:00 + 50 minutes. You need 10 more minutes to reach an hour.

$$
\begin{array}{r}
7{:}50 \\
+\ \underline{\ \ :10} \\
8{:}00
\end{array}
$$
   (50 + 10 = 60 = 1 hour)

So, we took 10 minutes from the 17 to add it to 7:50. How many are left?

$$
\begin{array}{r}
:17 \\
-\ \underline{:10} \\
:07
\end{array}
$$
   7 minutes left to add.

Add the 7 minutes to 8:00:

```
  8:00
+  :07
  8:07
```

So, what you did was break 1 hour, 17 minutes into small pieces and add the pieces on to 6:50 in three steps. Just remember, when you add regular numbers together, any time you pass 9, you carry over to the next digit. When you are adding numbers with time, when you reach 60, you carry it over as an hour.

28. What is the area of this rectangle?

3

6

(A)   9 square inches

(B)   18 square inches

(C)   12 square inches

Area is a calculation of the space inside of a flat, or two-dimensional, object. If you have a relatively simple figure, figuring out the area is simple. Let's start with the area of a four-sided figure, like the rectangle above.

The area of a rectangle = length (the long side) × width (the short side)

In the above example, the length was 6 and the width was 3.

Some other area formulas:

In a square all the sides are the same length. You can figure out the area by multiplying any two sides by each other—that's because in a square, length and width are exactly the same. Take a square that has all of its sides measuring 4.

definition

width

(width) *noun*, the distance from one side of something to the other side.

*The **width** of a regular piece of notebook paper is 8 1/2 inches.*

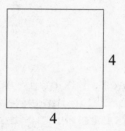

Area of square = side × side = 4 × 4 = 16

In a triangle, you have to figure out two measurements: the base and the height. To find this out, just plonk the triangle down on one of its sides (it doesn't matter which side). That side will now be the base. The height is the measure from the highest point of the triangle straight down to the base line. For example:

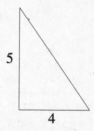

In this triangle, the base is 4 and the height is 5. To calculate the area, multiply the base times the height and then take one-half of that number.

Area of a triangle = $\frac{1}{2}$ base × height = $\frac{1}{2}$ (4 × 5) = $\frac{1}{2}$ (20) = 10.

What do you do if you want to get an idea of how big something is, but it's not a regular square or rectangle or triangle? You may be able to estimate using these formulas. Let's say you have a figure that looks like this:

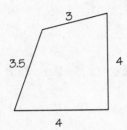

Well, if you just figured out the area as if it were a rectangle with sides 3 and 4, you'd actually come pretty close:

$$\text{Area} = \text{length} \times \text{width} = 3 \times 4 = 12$$

You can estimate (p. 168) that the area of that figure is really close to 12.

29. Maria needs to earn $30 to buy a new pair of jeans. On Monday she earned $8.00, and on Tuesday she earned $10. Which number sentence will help you figure out how much more money she needs?

(A) 30 x (8 + 10)

(B) 30 − 8 + 10

(C) 30 − (8 + 10)

Whenever you see a problem with more than one type of operation (for example, multiplication, addition, subtraction), you need to do these operations in the right order to get the right answer. Here is the order of operations:

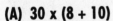 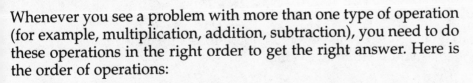

Parentheses, Exponents, Multiplication, Division, Addition, and Subtraction.

You can remember them with the nifty acronym:

P E M D A S

or

Please Excuse My Dear Aunt Sally.

What does this mean? It means that you should proceed in this order:

1. **Do any work inside of parentheses**
2. **Do any squares or cubes (called exponents—you'll learn about these soon)**
3. **Do the multiplication**
4. **Do the division**
5. **Do the addition**
6. **Do the subtraction**

Look at our example:

30 − (8 + 10)

If you do the addition inside the parentheses first, you get:

30 − (18)

Then do the subtraction (in this problem it's all that's left) and you get:

30 − 18 = 12

If you ignored the order of operations and just moved straight across you would have done:

30 − 8 = 22 + 10 = 32.

Wrong answer. It is important to follow the order of operations.

Because multiplication and division are the same thing, in reverse, you can do them in either order. For example: 30 x 10 ÷ 2 is the same whether you do the multiplication first:

$$30 \times 10 = 300 \quad 300 \div 2 = 150$$

or you do the division first:

$$10 \div 2 = 5 \times 30 = 150.$$

If all you have is multiplication and division, you can do them any which way.

When you get down to just addition and subtraction (your last two steps) simply move from left to right. Like reading:

$$8 + 5 - 6 + 2 - 3 =$$
$$8 + 5 = 13 - 6 = 7 + 2 = 9 - 3 = 6$$

It looks confusing, but just do it piece by piece and you'll be fine.

30. Which decimal has the greatest value?

(A) .1
(B) .01
(C) .0019

It's easy to compare decimals. Line them up , with all the decimals in the same place. Look at the choices you had above:

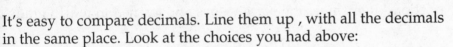

.1
.01
.0019

Now, if there were no decimal point, you'd probably think the last number, 0019, was the largest. But with decimals you read backwards, from the decimal point. The number closest to the decimal is the largest, and each place after that has a smaller and smaller value. So, .1 is larger than .01 or .0019. When you are comparing decimals, the largest one is the one that has the largest number closest to the decimal point.

You probably are most familiar with decimals from money. $4.51 is equal to 4 dollars and 51 cents.

Cents are $\frac{1}{100}$ of a dollar (remember, there are 100 pennies in a dollar), so you could write $\frac{51}{100}$ as the fractional equal of .51. 51 out of a possible hundred pennies is 51 cents. This is another good way to compare decimals—think of them as money—would you rather have .42 or .07?

Look at another example:

.239
.502
.03678

First, look at the number next to the decimal. Which is the largest number? Since 5 is larger than both 2 and 0, .502 is the largest decimal. Try another:

.250
.2091
.15789

Again, first look at the number next to the decimal point. 2 is larger than 1, so cross off the last choice immediately. It's between .250 and .2091. Look to the second number after the decimal point. Since 5 is larger than 0, .250 is larger than .2091.

Decimals are like fractions—they are parts of a number. The farther out you move from the decimal point, the more pieces you are chopping your number into. Decimals can always be written as fractions. Remember the place values you learned in fourth grade:

$$.1 = \frac{1}{10} \qquad .01 = \frac{1}{100} \qquad .001 = \frac{1}{1,000}$$

So, the farther away you are from the decimal point, the smaller the number. It's exactly the opposite as the other side of the decimal point. Imagine the decimal point is a mirror. Everything that moves away from it on the left gets bigger and bigger, while everything that moves away from it on the right gets smaller and smaller, just the way things get reversed in a mirror.

definition

decimal
(DES i mil) *noun,* based on the number ten.

Decimals are numbers based on fractions of ten, 1/10, 1/100, 1/1000.

31. Which figures are congruent?

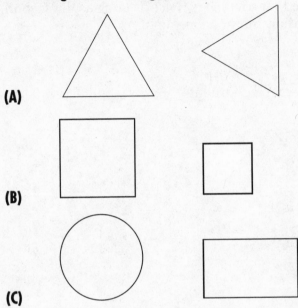

(A)

(B)

(C)

Congruent means that two figures have the same size and the same angles. These two triangles are congruent:

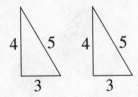

They have the same angles and the sides are the same length.

These two triangles are not congruent:

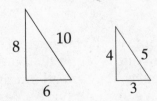

They are almost the same—the shapes are the same, the angles are the same, but the first triangle is twice as large as the second. These triangles are **similar**, but not congruent.

One more time!

These two figures are congruent:

Congruent figures are exactly the same. If you laid one over the other, it would be a perfect match. These two figures are similar:

Similar figures are the same in all ways except size. They are in proportion to each other, but one is larger than the other. If you look at the sides of similar triangles, they are all multiples of each other. In the similar triangles above, the first one's sides were 3–4–5 and the econd one's sides were 6–8–10. Can you see how in the second set, ach side is twice as long as its corresponding side in the first set?

32. What is the perimeter of the rectangle?

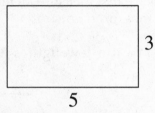

3

5

(A) 16
(B) 8
(C) 15

5

definition

perimeter
(pe RIM e ter) *noun*, the outer boundary of an area; the length of that boundary.

*Raoul and I figured out that the rectangular field with a length of 40 yards and a width of 20 yards had a **perimeter** of 120 yards.*

'ou've got a big yard and you come home one day with a cow. Hey, what are you going to do with that cow?" your mother emands. "Put him in the yard, Ma," you respond. But, of course, s cows are likely to do, old Elsie keeps wandering off. "You need o put a fence up, Jack!" your mother yells. So, off to the lumber ard you go.

"May I have some fencing, please?"
"How much?" the kindly lumber-yard salesperson inquires.
"Huh?" you ask.

There's the problem. You need to know he perimeter of the property you want to ence off. The perimeter is the length round a figure or thing. Here's a picture f your yard and your cow.

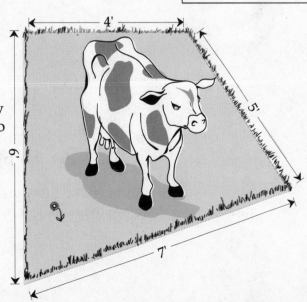

You measure each side of the yard and get the measurement shown in the picture. To fence off the whole area, you'd need fencing for 5 feet + fencing for 4 feet + fencing for 6 feet + fencing for 7 feet. In other words, you'd need 22 feet of fencing. That's the perimeter of the yard you have—22 feet.

To calculate the perimeter of any object, just measure all around the outside edges and add up all your measurements.

Perimeter is easy to figure out. Look at a few figures and write down the perimeters:

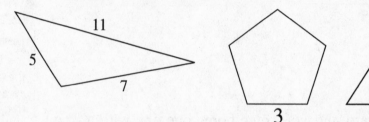

Think of perimeter as the amount of fence you'd need to completely go around the outside edge of your figure.

33. Which is smaller,

$$\frac{3}{8} \text{ or } \frac{5}{7}?$$

(A) $\frac{3}{8}$

(B) $\frac{5}{7}$

(C) **Neither, they are the same**

If you have fractions that have the same denominator, it is easy to compare them. Take a look:

The denominator represents how many pieces the pie is cut into. Here, it is five pieces. When the denominators are the same, you are comparing two pies that are cut up exactly the same way. So, if someone asks you which is more—three pieces or one piece, you'd have no problem telling him that three is more than one. Look at the shaded area: $\frac{3}{5}$ is definitely more than $\frac{1}{5}$.

But what if I take two pies and cut one into 7 slices and one into 8 slices? The pie with 8 slices has more slices, but each is smaller. When the denominators are different, it is not so easy to compare fractions, unless you remember that handy little trick we showed you on page 175. That's right, the bow tie!

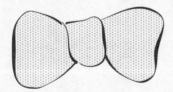

All you have to do is multiply the denominator of each fraction by the numerator of the other fraction. Write the answer above the numerator, like this:

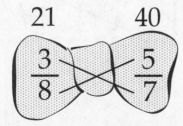

As you can see, the number 21 is above the fraction $\frac{3}{8}$ and the number 40 is above the fraction $\frac{5}{7}$. Simply ask yourself "which is greater, 21 or 40?" Since 40 is greater, the fraction it sits above, $\frac{5}{7}$, is greater than $\frac{3}{8}$. Try it again: which is greater $\frac{9}{10}$ or $\frac{10}{11}$?

The number 99 is above $\frac{10}{11}$ and the number 100 is above $\frac{10}{11}$. These two fractions are very close, as you can see, but $\frac{10}{11}$ is slightly larger than $\frac{9}{10}$.

You can use the bow tie to compare more than two fractions—just pair them off:

Which is greater?

$$\frac{3}{8} \text{ or } \frac{2}{3} \text{ or } \frac{4}{7}$$

First pair off $\frac{3}{8}$ and $\frac{2}{3}$:

Which is greater, 9 or 16? 16 is greater, therefore $\frac{2}{3}$ is greater. Now pair off the champion with the remaining fraction.

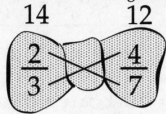

14   12

As you can see, 14 is greater than 12, so $\frac{2}{3}$ is still the champ, and the largest of the three fractions!

34. Which of the following is a 90 degree angle?

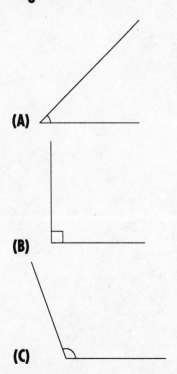

(A)

(B)

(C)

Before we get to angles, you need to understand two other things: lines and rays.

definition

vertex

(VER tecks) *noun,* the point at which two lines meet to form an angle.

*Pamela labeled each **vertex** on the triangle with a letter.*

LINE

A LINE JOINS TWO POINTS TOGETHER AND IT MOVES ON FOREVER IN BOTH DIRECTIONS.

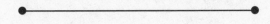

RAY

A RAY IS A LINE EXTENDING FROM ONE POINT. IT GOES ON FOREVER IN ONE DIRECTION ONLY.

ANGLE

AN ANGLE HAPPENS WHEN TWO RAYS OR LINES MEET.

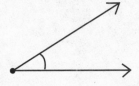

Angles are measured in degrees. A really cool thing to have to measure an angle is a protractor, which looks like this:

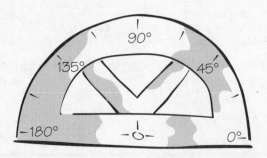

If you line a protractor up with one of the lines in the angle, you can read the measurement of the angle where the other line crosses the protractor.

Let's look at a typical angle:

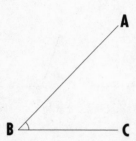

You would write $\angle ABC$. B is the vertex of the angle—that's where two points meet. The vertex is written as the middle letter in an angle. Sometimes an angle is written as just the letter of the vertex, $\angle B$. This angle, $\angle ABC$, measures 45 degrees.

ANGLES TO REMEMBER

90 DEGREE ANGLES

THESE LOOK LIKE THE LETTER "L." A 90 DEGREE ANGLE HAPPENS WHEN THE TWO LINES ARE PERPENDICULAR TO EACH OTHER. IT IS SIGNIFIED BY A LITTLE SQUARE WHERE THE ANGLE IS. HERE ARE A FEW 90 DEGREE ANGLES:

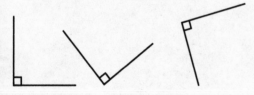

ACUTE ANGLES

NO, NOT CUTE ANGLES. ANY ANGLE THAT MEASURES LESS THAN 90 DEGREES IS CALLED ACUTE. THE FOLLOWING ARE ALL ACUTE ANGLES:

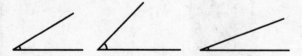

Obtuse angles

Angles that are greater than **90** are called obtuse. These are all obtuse angles:

A line has **180** degrees in it. Measure one with your protractor.
A circle has **360** degrees in it.

Supplementary Angles

Angles that add up to **180** degrees are called supplementary. These two angles are supplementary:

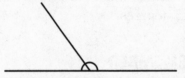

Complementary Angles

Angles that add up to **90** degrees are called complementary. These two angles are complementary:

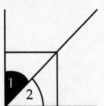

35. Sally scores 83, 86, and 92 on three
- math tests. What is her average
 score?

(A) 87

(B) 86

(C) 83

Many teachers do something called "taking the average" of the scores you receive on your tests in a subject to help them come up with your grade for the year. That means that if you get a really good score and then a really bad score, you don't deserve either a really good grade or a really bad grade, but probably something more in the middle.

Averages are used for all sorts of things. Meteorologists like to keep track of the temperature and rainfall for each month so they can tell you what the average temperature for July was, for example, and maybe compare it to the average temperature for July last year. You may keep track of your bowling scores and decide to figure out what your average score is. Let's look at how to figure out an average:

definition

range
(raynj) *noun*, the distance between two outside limits.

Kids who go to Cliff's school have ages that range from 6 to 12.

$$\text{Average} = \frac{\text{all the things added up together}}{\text{number of things}}$$

In the above example:

$$\text{Average} = \frac{83 + 86 + 92 \text{ (all the test scores added together)}}{3 \text{ (the number of test scores)}}$$

83 + 86 + 92 = 261, and 261 divided by 3 = 87. 87 is the average test score.

The average score should always fall into the middle of the group of numbers. When you are adding up your scores, or temperatures, or whatever you want the average of, you should know that it will always be smaller that the largest number there and larger than the smallest. Always try to estimate the average before you figure it out so you'll know where you're going.

Look at this list of temperatures for Indiana from last week:

Mon.	75°
Tues.	80°
Wed.	72°
Thurs.	84°
Fri.	79°

Now, if I take the average of those numbers, it should fall somewhere in the middle of all of them. If I put them all in order, I get:

$$72° \quad 75° \quad 79° \quad 80° \quad 84°$$

I know now that my average will be somewhere in between the low number (72°) and the high number (84°). If you get a number outside of this range, you've done something wrong. Let's do it together.

$$\text{The average} = \frac{\text{All the temperatures added together}}{\text{The number of temperatures}}$$

$$\text{The average} = \frac{72° + 75° + 79° + 80° + 84°}{5} \text{ or } \frac{390°}{5}$$

$$\frac{390°}{5} = 78°$$

78° is the average temperature. Can you see how it is right about in the middle of the range of temperatures on your chart?

36. Which price is about right for a new paperback book?

(A) 75 cents

(B) $7.95

(C) $27.95

Sure, a price tag is there to tell you what an item costs—but there are other reasons to know yourself the right price to pay for something. Probably the most important reason is that prices can be very different from one place to another. You may see a sign at the famous toy store I.M. POSH that says the following:

SALE !!!!!!!!!!!!!!!!!
THIS WEEK ONLY –
DISCOUNTED PREMIER
TRENDY BEARS
$89.99

If you are a smart shopper, you know that just because a sign says that this is a really low price doesn't mean it really is a really low price. The toy store downtown, CHEAP IZ US, has the same toy, but with this sign:

TRENDY BEARS
TODAY AND EVERYDAY
AT OUR LOW PRICE OF $59.99

Knowing what things cost is a good way to avoid getting ripped off. You probably do have a good idea of what things cost—at least the things you buy all the time. What does a pack of comic cards cost? Do you know where you can get them the cheapest? How about beads for necklaces? Do you know some place that has the best selection at a good price? When you are shopping, these are the things you should think about. Sometimes you are

---

definition

comparable

(kom PARE a bul) *adj.*, refers to things that can be compared to each other because they are similar.

*Our grades that year were **comparable**. Mattie got two B's and one A. I got two A's and one B.*

CAVEAT EMPTOR

Means "let the buyer beware" in Latin. As far back as ancient times, people were warned about getting ripped off. The idea here, though, is also that it is your responsibility to know about what you are buying and if it is worth the price. You cannot rely on stores or advertisements to supply all your information—remember, they're out there to make money from you.

"Buy Me That!" "Buy Me That Too!" and "Buy Me That 3!" (HBO). These specials explore the advertising geared towards kids. See how advertisers make things look better and watch a panel of kids deconstruct what they see on TV.

"Zillions TV" (PBS). Based on the *Consumer Reports* magazine for kids. Kids test products and decide which are worth the money and which aren't.

willing to pay more because it is convenient. Maybe the least expensive place is eight miles away. Even though the store on the corner is more expensive, you may go there anyway because it is convenient.

Why else should you bother knowing what things cost?

Maybe you don't see a price tag. You want to be sure you know about what something is going to cost.

You might want to estimate, before you go out, what you will need to spend. Let's say you want to buy your sister that Trendy Bear for her birthday. You need to know how much you have to save up before you head out to buy it.

How to Learn Prices

Check newspaper ads. BEWARE: things are not always as nice as they look in an ad. Read the "fine print"—all the writing that is tucked away in a corner or at the bottom of an advertisement. This will usually explain what is included with what you want to buy. You may see a great Super Nintendo system for sale and go to the store only to find out that it comes without controllers. Make sure the prices that you are comparing are for comparable items.

Shop without buying. This may sound crazy, but a good way to find out about prices is to shop around without necessarily buying anything. Then you can look at the item, decide if you want it, keep the price in your head, and look elsewhere to see if you can get a better deal.

Ask around. If a friend has something you are looking for, you may want to ask if he or she found it on sale. REMEMBER: it is NOT polite to ask someone how much he paid for something. But asking for a recommendation about where to buy an item is perfectly fine. "Wow, I love that Trendy Bear. Where did you get it?"

Unit Pricing

Some stores, especially supermarkets, post what is called unit pricing. This allows you to compare items that are not exactly the same. Suppose I asked you if you should buy a 12-ounce box of Raisin Branola for $3.50, or a 16-ounce box of the same cereal for $4.50. Would you know which is the better buy?

RAISIN BRANOLA		RAISIN BRANOLA	
On Sale		Everyday Low Price	
You Pay	Unit Price	You Pay	Unit Price
$3.50	$4.67	$4.50	$4.50
12 ounces	per pound	16 ounces	per pound

What does this tell you? The price under "You Pay" is, like it sounds, what you actually pay. The unit price tells you what the boxes would cost if they were the same size. So, even though the 12-ounce box is less expensive, you are not getting as much, and the price per pound is higher. Usually, larger packages of things are less expensive in the long run. You get sort of a discount for buying more. Compare the unit prices to see where the best bargain is.

37. What is 40% of 250?

    (A) 25

    (B) 1000

    (C) 100

Horton might have said "An elephant's faithful—completely," but it wouldn't have rhymed so nicely. When we talked about decimals, we found out they were just like fractions, but they always used multiples of 10. A percentage is a fraction with a denominator of 100. 100% means 100 parts of 100.

$$\frac{100}{100} \text{ or } 1$$

Remember that when the numerator and the denominator are equal, the fraction is always equal to one. Just like decimals, percentages work exactly like fractions. In fact, you can convert any percentage to a fraction by simply putting the number over 100:

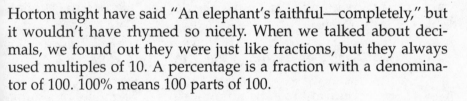

$$40\% = \frac{40}{100} \qquad 50\% = \frac{50}{100} \qquad 75\% = \frac{75}{100}$$

definition

equivalent
(ee KWIV e lent) *adj.*,
the same or equal.

40% is **equivalent** *to 40/100.*

If you want to figure out the percentage of any number, just turn the percentage into a fraction and multiply the fraction by that number. Let's look at our example above:

PERCENTS AND THEIR FRACTIONS

10%	1/10
25%	1/4
50%	1/2
66%	2/3
75%	3/4
100%	1

40% of 250?

$$40\% = \frac{40}{100}$$

$$\frac{40}{100}(250) = \text{what?}$$

It's not a bad idea to reduce $\frac{40}{100}$ before you multiply it by 250. It will make the multiplication easier.

$$\frac{40 \quad \text{divided by} \quad 20}{100 \quad \text{divided by} \quad 20} = \frac{2}{5}$$

Now, 2/5 (250) is equal to

$$\frac{2 \times 250}{5} = \frac{500}{5} = 100$$

There's a little rule we like to call the 10% rule—it goes like this. To take 10% of any number, just move the decimal place to the left one notch. For example:

10% of 250 = 25   10% of 300 = 30   10% of 94 = 9.4

Get it? So, if you want to get a rough idea of 20% or 30% of a number, just double or triple the 10% amount. For example:

If 10% of 250 = 25, then 20% is 50 (25 x 2) and 30% is 75 (25 x 3) and 40% is 100 (25 x 4).

If 10% of 300 = 30, then 20% is 60 (30 x 2) and 30% is 90 (30 x 3) and 40% is 120 (30 x 4).

The 10% rule is just a shortcut way to figure out basic percentages.

38. Convert the following into an improper fraction:

$$3\frac{5}{7}$$

(A) $\dfrac{26}{7}$

(B) $\dfrac{35}{7}$

(C) $\dfrac{7}{35}$

Some fractions are presented as mixed numbers. A mixed number is a number made up of an integer and a fraction, like $3\frac{5}{7}$. That means that I have 3 pies and 5 out of 7 pieces in the fourth pie:

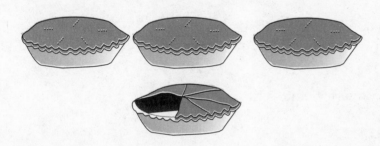

You may find it helpful to change a mixed number into an improper fraction. Why? Look at it this way. You may want to multiply $3\frac{5}{7}$ by $\frac{1}{2}$. It would be much easier to do that if $3\frac{5}{7}$ were just a fraction, not a whole number plus a fraction. To do that, you must think of this as an addition problem:

$$3\frac{5}{7} = 3 + \frac{5}{7} = ?$$

First, turn the whole number, 3 into a fraction: $\frac{3}{1}$.

6

MIXED NUMBERS

How many of these mixed numbers can you convert to improper fractions in 60 seconds?

$2\frac{3}{4}$	$3\frac{4}{5}$	$2\frac{7}{9}$
$1\frac{4}{7}$	$3\frac{2}{8}$	$9\frac{1}{4}$
$3\frac{8}{9}$	$7\frac{3}{5}$	$3\frac{5}{8}$
$3\frac{6}{9}$	$1\frac{7}{8}$	$6\frac{2}{5}$
$4\frac{5}{6}$	$5\frac{7}{8}$	$8\frac{3}{4}$
$7\frac{2}{3}$	$6\frac{3}{4}$	$2\frac{3}{8}$
$6\frac{4}{7}$	$7\frac{8}{9}$	$3\frac{2}{5}$
$2\frac{5}{7}$	$7\frac{1}{4}$	$8\frac{2}{3}$

IMPROPER FRACTIONS

Now, take a deep breath, and see how many of these improper fractions you can convert to mixed numbers in 60 seconds.

$\frac{23}{7}$	$\frac{56}{4}$	$\frac{23}{3}$
$\frac{33}{2}$	$\frac{44}{9}$	$\frac{24}{6}$
$\frac{12}{3}$	$\frac{34}{7}$	$\frac{56}{3}$
$\frac{67}{5}$	$\frac{45}{8}$	$\frac{24}{9}$
$\frac{13}{2}$	$\frac{11}{4}$	$\frac{45}{6}$
$\frac{67}{5}$	$\frac{45}{8}$	$\frac{26}{3}$
$\frac{59}{2}$	$\frac{99}{4}$	$\frac{12}{5}$
$\frac{67}{8}$	$\frac{45}{11}$	$\frac{38}{12}$

$$\frac{3}{1} + \frac{5}{7} = ?$$

Now, whenever you add together two fractions, the first thing you should be thinking is common denominator.

To change $\frac{3}{1}$ to a fraction with the same denominator as $\frac{5}{7}$, you can multiply both the top and bottom by 7:

$$\frac{3}{1} \times \frac{7}{7} = \frac{21}{7} \qquad \text{so,} \qquad \frac{3}{1} = \frac{21}{7}$$

Now, it's really easy to add together:

$$\frac{21}{7} + \frac{5}{7} = \frac{26}{7}$$

$\frac{26}{7}$ is $3\frac{5}{7}$ stated as an improper fraction.

But, you're saying, "that's such a pain in the neck." We agree. Luckily, there's a shortcut to converting mixed numbers. Here's how it works:

Let's convert $\frac{33}{7}$ into a mixed number.

Step 1

Divide the denominator into the numerator:

$$7\overline{)33} \quad \begin{array}{r} 4 \\ \hline -28 \\ \hline 5 \end{array}$$

4 is the whole number part of the mixed number

Step 2

What's the remainder? The remainder becomes the new numerator.

The denominator stays the same.

$$7\overline{)33} \quad \frac{4}{} \quad \text{remainder } 5$$

The new mixed number is $4\frac{5}{7}$.

39. Dianne bought 12 pounds of nectarines at $.69 a pound. How much was the total bill?

(A) $12.00

(B) $6.90

(C) $8.28

Multiplication with decimals is exactly like regular multiplication. In fact, you don't even pay attention to the decimals until you are completely finished with the problem. Take a look at our example. First of all, how did we get to the answer? Look at the facts:

12 pounds of nectarines
$.69 each pound

The question is how much was the total? (Remember to keep your eye on the question). You need to multiply .69 by 12 to figure out the total (.69, twelve times, is what she paid). Now, check it out. First we multiply as if there were no decimals at all:

$$
\begin{array}{r}
12 \\
\times \ .69 \\
\hline
108 \\
+ \ 720 \\
\hline
828
\end{array}
$$

Now, we're pretty sure she didn't spend 828 dollars, right? When you are all finished multiplying your numbers—

definition

divisor
(di VY zer) *noun*, the number you are dividing into another number.

If you divide 10 by 5, 5 is the divisor.

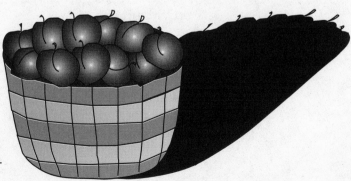

exactly like regular multiplication—and you are all the way down on the last step, then you add up all the decimal places in the original problem and put them in the answer. How many decimal places in 12? Zero. How many decimal places in .69? Two. So you have two decimal places all together. Starting at the right, count over two places; that's where you put your decimal point:

One more time. This time let's just multiply two numbers, both with decimals in them:

$$
\begin{array}{r}
3.48 \\
\times\ \ 1.3 \\
\hline
1044 \\
+\ \ 348 \\
\hline
4524
\end{array}
$$

Just multiply the two numbers, ignoring the decimal places. Now, add up the amount of decimal places in each number: Two places in 3.48 and one place in 1.3. You need to count over 3 places total in your answer:

4.524

Easy as pie.

DIVISION WITH DECIMALS

Now that you are a master of multiplication with decimals, you'll definitely want to know how division works. With division, there are two possibilities: decimals in the divisor and decimals in the dividend.

$$.8\overline{)240}$$

When this happens, before you start, you need to get rid of the decimal point in the divisor. To do that, you move it over as many places as you need to to get it all the way to the right (here, just one place). To keep everything equal, you add that many places to the dividend by adding zeroes:

$$\frac{300}{8 \overline{)2400}}$$

When there is a decimal in the dividend, as long as there is not a decimal in the divisor, just carry the decimal point up directly in the same spot to the answer. For example:

$$\frac{3.1}{8 \overline{)24.8}}$$

Just keep the decimal point lined up and you'll be fine. Now, put the two together:

$$.03 \overline{)23.403}$$

First step: move the decimal point in the divisor over to the right, this time, two places. Move the decimal point in the dividend the same number of places.

$$03 \overline{)2340.3}$$

You still have a decimal point in the dividend, so just carry it up to the same spot in the answer and divide:

$$\frac{780.1}{03 \overline{)2340.3}}$$

Be sure to keep everything neat and lined up when you work with decimals. The most common mistakes occur when decimal points are carried to the wrong spot.

40. What is the value of b in this equation?

$$15b = 60$$

(A) 4

(B) 20

(C) We need more information

definition

algebra

(AL je bruh) *noun*, a form of mathematics that uses letters to stand for numbers that are not known or numbers that may change.

*Even though **algebra** is a difficult subject, Valerie preferred it to geometry.*

When you first learned math, you learned how to express mathematical concepts using numbers. You learned how to relate those numbers to each other and how to see patterns in the number system. There is another, more abstract way to do math. It is called **algebra**. Sometimes you want to figure out the relationship between numbers even if you don't have specifics. Let's say, for example, that your father tells you that every time you mow the lawn, he'll give you 3 dollars. You can make up a neat formula for how much you will earn this summer:

$$3m = s$$

In this formula, m stands for the number of times you mow the lawn and s stands for how much you will save. So, you can plug in for one number to figure out the other. Here, if you mow the lawn 5 times,

$$3 (5) = s$$
$$15 = s$$

You will earn 15 dollars.

Algebra tells you the relationship between things if you don't have specific numbers. In algebra, you can stick a letter right next to a number to indicate that you multiply the two together. The letter is called the **variable**. That simply means that it is not a fixed number—it could stand for any number at all.

The number next to the variable is called the **coefficient**.

Look at a few others:

> **"There are twice as many boys as girls in our class."**
> **B = 2G**
> **"Su-jeung earned three dollars more than José."**
> **M = J + 3**

Now, you can plug in a number for one variable and solve for the other. For example, if I tell you that there are 10 girls in our class, you can figure out how many boys there are, using the class formula:

> **B = 2 (10) = 20. There are 20 boys.**

If I tell you that José earned 15 dollars, you can figure out how many dollars Su-jeung earned, using that formula:

> **M = 15 + 3 = 18. Su-jeung earned 18 dollars.**

41. If Martin drives 50 miles in 2 days, how many miles will he travel in 6 days?

(A) 100 miles
(B) 200 miles
(C) 150 miles

A proportion is the relation between two things. You can use proportions to figure out how big or small something will get under different conditions. For example, here, as long as Martin drives at that constant rate of 50 miles in 2 days, you can figure out how many miles he will drive other numbers of days by setting up a proportion:

$$\frac{50 \text{ miles}}{2 \text{ days}} = \frac{? \text{ miles}}{6 \text{ days}}$$

definition

proportion
(proh POHR shun)
noun, the relationship
between numbers or
things.

*We wanted to make sure
the **proportion** of how
much money we spent
was not too much
compared to how much
food we got.*

Now, if Martin were to speed up, or slow down, this wouldn't work. We'll say he stays at the same speed.

You figure out a proportion through a process called cross-multiplying. That means you multiply diagonally, like this:

$$\frac{50}{2} \diagdown = \diagup \frac{?}{6}$$

And you end up with a problem that looks like this:

$$50 \times 6 = ? \times 2$$
$$300 = ? \times 2$$

What do you have to multiply by 2 to get 300? 150 is the answer. You can just divide by 2 on both sides to solve for the ?

As long as you keep the same types of things on the top on both sides and the same types of things on the bottom of both sides you'll be fine. Here, miles are on the top and days are on the bottom. Let's try one more proportion problem:

If you need 3 bottles of soda for every 5 people at a party, and 30 are coming to the next party, how many bottles of soda should you buy?

Set up your proportion. It doesn't matter which thing you put on top or bottom, as long as the same things are on the top and bottom on both sides. Let's put people on top and soda on the bottom:

$$\frac{3 \text{ bottles}}{5 \text{ people}} = \frac{? \text{ bottles}}{30 \text{ people}}$$

Now, cross-multiply and you get:

$$3 \times 30 = ? \times 5 \quad \text{or} \quad 90 = ? \times 5$$

divide both sides by 5 and you get:

$$18 = ?$$

You'll need 18 bottles of soda for your party. Keep your proportions straight. You'll find them very useful.

42. Which of the following is an equilateral triangle?

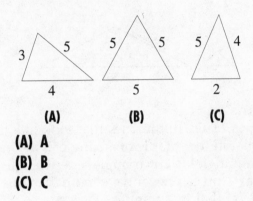

(A)   (B)   (C)

(A) A
(B) B
(C) C

 Math Smart Jr. In this entertaining book the reader learns math while following the adventures of four strange friends.

There are a few special triangles that you should be able to recognize:

EQUILATERAL TRIANGLES

These are simply triangles in which all the sides are the same length. When all the sides are the same length all the angles are the same—60 degrees each. Look at the word equilateral. "Equi-" is a prefix that means the same or equal and "lateral" means sides. You can figure out that "Equilateral" means having equal sides. These are equilateral triangles:

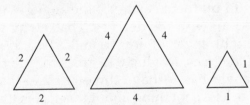

ISOSCELES TRIANGLES

Triangles are called isosceles when 2 out of the 3 sides are equal to each other. In these triangles (you may have guessed this already), two of the angles will be equal as well. Which two angles?

definition

isosceles
(eye SAHS i lees) *adj.*, a figure (especially a triangle) in which two of the sides, and the two angles opposite them, are equal in measure.

The two equal sides of the isosceles triangle measured six inches.

The angles opposite the equal sides will always be equal. Check out a few:

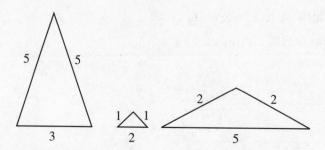

RIGHT TRIANGLES

Remember right angles? They're the ones that look like this. If you see a little box like that in the middle of an angle, it means that it is a 90 degree, or right, angle. Right triangles are triangles that have a right angle in them. You can never have more than one right angle in a triangle (more on that in a minute). Here are some right triangles:

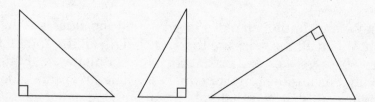

Whenever you add up the measure of the angles within a triangle you'll always end up with 180 degrees. That's why you can't have more than one right angle in any triangle: two 90-degree angles would equal 180 degrees, leaving 0 degrees for the third angle. By definition, a triangle has to have three angles—that's where the name comes from. The cool thing about this fact is that you can figure out the measure of the third angle if we tell you the measure of the other two.

43. What is the area of this circle?

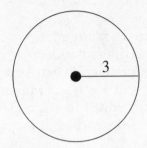

(A) 9π
(B) 9
(C) 3.5π

How do you figure out the area and circumference of a circle? First, let's take a look at a circle:

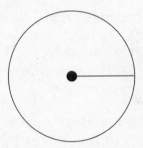

The radius of a circle is any straight line from the center of the circle to any point on the edge. A straight line that goes from edge to edge of the circle, passing through the center, is the diameter. The diameter of a circle will always be equal to twice the length of the radius. If, for example, a circle has a radius of 3, the diameter will be 6.

If you measure all the way around the outside of a circle, you will get the circumference of that circle. The circumference is what we call the perimeter of a circle. Now, if you measured the circumference of the circle exactly, and then you measured the diameter of the circle exactly and divided the circumference by the diameter, this would happen:

definition

diameter

(dye AM et er) *noun,*
the width of a circle;
the length of any line
that goes from edge to
edge passing through
the center.

*We know the **diameter**
of the circle, because the
radius was 2.*

$$\frac{\text{Circumference of any circle}}{\text{Diameter of that same circle}} = 3.1416$$

How did we know this? In ancient Greece a mathematician discovered that no matter what size a circle is, its circumference always has the exact same relationship to its diameter. When you divide the circumference by the diameter you will always get the number π. That symbol represents pi (pronounce it just like "pie") or 3.14. All you have to know is the diameter or the radius of a circle and you can calculate its circumference.

Circumference = Diameter $\times \pi$

you may also see this written as:

Circumference = 2 π r

where r is the radius. Remember that 2r = diameter.

When you calculate the circumference of a circle, you can just leave the π symbol there—if you have a circle with a diameter of 6, you just say that the circumference is 6 π.

To calculate the area of a circle, you only need to multiply the radius by itself—r^2. This is called "squaring the radius," since to square a number means to multiply it by itself. Now, take that square and multiply it by π.

Area = πr^2

ANSWERS:

1. B	2. C	3. C	4. C	5. B	6. A	7. ◐	8. C	9. B	10. B
11. B	12. A	13. A	14. C	15. A	16. C	17. A	18. B	19. A	20. C
21. C	22. C	23. A	24. A	25. C	26. B	27. A	28. B	29. C	30. A
31. A	32. A	33. A	34. B	35. A	36. B	37. C	38. A	39. C	40. A
41. C	42. B	43. A							

1. Name three planets in our solar system.

1. _____
2. _____
3. _____

A **solar system** consists of a sun and all the objects that revolve around it. Our solar system is made up of our sun, planets, moons, asteroids, and comets. It was formed about 4.5 billion years ago. There are **nine planets** in our solar system, including the Earth. So far, there is no evidence of life on any of the other planets in our solar system, but we're still looking.

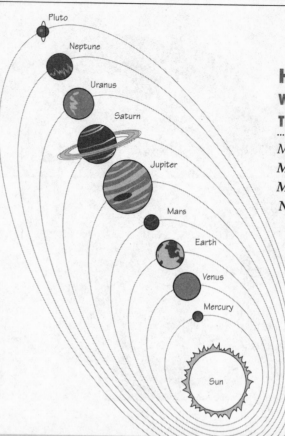

Pluto
Neptune
Uranus
Saturn
Jupiter
Mars
Earth
Venus
Mercury
Sun

definition

asteroid

(AS ter oyd) *noun*, a small planet-like object in space.

Most **asteroids** *in our solar system are between the orbits of Mars and Jupiter.*

HERE'S AN EASY WAY TO REMEMBER THE NINE PLANETS.

Memorize this sentence: **My Very Educated Mother Just showed Us Nine Planets.**

The first letter of each word matches the first letter of each of the nine planets.

COOL FACTS ABOUT THE PLANETS OF OUR SOLAR SYSTEM

PLANET	TEMPERATURE	YEAR	YOUR WEIGHT (IF YOU WEIGH 50 LBS. ON EARTH)	DISTANCE FROM EARTH
Mercury	-279F to -801F	88 days	19 lbs.	57 million miles
Venus	864F	225 days	45 lbs.	25.7 million miles
Earth	-128F (record low) to +136F (record high)	365 1/4 days	50lbs.	0 miles
Mars	-225F to -163F	687 days	19 lbs.	48.95 million miles
Jupiter	-234F to +70	12 years	133 lbs.	392.9 million miles
Saturn	-288F	29.5 years	54 lbs.	799.87 million miles
Uranus	-357F	84 years	46 lbs.	1.6 billion miles
Neptune	-353F	165 years	60 lbs.	2.7 billion miles
Pluto	-369F to -387F	248 years	31 lbs.	3.6 billion miles

As big as our solar system is, it is only a tiny part of the universe. It's hard to describe how big the universe is, but let's give it a try:

- YOU ARE ONLY ONE SMALL PART OF YOUR COMMUNITY.
- YOUR COMMUNITY IS ONLY ONE SMALL PART OF YOUR COUNTRY.
- YOUR COUNTRY IS ONLY ONE SMALL PART OF THE EARTH.
- THE EARTH IS ONLY ONE SMALL PART OF THE SOLAR SYSTEM.
- THE SUN IN OUR SOLAR SYSTEM IS ONE OF MORE THAN 200 BILLION STARS IN OUR GALAXY, THE MILKY WAY.
- THE MILKY WAY IS ONE OF MANY BILLIONS OF GALAXIES IN THE UNIVERSE.

In other words, there's much more out there than you can imagine. Can you even think about how many a **billion** is? You'd have to count to a hundred 10,000 times to count to a million. And you'd have to count to a million 1,000 times before you'd count to a billion. A billion looks like this written out:

$$1,000,000,000$$

Remember, there are billions of galaxies, each of which has billions of planets. Our universe is a very big place.

2. What happens when you heat up ice?
   (A) It becomes water, then steam.
   (B) It becomes steam, then water.
   (C) It becomes a Snickers bar.

Everything in the world exists in one of three different ways:

SOLID, LIQUID, or GAS.

HOW BIG IS A BILLION?

Let's say a kind bank manager gave you a really big stack of one-dollar bills, with one catch. You have to spend one dollar every minute of every day. After one day, you'll have spent 1,440 dollars. If you spend 1,440 dollars a day, you would spend a million dollars in a little less than two years. It would take you 1,902 years to spend a billion dollars if you spent a dollar a minute.

definition

state

(stayt) *noun*, one of the three ways in which all matter exists.

*Water can be any one of three **states**: liquid (water), solid (ice), or gas (steam).*

Water is something that can be solid, liquid, or gas, depending on its temperature. At normal room temperature, water is a liquid. You can pour it, drink it, put it in a squirt gun, bring it outside (as long as it's not too cold), and the water will still be a liquid.

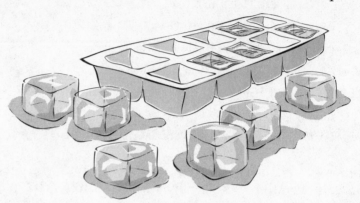

 The Magic School Bus Lost in the Solar System, by Joanna Cole and Bruce Degan. Miss Frizzle and her class take a magic bus into space.

If you pour the water into an ice-cube tray and put it in the freezer, in a few hours you'll have **ice**. Now the water is a solid— you can't pour it any more. It will be ice for as long as it stays at a very cold temperature.

When water is heated up, it becomes a gas called **steam**. If someone boils water for you, you can watch the steam coming off the top of the boiling water. You also may have noticed steam forming when you take a very hot shower. Gas doesn't have any shape or stay in any one place for long. Air is also a gas.

Different types of liquids freeze at different temperatures. Regular water from the faucet will freeze at 32 degrees (your freezer is probably about 0 degrees). Salt water must be a lot colder to freeze. That's why, in places where it's very cold in the winter, they pour salt onto the roads to melt the ice. That's also why a pond, which is regular fresh water, will be frozen in a cold climate in the winter, but the water in the ocean very rarely freezes.

 Mr. Wizard's World (Nickelodeon). Don Herbert, also know as Mr. Wizard, performs amazing science tricks and experiments.

See if you can classify other stuff around you as solid, liquid or gas. Here are some examples:

SOLIDS	LIQUIDS	GASES
desk	*juice*	*air*
glass	*milk*	*neon*
balloon	*soda*	*helium in a balloon*

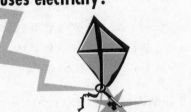

3. Which of the following things uses electricity?

    (A) A bicycle

    (B) A book

    (C) A lamp

definition

charge
(charj) *verb*, To fill
with electricity.

*I **charged** all sixteen
batteries for my new
remote-controlled car.*

Energy makes things happen. Lots of different things can provide energy. You give a pen the energy it needs to write by picking it up and pushing it across a page. Batteries give energy to some toys and things like flashlights and Walkmans.

Electricity is a type of energy. Over 200 years ago, **Benjamin Franklin** (p. 316) studied lightning and discovered that it was electricity. It took a few years after Franklin's discovery for people to figure out how to produce electricity. Think of all the things around your house that run on electricity. Without electricity, there'd be no lights, television, or refrigerators.

There are two types of electricity: current and static electricity. **Current** electricity can move from a battery to a toy, or from a power station to your house. **Static** electricity stays in one place.

Chemicals can also produce electricity. A reptile called an electric eel has chemicals in its body that produce electricity, and the eel uses that electrical power to shock its enemies. Chemicals are what a battery uses to produce electricity. The electricity that comes into your home is produced by large machines at a power station.

Have you ever brushed your hair in the middle of the winter and noticed that wisps of it are standing straight up? This happens because of static electricity. Since static electricity does not move, the charge on the brush doesn't flow through your whole body, so your electrified hair stands on end.

1

4. How is Paul's mother's brother related to Paul?

(A) He is Paul's grandfather.

(B) He is Paul's brother.

(C) He is Paul's uncle.

All **families** are different. Some have a mother and a father, a sister and a brother. Others have a grandmother and two sisters. Some have no father; some have no mother. Some families don't even have kids! You should know how the people who live in your house and the people who make up the rest of your family are related to you. One way to understand family relationships is to look at a family tree. Here is our friend Christy's family tree:

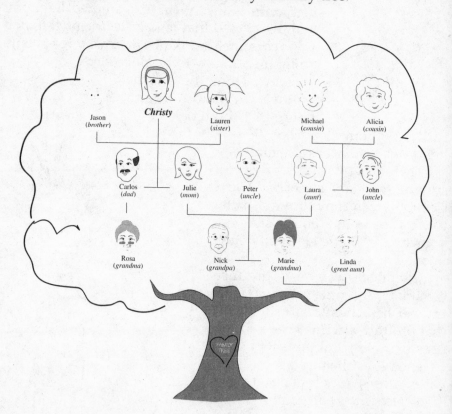

See if you can follow this on the tree. First find Christy, and start from there. Julie and Carlos are Christy's parents. Jason and Lauren are her brother and sister. Laura and Peter are Christy's Mom's sister and brother, so they are Christy's aunt and uncle. John, who is married to Christy's Aunt Laura, is considered Christy's uncle, too. Aunt Laura and Uncle John's children, Michael and Alicia, are Christy's cousins. Christy's grandparents are her Mom's parents, Marie and Nick. Grandma Marie has a sister, Linda, who is Christy's great aunt. Christy also has another grandmother—Rosa, Christy's dad's mother.

Make a Family Tree

See if you can draw your own family tree. Use this space to sketch the tree first with all the names. Once you've done that, copy it onto a big piece of paper or cardboard and make it look really neat. This is a great thing to do for a special day—like your grandmother's seventieth birthday or your parents' anniversary. Decorate it like a tree, and add pictures if you can. If you are bringing your family tree to a party, ask the people at the party to sign it for you.

5. What does gravity do?

(A) It makes things go fast.
(B) It pulls smaller objects towards larger objects.
(C) It makes things stronger.

DEFY GRAVITY!

Take a 5 x 7 index card and a straw. Suck in through the straw and gently place the index card on the bottom of the straw. The card will stay in place. Why doesn't it fall? Remember that gravity grows

stronger as an object gets heavier. An index card is not very heavy, so almost any force you exert on it will be stronger than gravity. That's why tissues blow away on a windy day, but your dog doesn't.

Explorabook, by John Cassidy of the Exploratorium in San Francisco. A fun book filled with scientific facts, phenomena, and experiments.

Take a look at a globe. Did you ever wonder why people don't just fall off the earth? Or why all the water stays in the oceans? Gravity is a force that attracts all objects to each other. The larger the object, the stronger the gravity. OK, people don't stick together, but we all stick pretty close to the earth, since the earth is so big. Sure, you can jump off the ground, but it's hard to stay there for long because gravity pulls you back down.

Hold a ball in your hand. If you let go, it will fall to the earth. That's gravity in action. Gravity is also at work in our solar system. The moon revolves around the Earth because of the pull of the larger object (the Earth) on the smaller object (the moon). The Earth and all the other planets revolve around the sun because of the pull of the sun, which is much larger than all the planets that circle it.

GRAVITY MAKES EVERYTHING FALL AT THE SAME SPEED

It's true! Take a penny and a book. Stand on a chair and drop them both. Which do you think will hit the floor first? You'd think the book, since it's so much heavier—but you'd be wrong. Both the penny and the book fall at the same speed, so they should reach the ground at about the same time. Try this with a bunch of different objects.

6. What will a kitten be when it grows up?

(A) A dog
(B) A guinea pig
(C) A cat

In order to survive, animals need many of the same things humans need to stay healthy and happy. Nutritious food (p. 245), plenty of water, and shelter from bad weather are just some of these things.

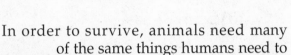

Pets need love and protection while they are young, because they are too small to find their own food or defend themselves against hungry predators.

If an animal gets hurt or sick, a **veterinarian** can be a big help. Veterinarians are just like doctors, helping animals the same way doctors help people. Just like people, most tame animals need regular check-ups just to make sure everything is OK. Veterinarians give pets and livestock their check-ups, help them out when they're sick, and sometimes even help deliver their babies.

ANIMALS AND THEIR BABY NAMES	
DOG	PUPPY
ELEPHANT	CALF
DEER	FAWN
FISH	FRY
KANGAROO	JOEY
SEAL	WHELP
SWAN	CYGNET
COCKROACH	NYMPH
TURKEY	POULT
WHALE	CALF
ZEBRA	COLT
CHICKEN	CHICK

7. What do we call a group of animals that no longer exists?

(A) Mammals

(B) Extinct

(C) Species

Since the beginning of animal life on this planet, there have been **species** that die out. A species is a type of animal. When a species dies out and there are none of them left, then that species is **extinct**. Dinosaurs (p. 267) are an example of a species that became extinct. Something happened millions of years ago that caused all the dinosaurs then living to die. Today, there are no dinosaurs anywhere.

A number of things can make a species die. It's a normal part of nature for some species to become extinct. It can happen because the animal's food supply or home is destroyed in some way. Unfortunately, in the last hundred years, many more species have become extinct than in the past. For one thing, human interference in nature is greater now than it ever was. Pollution (p. 255) can kill animals. When a crop or food supply gets sprayed with chemicals, those chemicals can make the animals who eat the food sick. If forests are cut down for farmland or houses, large numbers of animals often lose their homes. Some species become extinct when people hunt them until there are none left.

In recent years, people who are concerned about the rising rate of extintion have tried to protect certain animals that

definition

extinct

(ek STINKT) *adj.*, a type of animal or group of people that has completely died out.

The dodo was a large, hook-billed bird that is now extinct.

The Dodo bird

Passenger pigeons

The California Condor

seem to be in danger of extinction by calling the species endangered. An **endangered species** may become extinct if its home or food supply is threatened, or if it is hunted too heavily, so people try to protect them from these things by passing laws. Perhaps we can still save some endangered species.

8. Which of the following animals is a mammal?

(A) A lizard

(B) A hamster

(C) A guppy

The **animal kingdom** is the group of animals on the earth. **Scientists** believe that there are over ten million species of animals on the planet, in all shapes and sizes. Cats, dogs, birds, fish, spiders, worms, snakes, buffaloes, bats, people: we're all animals. To make it easier to talk about animals, scientists group them together into different categories according to certain characteristics the animals may share. The scientists who decide which group, or class, an animal will belong to are called **zoologists**. There are many different classes of animals. Some of the classes into which animals are categorized are reptiles, birds, insects, and mammals.

All Mammals Have These Four Main Characteristics:

1. MAMMALS ARE WARM-BLOODED (UNLIKE REPTILES).

2. MAMMALS ARE COVERED IN FUR OR HAIR (YES, YOU TOO).

3. MAMMALS FEED THEIR YOUNG WITH THEIR OWN MILK.

4. MAMMALS HAVE A PARTICULAR TYPE OF JAWBONE JOINT.

CULTURESCOPE

Homeward Bound—The Incredible Journey. Two dogs and a cat, stranded far from home, make an unbelievable trek back to their family.

The tallest, the fastest, and the noisiest animals on Earth are all **mammals**. The fastest land animal on Earth is the cheetah. In the open fields of its home in Africa, the cheetah reaches a speed of sixty miles per hour. That's as fast as a car on a highway The tallest animal on Earth is the giraffe, which also lives in Africa. Giraffes can grow to be twenty feet tall. The noisiest animals on Earth are the Howler monkeys of Central and South America. They make so much noise that they can be heard clearly from two miles away.

The sperm whale is a mammal.

9. The Big Dipper is a group of
- **(A) stars**
- **(B) numbers**
- **(C) toys**

MORE STUFF ABOUT ANIMALS

- A SLUG HAS FOUR NOSES.
- CRANES ARE REVERED IN ASIA AS SYMBOLS OF LONG LIFE.
- THE FATHER SEAHORSE HAS A POUCH IN WHICH THE MOTHER LAYS HER EGGS. HE CARRIES THEM AROUND FOR TWO MONTHS UNTIL THEY HATCH, AND THEN HE WATCHES OVER THEM.
- AN AFRICAN ELEPHANT IS PREGNANT FOR 1 3/4 YEARS.
- THE BALD EAGLE IS NOT BALD—IT JUST HAS WHITE FEATHERS ON ITS HEAD.
- A CHAMELEON CAN MOVE ITS EYES IN TWO DIFFERENT DIRECTIONS AT THE SAME TIME.
- THE LARGEST BRAIN BELONGS TO THE SPERM WHALE—IT WEIGHS TWENTY-TWO POUNDS.

About 6,000 stars are visible in the night sky without a telescope—3,000 in the northern sky and 3,000 in the southern sky. Visibility of stars depends on a lot of different factors. If you live in a big city or in an area with lots of street lamps, it is difficult to see the stars because of all the lights around you. Since the earth revolves around the sun, the stars appear in different places in the sky at different times of the year. Only one star remains constant: **Polaris**, the **North Star**.

Because Polaris is always in the same place, sailors and travelers have used it for years to find their way through the night.

When ancient peoples saw the stars at night they imagined that the groups of stars were things such as bears or hunters. We still identify stars as parts of these patterns, which are called **constellations**.

A great place to learn more about stars and constellations is a **planetarium**. A planetarium is like a movie theater, but instead of watching a movie, you watch the night sky, which is projected above your head onto a big, curved ceiling. When the lights in the planetarium are turned out, it's just like you're outside on a clear night, with thousands of stars and constellations overhead.

definition

constellation
(kahn ste LAY shun)
noun, a group of stars that form a pattern.

Julian pointed out the Big Dipper and Orion as his favorite constellations.

Glow-In-The-Dark Constellations: A Field Guide for Young Stargazers, by C.E. Thompson. Read about the constellations, then turn out the lights and see them twinkle.

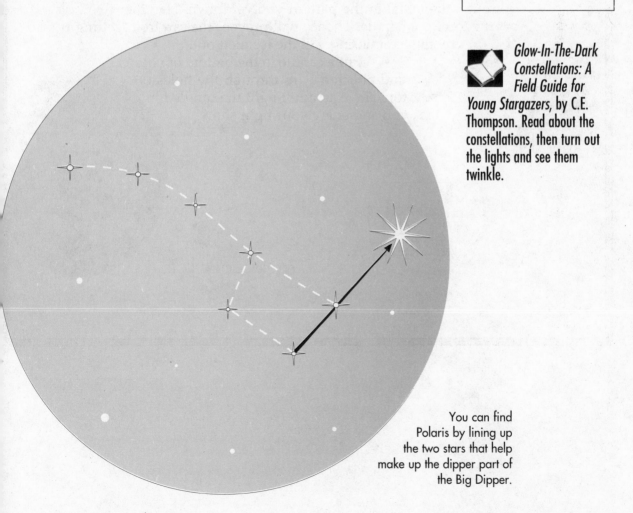

You can find Polaris by lining up the two stars that help make up the dipper part of the Big Dipper.

Tin Can Lantern

This is a great way to illuminate the night while camping out.

- Find a can with a smooth surface. A coffee can works best. Draw a pattern of dots with a felt marker on the outside. Fill the can with water and freeze for 24 hours.

- Have a parent or helper hammer nails to pierce through the metal in the pattern you've drawn. Hammer two holes at the top for a handle. The ice will prevent the can from getting ruined by the hammering. Let the ice melt out.

- Put a candle in the bottom of your can and attach a wire through the holes on top. Have an adult light the candle for you and enjoy your light show!

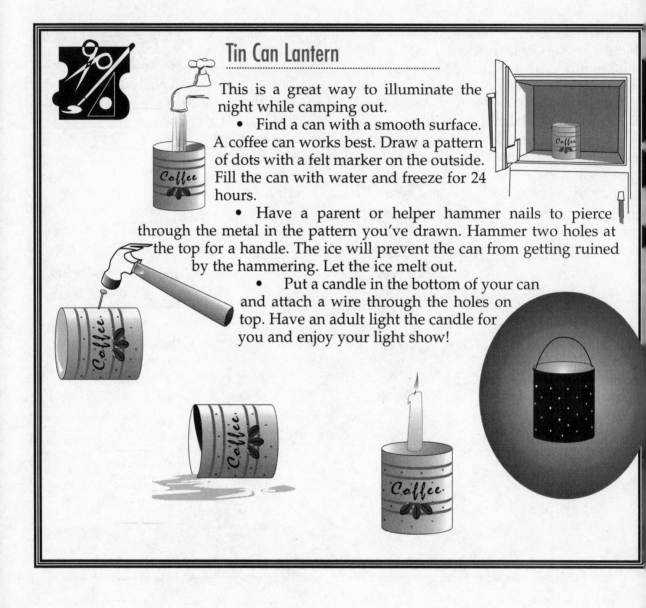

10. Which of the following foods gives you the most vitamin C?

(A) Milk

(B) Candy

(C) Orange juice

An important part of caring for yourself is knowing about good **nutrition.** Eating right, exercising, and staying safe all help make you strong and well. To help people make good decisions about what to eat, the Food and Drug Administration, the part of our government (p. 295) that figures out which foods and drugs are good for you, has made this food pyramid.

As you can see, you should be eating mainly grains, vegetables and fruits. Meats are not as big a part of people's meals as they once were, becuse now we know more about what's good for you. Think about what you ate today. Did you eat the right amounts from each group?

All of the following make great snacks:

Fruit, pretzels, cut up vegetables, peanut butter on bread or crackers, leftovers from dinner, cold pizza, toast with jelly, low-fat crackers, graham crackers.

The FDA food pyramid

government (p. 295)

definition

Nutritious
(noo TRISH us) *adj.*, nourishing; good for you.

*Raw carrots and yogurt dip make a **nutritious** snack.*

Healthy Kids (Family Channel). The "Healthy Kids" series has pediatricians and families who talk about health and nutrition.

Recipe

Here are some great-tasting, nutritious snacks and meals that you can make.

ANTS ON A LOG

Take as many stalks of celery as you think you could possibly eat.
Wash them off and ask someone older to help you cut them into 2-3 inch pieces.
Fill each piece with peanut butter, smoothing off the top as you go.
Top with raisins (that's the ant part) and enjoy!

FRUIT KABOBS

Fresh fruit is best, but canned fruit is good in a pinch.
If you have canned fruit, you can just take the pieces out of the can and skewer each on a wooden skewer (like you might use for a barbeque—ask a parent).
If you have some good fresh fruit, wash it all off and ask someone to help you cut it into bite-sized pieces.
The best fruit to use:

Grapes, bananas, peaches, melon, pineapple, apple.
Put all your favorites together and alternate different fruits as you skewer. Try to make it look pretty. Present to your favorite people as an elegant and delicious snack.

QUICKIE QUESADILLAS

For those of you who like a Mexican flair to your snacks.
You'll need some flour or corn tortillas, shredded cheese (cheddar or Monterey Jack are best, but any of your favorites is fine) and, if you like, some tomato, salsa, or sour cream.
Ask a grown-up to help. Preheat either the toaster oven, if you have one, or the oven to 375 degrees. Put a couple of tortillas on a sheet of aluminum foil, or a small cookie sheet. Sprinkle with cheese and pop in the oven or toaster oven for about 5 minutes, or until all the cheese melts. Top with the tomato, salsa or sour cream if you have them, and enjoy.
Heathful Snacking!

11. Name two dairy products.

1. _____

2. _____

Most of the **dairy products** we eat come from cows. Cows are a member of the cattle family. Cattle include cows, bulls, buffalo, and bison. Dairy cows are domesticated animals raised for their milk, and they produce lots and lots of it —millions of gallons a year. That milk goes through many different steps to get from the cow to your glass.

On most large dairy farms, cows are milked by milking machines. The milk that comes from a cow is called "raw milk." It must be **pasteurized** to prevent bacteria from growing in the milk. It is then stored in a refrigerator until it can be processed into the following products:

BUTTER	CHURNED MILK FAT
CHEESE	MILK CURDS (THE SOLIDS IN THE MILK) WITH THE LIQUID PART PRESSED OUT
CREAM	THE RICH FAT OF THE MILK THAT IS REMOVED TO MAKE THE MILK LOW-FAT OR SKIM
SKIM MILK	MILK FROM WHICH THE FAT HAS BEEN REMOVED
YOGURT	MILK TO WHICH A CERTAIN KIND OF BACTERIA IS ADDED, FORMING TANGY CURDS, OFTEN MIXED WITH FRUIT AND SUGAR
ICE CREAM	CREAM, MILK, AND FLAVORING MIXED TOGETHER AND FROZEN. ICE CREAM MUST BE STIRRED WHILE IT IS FREEZING TO GIVE IT ITS CREAMY TEXTURE.

RECIPE

MAKE YOUR OWN BUTTER

You'll need:

• *A jar*

• *A cup of whole milk*

Put the milk in the jar and shake it like crazy. After few minutes, you should see little bits of something solid floating around. Strain those out of the remaining milk. That's the butter! You can spread it on some bread and enjoy.

definition

domesticate
(doh MES ti kayt) *verb*
to tame a wild animal.

*Some animals, like dogs
and cats, are easier to
domesticate than
others; like wolverines.*

Dairy products are considered an important part of a good diet because they provide so many nutrients. They are a good source of protein, minerals, vitamins and carbohydrates. **Calcium,** a mineral, is found in large quantities in dairy products, and helps you develop healthy bones and teeth.

Usborne Book of Science Tricks and Magic, by Gaby Waters. Fun science tricks to perform for your friends.

12. Which of the following covers most of the Earth?

(A) Land
(B) Water
(C) Cereal

Every living thing on earth needs water to survive. Thankfully, more than 70 percent of the surface of the earth is covered with it. When you look at a globe, most of it is blue, representing water. 70 percent of the planet is much more than half of the planet.

Most of the water that covers the earth is the salt water of the

oceans. A small amount of water is frozen into ice and snow at the **North and South Poles**. The rest is the fresh water that makes up the lakes, rivers, streams, ponds, and all other water in the ground.

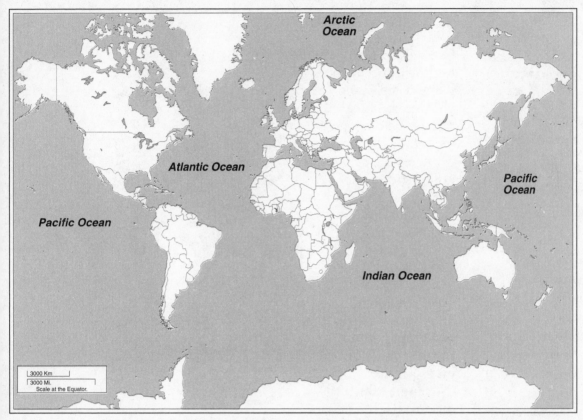

The world's four oceans: the Arctic, Atlantic, Indian, and Pacific.

The earth is mainly made up of water, and so are we! More than two-thirds of your body is water. Without water, no one could survive. You can live without water for about four days—that's it. Drinking lots of pure water and liquids such as juice and milk (not soda!) is absolutely essential to good health. On a hot day, your body loses even more water through sweat, so you should be sure to drink extra water to keep yourself healthy.

definition

hydrate
(HI drayt) *verb*, to fill with water.

"OK, everybody hydrate!" yelled Tim's soccer coach as the water bottles were passed around.

3

You can see for yourself how this works.

All you need is:

- *A tennis ball, or similar sized ball (the moon)*
- *A beachball, or basketball (the earth)*
- *A lamp, without the lamp shade (the sun)*

Now, have someone hold up the basketball or beachball with the lamp shining light on it. Move the tennis ball around the basketball. Do you see how, depending on the position of the tennis ball, different amounts of the lamp's light shine on it?

13. How often does a full moon appear?

(A) Every night
(B) Once a week
(C) Once a month

On a clear night, the brightest, largest thing in the sky is usually the **moon**. But you've probably noticed that as the days go by, the moon changes shape, going from a big round circle (called a full moon) to a skinny **crescent** shape.

When you see the moon glowing in the sky, you might think that it gives off light like the sun. But the moon itself doesn't have its own source of light. What you're seeing is the sun's light bouncing off of the moon.

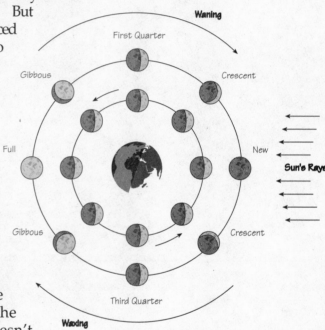

As the moon moves around the earth, differing amounts of sunlight reach the moon and bounce off of it. A full moon happens when the moon is completely lit up by the sun.

It takes a little less than a month for the moon to revolve around the earth one time. So it's about a month from one full moon to the next. Halfway in between there's a "new moon." That's when the moon is completely dark. When it's not a full moon, and it's a clear night or you're using **binoculars**, you can just make out the dark part of the moon.

LUNAR FACTS

- THE MOON IS 238,855 MILES FROM EARTH.
- IT TAKES THE MOON 27 DAYS, 7 HOURS, AND 43 MINUTES TO REVOLVE AROUND THE EARTH ONE TIME. THE MOON HAS NO ATMOSPHERE (YOU COULDN'T BREATHE THERE).
- THE TEMPERATURE ON THE MOON RANGES FROM 240 DEGREES F, TO -260 DEGREES F. THERE ARE LOTS OF MOONS ORBITING AROUND OTHER PLANETS IN OUR SOLAR SYSTEM.
- THE MOON'S PULL ON THE EARTH CAUSES OUR TIDES TO RISE AND FALL.

14. March comes in like a lion and goes out like a _____.

(A) Bear
(B) Lamb
(C) Hermit Crab

The change of **seasons** can be pretty radical in some parts of the country. Take the month of March, for example. Often March begins with very cold, blustery weather. As the month goes on, the weather tends to warm up. By the end of March, we are firmly into spring.

You only have to look at pictures of tropical islands in the middle of winter to figure out that the climate is different all over the

 The Magic School Bus at the Waterworks, by Joanna Cole and Bruce Degan. Ms. Frizzle and her class get to see first-hand how water gets from one place to the next.

CULTURESCOPE

National Geographic Video: For All Mankind. This video covers the flights to the moon and includes rare narration by the Apollo astronauts.

The Four Seasons, by Vivaldi. Four concertos that beautifully evoke the seasonal cycle.

world. Some places are always cold, like the North Pole, some are always hot, and some have real changes in weather from one time of year to another. It all has to do with the way the Earth is tilted toward the sun. In the picture below, you can see that the Earth is tilted slightly. Because of that tilt, and the fact that the Earth revolves around the sun, at certain times of the year a part of the earth is closer to the sun, and at other times of the year that part is farther away. The farther you are from the sun, the colder it becomes. When the sun is closer, the **temperature** warms up and it becomes summer. The **equator,** an imaginary line that goes around the middle of the Earth, is closest to the sun no matter how the earth is tilted, so anything around the equator is hot all year round.

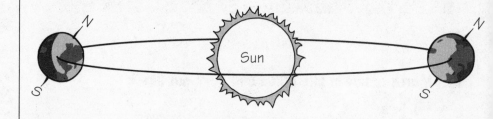

When it's summer in the northern part of the world, it's winter in the southern half. When it's winter in the northern part, it's summer in the southern part.

15. Which of the following places isn't like the other two?

(A) Desert

(B) Swamp

(C) Bog

The **wetlands** are the freshwater habitats of many swamp and marsh animals. Many birds, mammals, and reptiles, as well as different types of plant life, make their home in the wetlands of the world.

Swamps, marshes, and bogs generally form in an area near a lake where the water

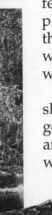

cannot drain away properly. They may also form in an area where the land is generally dry, but the water from rain can't drain away from a particular place. The amount of water in a swamp usually changes from season to season. Sometimes the water level may be

CULTURESCOPE

"Wildlife Chronicles" and *"Nature Watch"* (The Discovery Channel). Both of these Discovery series bring wild animals from all over the world into your living room (or wherever you watch TV).

quite high, while at other times the swamp may be totally dry.

The **Florida Everglades** is one of the largest swamps in the country, covering 5,000 square miles. It is an important part of the ecology of Florida, and many animals and plants depend on the Everglades to stay alive.

A pelican

SWAMP THINGS

Pelicans
Pelicans build their nests in marsh areas. Some breeds of pelican have become rare due to the destruction of their nesting sites.

Crocodiles
Crocodiles can reach lengths of twenty-one feet. One way to tell a crocodile from an alligator is that crocodiles have pointier noses than do alligators.

Proboscis Monkey
This monkey, so named because of its funny nose, lives in the mangrove tree and is a good swimmer.

The Mangrove Tree
The Mangrove tree grows in tropical swamps. Its roots grow into the mud, and its seedlings establish quickly so they are not washed away. The roots of this tree stick up above mud to get the oxygen the tree needs to grow.

A Probiscus Monkey and her baby

16. Which of the following gases pollutes the air?

(A) Oxygen

(B) Nitrogen

(C) Carbon monoxide

Pollution is something that makes the air, earth, or water dirty and harmful to living things. Pollution is an old problem—it has been around for hundreds of years. In the past, when factories burned coal, the smoke contained lots of harmful chemicals that were released into the atmosphere. Today, even though people are much more aware of what is harmful to the environment, pollutants still enter the air, ground, and water all the time.

Smoke from cars and trucks and factories contains lead, carbon monoxide, carbon dioxide, and other pollutants. Farmers spray crops with **pesticides** to keep insects away, but the leftover chemicals wash into the soil. Oil and gasoline leak from ships, polluting the water and making it uninhabitable for fish and other marine life.

People throw garbage on the ground. Not only is garbage ugly to look at, it is not good for animals or the environment. In many places around the country, there's hardly any room left to store all the garbage that we make. Pollution is a big problem that reaches into all different parts of our society. But all of us can do our share to help slow down the pace of pollution and keep our environment beautiful.

Recycling takes certain types of garbage, like newspapers (p. 123) or glass, and reprocesses them so they may be reused. Find out if your neighborhood recycles. If not, ask if a recycling program could be started.

definition

environmentalist
(en vy ren MENT ul ist)
noun, someone concerned about the environment.

Rickie, worried about the city's water pollution problem, rallied every **environmentalist** *in her school to protest the nearby chemical plant.*

HERE ARE SOME ORGANIZATIONS THAT ARE HELPING THE ENVIRONMENT.

Write to them and they'll send you information about how to make the world a cleaner place.

The Children's Rainforest
P.O. Box 936
Lewiston, ME 04240

The Cousteau Society
870 Greenbriar Circle
Suite 402
Chesapeake, VA 23320

Greenpeace, USA
1436 U St. NW
Washington, D.C. 20009

Don't buy things you won't use. Write on both sides of the paper in your notebooks. Rather than throwing them away, swap toys and clothes with friends, or ask a parent to donate them to people who could use them.

Car pooling can also help. The more people in each car, the fewer cars there are on the road. If your parents are driving, ask them to pick up a friend if you have room. If you can, take a bus or a train instead of driving. Clean up the litter around your house or apartment. If everyone cleaned up the litter on his own street, we'd have much cleaner neighborhoods.

17. Name three colors in the rainbow.

1. _____
2. _____
3. _____

Color comes from light. A **prism**, a special triangular-shaped piece of glass, "breaks up" a stream of light into its colors. These colors are called the **spectrum**.

When you see a rainbow in the sky, you are seeing small drops of water in the air acting like prisms. The drops of water take light and break it up into its many pieces. No matter what, light will always break into the same spectrum, and the colors will be in the same order. One way to remember the colors of the rainbow or spectrum is by remembering this name:

ROY G. BIV

Who is Roy G. Biv? His name is made up of all the colors of the rainbow in order—Red Orange Yellow Green Blue Indigo Violet.

Sunlight, which looks perfectly white to you, is a combination of many different colors of light. We see color in things because some things absorb certain of those bands of light and reflect the others.

---

definition

spectrum
(SPEK trum) *noun*, the bands of color that appear together in a rainbow.

Sometimes a rainbow is so clear you can see every color in the spectrum.

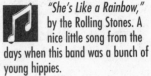

"She's Like a Rainbow," by the Rolling Stones. A nice little song from the days when this band was a bunch of young hippies.

This car looks purple because purple paint absorbs every color in the spectrum *but* purple. The purple bounces back, so that's what your eyes see. That's also why the purple words in this book are purple—the purple ink absorbs every color except purple.

PRIMARY COLORS

The primary colors are red, blue and yellow. These three colors can be used in different combinations to create any other color (except white).

18. Which of these states borders the Pacific Ocean?

(A) California
(B) Illinois
(C) Florida

There are four main bodies of water, or **oceans**, in the world. In order of largest to smallest, they are the Pacific Ocean, the Atlantic Ocean, the Indian Ocean, and the Arctic Ocean.

The **Pacific** is the largest and deepest ocean in the world. It is located between North America and Asia, and in total covers more than a third of the whole globe. The deepest spot in the world is the Marianas Trench in the Pacific Ocean. In 1960, a diving vessel called a **bathyscaphe** dived almost seven miles to the bottom of the Marianas Trench. It took about five hours to get all the way to the bottom.

The Bathyscaphe

definition

ocean

(OH shun) *noun* the large body of salt water that covers almost 3/4 of the earth's surface, or one of the four main divisions of this body of water: Pacific, Atlantic, Indian, or Arctic.

Denise wrote a funny song about sailing across the ocean in a paper cup.

The **Atlantic Ocean** separates Europe and Africa to the east and Europe and the Americas to the west. The Atlantic was probably named after Atlantis, a legandary island nation said to have sunk around 10,000 B.C. The North Atlantic is the saltiest of all the four major oceans and also has the highest waves, reaching heights of almost sixty feet!

Betweeen Africa and Australia, with India to the north, lies the

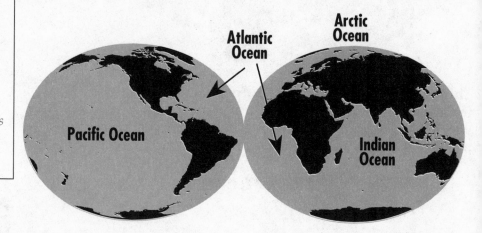

WHERE DOES SALT WATER COME FROM?

Ocean water is salty because of the dissolved salt and minerals that come from the rocks lining the rivers that flow into the ocean. The amount of salt in the ocean, or anything for that matter, is called its salinity.

Indian Ocean. Its deepest spot is the Java Trench, at over four miles deep, which gives you an idea of just how deep the Pacific's Marianas Trench is—almost twice as deep as the Java.

The Arctic Ocean surrounds the North Pole and, because of the frigid climate and low **salinity** of the Ocean, freezes easily and often.

WHY DO ICEBERGS FLOAT?

Ice weighs less than water. When water freezes, it expands as air bubbles get trapped inside. Because there is air trapped in with the water (that's what the little white dots are), the ice is lighter and floats. Test this for yourself: Put an ice cube in a glass of water. Now, if you add salt to the water, the ice will float even higher because salt makes the water heavier.

19. Which of the following is NOT a part of a plant:

(A) Roots

(B) Lungs

(C) Leaves

Different parts of the plant perform different functions.

The **flower** of a flowering plant is the reproductive part of the plant. All the things necessary to produce seeds are in the flower. The **leaves** of a plant produce the food for the plant. They absorb sunlight and carbon dioxide from the air and combine them with nutrients from the soil to produce plant food. The **fruits** of a plant contain its **seeds**. Some plants' seeds are called **pits** (the seed of a peach, for example), and some are called **beans**. The **stem** of the plant (the trunk, if the plant is really big) carries the water and food up and down the plant—to and from leaves and roots—and holds the plant up. The **roots** anchor the plant into the ground and absorb water and minerals from the soil.

Flower

Leaves

Stem

Roots

definition

photosynthesis (foh toh SIN tha sis) *noun*, the process a plant uses to produce its own food; the formation of sugars in a plant using sunlight, water, and carbon dioxide.

In biology Sheila learned all about photo-synthesis by studying ferns.

HOW DO ROOTS WORK?

The ingredients:

- A PIECE OF CELERY (MAKE SURE IT HAS LEAVES ON IT)
- A CLEAN JAR
- BLUE OR RED FOOD COLORING (DON'T USE GREEN OR YELLOW)

1. Fill the jar with water and add a few drops of food coloring—enough to make the water a nice color.

2. Carefully cut about an inch or two off of the bottom of the celery stalk.

3. Place the stalk in the colored water.

4. After about an hour, check the stalk. What do you see? Cut another 1/2 inch off of the bottom. Those red or blue dots are the veins that lead through the stalk of the celery. Put the celery back into the water and leave it for a few hours or overnight. What do you think will happen eventually?

When you are all finished, cut open the stalk. Those tubes you see are called **xylem**. They carry the water from the root to the leaves. You can eat the celery if you like—food coloring is harmless and won't change the taste of celery.

20. In what season are days the shortest?

(A) Summer
(B) Fall
(C) Winter

You already know that it is winter when our part of the world (the northern hemisphere) is tilted farthest from the sun. Look at the way the sun hits us in the winter and in the summer:

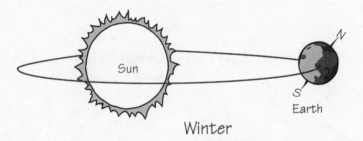

Winter

In the winter, remember that one rotation of the earth happens every day. We are tilted away from the sun, so the amount of time we spend in sunlight during our daily rotation is very little, compared to the rest of the year. The shortest day of the year, the day we are tilted farthest away from the sun, is December 21. This day is called the **winter solstice**.

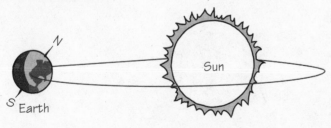

Summer

During the summer, we are tilted towards the sun. As a result, we are in the sun for a longer time as we make our daily rotation. Days in the summer are longer. The longest day of the year is June 21, the **summer solstice**.

In spring, days get longer and longer after the short winter days. On March 21, the **spring equinox**, we get exactly the same amount of day as night. The **autumnal equinox** falls on September 21, another day when day and night are exactly the same length.

21. Name the five senses:

1. _____
2. _____
3. _____
4. _____
5. _____

The **senses** are what people and animals use to find out about the world. You get information about the things around you by looking at, hearing, touching, tasting, or smelling them. There's really no other way for your body to find out about things. You learn if the food you are eating is good or bad by tasting it. You learn if it is cold outside and you need a coat by the sense of touch, the feel of cold on your skin. You learn in school by hearing things and seeing things. You can sense the danger of a fire by smelling smoke.

Taste

Hearing   Sight   Smell

Touch

4

definition

acute

(uh kyoot) *adj.*, very sensitive.

*Patrice had an **acute** sense of hearing; she could hear things that happened on the other side of the house.*

THERE'S A COMPASS IN YOUR NOSE

We all have a trace of iron in our noses, and that makes a sort of basic compass in the bone between our eyes. Many people can use this to orient themselves—even if they are blindfolded— towards the North Pole!

Some people can't use all their senses: a blind person cannot see; a deaf person cannot hear; some people lose some of their sense of touch if their skin is burned or frozen in an accident. Yet often, if one of the senses is not working well, another will become stronger to make up for the loss. Many blind people have very good senses of smell or hearing, for example, because they have to compensate for not being able to see.

Animals have senses that are often much more acute than ours. **Sharks**, for example, can smell blood in water over a hundred yards away. Dogs also have very strong senses of smell. **Bloodhounds** are used to track down lost people and things because their sense of smell is extremely sensitive. Some animals even have a magnetic sense. **Monarch butterflies** have a built-in compass that allows them to migrate thousands of miles when they are only a few weeks old.

YOUR NOSTRILS TAKE TURNS!

That's right—they take turns every three hours or so—one breathes and smells while the other takes a rest.

Tommy, by The Who. A "rock opera" about a "deaf, dumb and blind kid" who "plays a mean pinball." Includes the classic "See Me, Feel Me."

22. Which of the following is NOT an insect?

(A) A spider
(B) A beetle
(C) A butterfly

A spider sure seems like an **insect**—it can climb anywhere, it's got lots of legs, and it crunches when you step on it. But a spider is not an insect. An insect has six legs, while spiders have eight. Spiders are classified as **arachnids**.

4

Insect, by Laurence Mound. This entertaining book has tons of great pictures.

definition

exoskeleton

(eks oh SKEL a ten) *noun*, the hard outside skeleton of an insect.

Samantha couldn't help being amazed at the strength of the exoskeleton of a beetle she watched fall from a tree.

HERE ARE SOME OF THE FEATURES THAT CHARACTERIZE AN INSECT

- SIX LEGS
- NO BACKBONE
- JOINTED LEGS
- HARD, PROTECTIVE EXOSKELETON (ON THE OUTSIDE OF THEIR BODIES)
- WINGS (USUALLY)
- THREE BODY SECTIONS: HEAD, THORAX, ABDOMEN

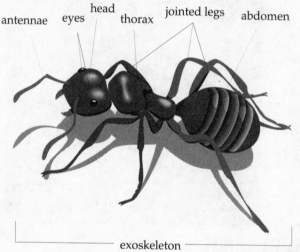

antennae   eyes   head   thorax   jointed legs   abdomen

exoskeleton

OUR SIX-LEGGED FRIENDS

One beehive can contain 80,000 bees.
There are 200 million insects for each person on earth.
There are over 14,000 species of ants.
The Goliath Beetle is the heaviest living insect at an average weight of 3.5 ounces.

To get a clearer idea of the parts of an insect, check out this ant.

Hard exoskeleton. Made of chitin, the exoskeleton protects the insect. When the insect is young it must shed, or molt, its exoskeleton to allow its body to grow.

Abdomen. The first body part of the insect—usually the largest. It's where the guts, the sex organs, the heart, and the digestive system are all located

Thorax. The middle body part. It is where the six legs join, and where the wings, if there are any, are attached.

Head. The head is where the insect's brain, eyes, and antennae are located.

Compound eyes. An insect's eyes are

Bees in their hive

made up of hundreds of tiny eyes put together. Because of this, insects can detect movement from all around them (that's why it's so hard to swat a fly).

Antennae. An insect uses antennae to feel and smell.

Jointed legs. Insects' legs consist of four main parts jointed together. They use their legs to scamper, crawl, or even jump, depending on the species.

Wings. Though not all insects have wings, most do. There are no muscles in the wings themselves; instead, they are controlled by muscles in the thorax.

Some insects are harmful to man. Flies can spread sickness, and other insects, like locusts, can destroy the crops that we depend on to eat. But most insects have a very important role to play in the world. Bees pollinate flowers. Others are crucial sources of food for mammals and reptiles. There are a lot of insects in the world—over one million different species. Bugs outnumber people, so we might as well learn to live with them.

The Fly. This movie has been recently remade, but you should see the old one. It's about a man who starts to turn into a you-know what.

23. Which of the following is a type of rock?

(A) Aluminum
(B) Sedimentary
(C) Voluminous

Rocks are classified into three groups, depending on how they were formed: sedimentary, igneous, and metamorphic.

Sedimentary rocks are formed as small pieces of rock and minerals called sediment are deposited in layers, usually along a river bank or near a body of water. Each successive layer pushes down the previous one, until all of them combine to form a rock. You can usually see the layers in sedimentary rock. Some examples are limestone, conglomerate, and sandstone. **Igneous rocks** start off deep within the earth, where the temperature is so hot that the rock melts. This liquid rock is called magma. As the magma cools, it forms the rock. Some common examples of igneous rocks are granite, basalt, and obsidian.

Metamorphosis means change, like when caterpillars turn into butterflies. **Metamorphic rocks** start out as either sedimentary or

definition

mineral
(MIN er el) *noun*, the substance that makes up rocks.

Lead, iron, and gold are minerals.

Rocks and Minerals, by Dr. R.F. Symes and the staff of the Museum of Natural History, London. Great pictures, interesting rock facts— what more could you want?

igneous and then change form. Two things can make a rock change: heat and pressure. Buried rocks may be squeezed and baked to actually form new minerals and crystals. Some examples of metamorphic rocks are marble (changed from limestone), slate (comes from mica, and schists.

Rock collecting is a fun hobby. You can start by finding rocks in your neighborhood and trying to identify them. You may also want to buy rocks to add to your collection. To keep your collection in good order, you should store your rocks in trays with dividers or small boxes, and get a rock tumbler to polish up your stones. The rocks that are used to make jewelry are highly polished stones. Many rock tumblers come with kits for making jewelry or key chains.

Often, when basaltic lava cools, it forms **hexagonal** columns—columns with six sides. An example of this is the Giant's Causeway in Northern Ireland, a naturally occurring rock formation.

24.   A fossil is

(A) a living plant or animal
(B) the remains of a dead animal or plant preserved in rock or ice
(C) a very old stone

Ancient Journey's "Searching for Dinosaurs" (The Learning Channel). Archeologists figure out a dinosaur's age, diet, and appearance from its fossilized remains.

Sometimes when a plant or animal dies it falls into mud, dead leaves, or water and is covered by stuff before it decays. As the years go by, the layers of dirt and rock build up over the remains and most of the animal or plant finally does decay. What is left is the fossilized remains of the animal or plant, usually the bones or shells of an animal or the leaves of a plant. The impression often gets filled in by a mineral—so you end up with a mold of the animal's bones or shell. A **fossil** can also be the remains of a plant or animal frozen in ice. **Woolly mammoths** have been discovered intact as the glaciers they became trapped in melted.

Scientists look at fossils for clues about ancient life. Rocks preserve remains from millions of years ago. There are fossils of dinosaur bones and eggs, ancient plants that no longer exist, and all sorts of now-extinct creatures.

Fossils also help scientists date particular rocks. If a scientist sees the fossil of a dinosaur that lived during a certain time period, then the rock surrounding it must have formed during that time period.

The largest land predator ever may have been an alligator found fossilized along the banks of the Amazon River in rocks dated at eight million years ago. It had a five-foot-long jaw (bigger than you!) and four-inch-long teeth. From these measurements, scientists estimate that he was about forty feet long and weighed in at thirteen tons—larger than **Tyrannosaurus Rex**! Imagine if that one never became extinct.

definition

decay
(dee KAY) *verb*, to decompose or rot away.

If your diet consists of candy bars, taffy, and jelly beans you might have trouble with tooth decay.

JURASSIC BIGFOOT?

....

The largest fossilized footprint of a dinosaur was found in Salt Lake City, Utah. It measured 53.5 inches long and 32 inches wide. It was believed be made by a hadrosaurid *or* duckbill dinosaur.

4

25. Which of the following is a type of cloud formation?

(A) Cirrus

(B) Styrofoam

(C) Barometer

You may think all clouds are pretty much the same, but if you look at the sky closely, you'll notice lots of variations. There are three main types of clouds .

Cirrus clouds are those feathery stringy clouds that float highest of all in the sky. They are so high up, around ten miles above sea level, that they contain only ice crystals. **Cumulus clouds** are the next highest, usually between about two miles and about eight miles up. Cumulus clouds are the ones most people think of when they think of clouds. They're the thick, fluffy ones that may be patchy or really thick and dense. **Stratus clouds** make thunderstorms.

"Both Sides Now" by Joni Mitchell. Joni "looks at clouds from both sides now," and she's not even in a plane!

Cirrus

Cumulus

Stratus

Stratus are the closest to the ground. They lie low in the sky and form in thin sheets. If you see lots of gray stratus clouds, it's probably going to rain.

Now that you know the cloud formations, here's how they develop. Water evaporates from the earth's seas, lakes, rivers—even from the ground itself. As evaporated water moves up into the atmosphere, it begins to cool. The evaporated water then forms droplets that make up clouds. When the droplets become too heavy to stay up in the sky, they make some form of **precipitation**: rain, snow, sleet, or hail.

Hail is definitely one of the strangest things a cloud drops on us. When a strong wind carries ice back up into a cloud over and

over again, the ice builds up into balls called hailstones. When they become too large, they fall to the ground. Hail-stones can be as small as a super-ball or as big as a baseball, making everyone run for cover, or the batting cages.

definition

precipitation
(pree SIP i tay shun)
noun, rain, snow, sleet or hail; any type of water that falls from the sky.

*The newspaper forecasted over three inches of **precipitation** for the holiday weekend.*

4

26. At what temperature would you most likely set your oven to bake cookies?

(A) 200 degrees

(B) 350 degrees

(C) 500 degrees

By the time you're in fourth grade, you can take a very active role in cooking for yourself or for your family. But you'll need to know some cooking basics.

To begin with you'll need the right equipment. When a **recipe** calls for a teaspoon or a tablespoon, it is talking about measuring spoons. Don't use a regular spoon—it's not as exact. The same thing holds true for cups and half cups. Use a measuring cup to measure out liquids, flour, rice, sugar, etc. To get a "level" cup, put a little extra in the measuring cup and then sweep across the top with the flat side of a knife to make whatever you're measuring lie flat at the top of the cup. You'll probably need mixing bowls and pans to cook up your concoctions. Before you begin cooking, make sure to read the recipe all the way through to make sure that you've got all the

Kids Get Cooking (Kid Vidz). This Kid Vidz video is a great introduction to cooking.

equipment you need. If you don't have the right sized pan, you can try to borrow one, or you can buy a disposable pan from the grocery store.

You'll also need to read through the whole recipe first to make sure you have all the ingredients you need. Be careful about substituting anything. Once you know your way around a kitchen, you'll learn that you can substitute margarine for butter, for example, without too much change. But for now, follow the recipe exactly. There's a big difference between baking soda and baking powder, and between medium and jumbo eggs. Different oils have different flavors. Semisweet chocolate and baker's chocolate are also two completely different things. So, what seems to you like a completely harmless change can ruin all your hard work.

RECIPES

CHOCOLATE CHIP COOKIES

Preheat oven to 375 degrees F.
2 1/4 c. all-purpose flour
1 tsp baking soda
1 tsp salt
1 c. (2 sticks) butter, softened
3/4 c. granulated sugar
3/4 c. brown sugar, packed
1 tsp. vanilla extract
2 eggs
2 c. chocolate chips
1 c. chopped nuts (optional)

Combine flour, baking soda and salt in a bowl and set aside. Beat butter, sugar, brown sugar, and vanilla in a large mixing bowl. Add eggs one at a time, beating well after each addition. Gradually beat in flour mixture. Stir in chocolate chips and nuts. Drop rounded tablespoonfuls onto ungreased baking sheets. Bake for 9-11 minutes or until golden brown. Let stand for 2 minutes, then remove and put on a wire rack to cool completely. Makes about 60 cookies.

HERE ARE A FEW MORE THINGS TO CONSIDER BEFORE UNDERTAKING ANY RECIPE, FROM TOAST TO TOSTADAS

- LAY OUT ALL YOUR INGREDIENTS BEFORE YOU BEGIN.
- HAVE AN ADULT HEAT THE OVEN TO ITS PROPER TEMPERATURE BEFORE YOU BEGIN MIXING YOUR INGREDIENTS. IT GENERALLY TAKES ABOUT TEN MINUTES FOR THE OVEN TO REACH THE TEMPERATURE YOU SET. MOST OVENS HAVE A LITTLE LIGHT THAT GOES OFF WHEN THE PROPER TEMPERATURE IS REACHED. ASK A PARENT IF YOURS DOES.
- ALWAYS USE OVEN MITTS, OR ASK AN ADULT TO HELP WHEN YOU TAKE ANYTHING OUT OF THE OVEN OR PUT ANYTHING IN. OVENS ARE VERY HOT. MAKE SURE AN ADULT IS IN THE ROOM WITH YOU WATCHING WHENEVER YOU ARE NEAR THE STOVE OR OVEN.
- WHEN YOU BAKE A CAKE, YOU NEED TO LET YOUR INGREDIENTS WARM UP BEFORE YOU START. DON'T USE COLD EGGS, MILK AND BUTTER STRAIGHT FROM THE FRIDGE. LET THEM SIT OUT UNTIL THEY ARE AT ROOM TEMPERATURE.
- AFTER YOU'RE DONE BAKING SOMETHING, LET IT COOL DOWN FOR A FEW MINUTES. DON'T TRY TO REMOVE A CAKE OR COOKIES FROM A PAN RIGHT AWAY—THEY'LL JUST BREAK APART. READ THE DIRECTIONS.
- DON'T EAT ANY BATTER THAT CONTAINS RAW EGGS. RAW EGGS CAN MAKE YOU SICK. STICK TO THE FROSTING IF YOU WANT TO LICK THE SPOON.
- YOU CAN USUALLY DOUBLE A RECIPE PRETTY EASILY (JUST DOUBLE THE AMOUNT OF EACH INGREDIENT), BUT DON'T TRY TRIPLING A RECIPE. FOR SOME REASON, IT USUALLY DOESN'T WORK.
- YOU CAN CHECK TO SEE IF A CAKE IS DONE BY STICKING A TOOTHPICK INTO THE CENTER OF IT. IF THE TOOTHPICK COMES OUT CLEAN (NOT COVERED WITH CAKE CRUMBS OR LIQUID OF ANY SORT), THE CAKE IS READY.
- A GREAT PLACE TO FIND RECIPES IS ON THE BOXES AND BAGS OF THINGS YOU BUY IN THE STORE. CHECK OUT RICE KRISPIES™ (RICE KRISPIE TREATS) NESTLE'S SEMI-SWEET MORSELS™ (TOLL HOUSE COOKIES™) AND OTHERS.

definition

whip (wip)
verb, to beat something (usually cream or eggs) until it is a foam.

*Mitch's arm grew tired while **whipping** the cream for his strawberries.*

27. Which part of a computer do you type on?

(A) The monitor
(B) The hard drive
(C) The keyboard

definition

cursor

(KER ser) *noun,* the movable flashing line or square on the monitor screen that shows where you are inputting information.

Jennifer moved the **cursor** *on the screen to the heading marked "file" in order to save her program.*

It's hard to imagine life without **computers**. They're everywhere: cars' engine systems are run by computers; automatic cameras have little computer chips; washers and dryers even have computers in them these days. Everyone needs to have a basic understanding of computers.

The **keyboard** looks just like a typewriter's keyboard, but the difference is that each key here sends a different signal to the computer's memory. Sometimes you need to press a combination of keys to perform a certain function. The **monitor** is the screen on which the information is displayed. If you are playing a game or typing a paper, you can track your progress on the computer's monitor.

Memory is contained in the computer's **microchips**. There are two types of memory: **RAM** (random access memory) and **ROM** (read only memory). ROM contains the permanent instructions that tell the computer how to run. It cannot be erased and remains even when the computer is turned off. RAM holds a program or information as it is needed, just on a temporary basis. The computer chip that controls

Monitor

Keyboard

Mouse

the computer is called the microprocessor or CPU (Central Processing Unit). This microchip is made from **silicon** or sand.

Computers use two types of disks: **hard disks** and **floppy disks**. The hard disk stays permanently in the computer and stores a lot of information. Floppy disks are portable and store less information. You can copy information onto a floppy disk and carry it to another computer.

"Schoolhouse Rock" (ABC). You know, those little in-between-the-shows cartoons on the ABC Saturday morning lineup. There's a new episode called "Computer Rock" that is particularly enlightening.

28. How many lungs does the average person have?

(A) One
(B) Two
(C) Sixteen

5

Every part of your body is part of a system. Each system does something different, and they all work together to keep you alive.

The **nervous system** consists of the **brain** and all the **nerves** in your body. The nerves detect signals all over your body and send the information to your brain. So, if you touch a flame, the nerves in your finger send an impulse to your brain, which interprets the signal and sends back to your finger a message to pull away from the flame.

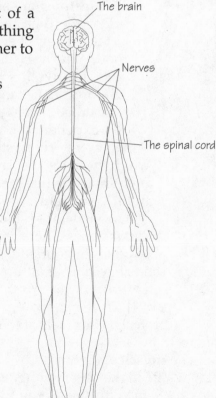

The brain

Nerves

The spinal cord

The human nervous system

BODY TALK

- *Your body contains 8 pints of blood.*
- *You use 14 muscles to smile.*
- *Your small intestine is 20 feet long.*
- *You shed 40 pounds of skin over a lifetime.*
- *Your body is 70% water.*
- *400 gallons of blood flow through your kidneys in one day.*
- *Your heart beats over 100,000 times per day.*
- *You blink your eyes 20,000 times per day.*
- *You have about 120,000 hairs on your head.*

CULTURESCOPE

The **respiratory system** consists of your **lungs** and air passages (**throat, nasal passages**). The sole purpose of respiration is to bring oxygen into your system to feed your cells, and to expel carbon dioxide, which is a toxin that your body creates.

The **digestive system** consists of all the things you need to digest your food and get rid of waste. Your **mouth**, **stomach**, and **intestines** are all part of the digestive system. They chew up the food, churn it around, and dissolve it so that the nutrients can be absorbed. The rest is expelled through the **excretory system**, which includes the **large and small intestines**, **urethra**, and **anus**.

The **skeletal system** is your bones. There are 206 bones in your body, and they hold it all up and protect it. Your skull, for example, protects your delicate brain.

The **muscles** in your body are what make everything move. Some muscles you move by thinking about it (the muscles in your fingers,

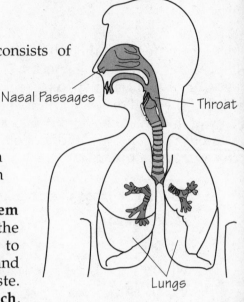

The human respiratory system

Nasal Passages

Throat

Lungs

The skeleton

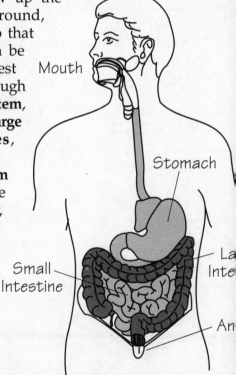

The human digestive system

Mouth

Stomach

Small Intestine

La
Inte

An

for example) and some are controlled by your brain automatically—you don't need to think about breathing to do it, right? The muscles in your heart move automatically, even when you sleep.

Each system in your body is made up of **organs**. Each organ is made up of **tissues**, and tissues are made up of **cells**. Each cell does its own job. Cells in your heart are different than cells in your brain. Every second of every day, your body is working, producing more cells, bringing in nutrients for energy and fuel, and expelling all the toxic waste. You can see why proper nutrition (p. 245) is so important—it's the fuel that keeps the whole body running.

29. Which of the following is a way you can get AIDS?

(A) Sharing a drinking glass with an infected person

(B) Going to school with someone who is infected

(C) None of the above

AIDS has been in the news for a long time now—probably as long as you've been alive. You may have heard about people who have had AIDS and people who have died from AIDS. It can be very frightening, but the more you know about it the better off you are.

AIDS is a condition that attacks the body's ability to fight off sickness. It is caused by a germ called a virus. The name of the virus that causes AIDS is the **human immunodeficiency virus (HIV)**.

Colds are also caused by viruses. Chicken pox is caused by a virus. But you cannot catch HIV the way you catch a cold. You cannot get AIDS from doing things like going to school, using a bathroom, or riding in a bus.

It is important to know the facts about AIDS, because a lot of people who talk about it do not have their information straight. All of the following information about AIDS come from the Centers for Disease Control. That's the U.S. Government agency reponsible for the control and prevention of diseases. When you hear something about AIDS that isn't true, speak up.

You cannot get AIDS from the things you do every day, such as going to school, using a toilet, or drinking from a glass.

You cannot get AIDS from sitting next to someone in school who has AIDS.

> **definition**
>
> **cell**
>
> (sel) *noun*, the basic unit that all living things are made from.
>
> *All the parts of the body are made up of cells, from the blood to the brain.*

> **definition**
>
> **virus**
>
> (VYE rus) *noun*, a tiny germ, smaller than bacteria, that can enter the cells of a living thing and cause a disease.
>
> *Antonio missed his basketball game, because he had a fever from the virus going around school.*

You cannot get AIDS from living in the same house with someone who has AIDS.

You cannot get AIDS from a kiss on the cheek, or from touching or hugging someone who is infected.

You cannot get AIDS from a mosquito or any other kind of insect. The virus that causes AIDS dies inside of bugs, so there is no way bugs can give it to you.

You can become infected with HIV either by having sexual intercourse (p. 280) with an infected person or by sharing drug needles or syringes with an infected person. Also, women infected with HIV can pass the virus to their babies during pregnancy or during birth.

A person who is infected can infect others in these ways even if no symptoms are present. You cannot tell by looking at someone whether he or she is infected with HIV. An infected person can appear completely healthy.

You can play with someone who has AIDS just as you can with any of your other friends, and you won't get sick.

All types of people have AIDS—male and female, rich and poor, white, Black, Hispanic, Asian, and Native American.

As of the end of 1994, more than 82,081 people age twenty to twenty-nine have been diagnosed with AIDS. Because a person can be infected with the virus that causes AIDS for as long as ten or more years before the signs of AIDS appear, scientists believe that a significant number of these young people would have been infected when they were teenagers.

30. What is the name of the force that holds water molecules together?

(A) Surface tension

(B) Magnestism

(C) Electricity

"Newton's Apple" series (PBS). This great series explores scientific and technological phenomena. Watch for it.

If you've ever watched a bug (p. 263) walk across the surface of a lake, you've observed a phenomenon known as **surface tension**. You can also see surface tension at work if you look at the top of a glass of water—it may appear to look like a skin. The molecules in the water stick together because of a force know as **cohesion**. It is because of surface tension that water forms in droplets.

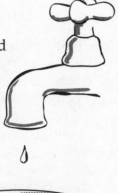

Take a small plate or a piece of waxed paper. If you drop water onto it a little bit at a time you can watch it form drops and roll around. How easy is it to break a droplet of water? Just raise up your hand and drop the water from a greater height. It will splatter pretty easily. Surface tension is not a very strong force—it can be easily broken.

Fill a glass to the top. Slowly drip water into the glass and you'll see that it will fill to a point where it bulges above the rim (this works best with a narrow glass). The surface of the water is holding it together. Since surface tension is not that strong, it will only take a few extra drops until the water begins to spill out.

Float a paper clip on the surface of a cup of water. How many clips can you pile on before they sink? Notice that you have to lay the clip down flat to make it float. If you try to float it on its end, it will sink.

Now, get a cork from a bottle. If you fill your glass all the way to the top again (so that it is almost overflowing) and try to float your cork in the water,

HOW DO YOU MAKE A SQUARE BUBBLE?

Blow lots of bubbles, attaching each new one to the previous one. Once you have gotten about five or more, look deep inside. Any bubble trapped in the middle will be square.

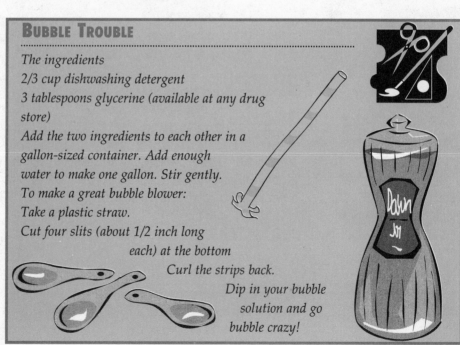

BUBBLE TROUBLE

The ingredients
2/3 cup dishwashing detergent
3 tablespoons glycerine (available at any drug store)
Add the two ingredients to each other in a gallon-sized container. Add enough water to make one gallon. Stir gently.
To make a great bubble blower:
Take a plastic straw.
Cut four slits (about 1/2 inch long each) at the bottom
Curl the strips back.
Dip in your bubble solution and go bubble crazy!

you'll notice that the cork always floats to the outside rim. When something is going to break the surface of the water it goes to where the surface is weakest. Right now, it is weakest at the edge.

If you fill the same glass halfway with water and drop in the cork, it will float in the middle. That's where the surface tension is weakest now. Both of those spots (the edge when the glass is overflowing full and the middle when the glass is halfway full) are where the water level is lowest. Look closely. Things in general will always take what is called "the path of least resistance." The cork will float wherever the least effort needs to be made.

6

31. How long does the average star live?

(A) A million years
(B) A billion years
(C) Ten billion years

There are billions of **stars** in the galaxy. Stars are constantly dying out, and new ones are being born. How do stars come about?

Stars begin as huge clouds of dust and hydrogen gas called nebulae. The word nebula means "mist" in Latin (p. 92). Gravity (p. 238) pulls these particles together until they form a globule. The globules pack together until they begin to spin off into smaller pieces. Each of these mini-globules turns into a star.

PROTOSTARS

As the gas in each mini-globule begins to pack even closer, it begins to spin and become even hotter. When it reaches a temperature of more than eighteen million degrees, it begins to glow. Nuclear reactions in the core turn the hydrogen to helium. In this phase the developing star is called a **protostar**.

RED GIANTS and RED SUPERGIANTS

As the star begins to cool down (billions of years later) it actually gets a little larger and turns a reddish color. This is called a **red giant**. Sometimes these red giants swell into huge stars, called **red supergiants**, which can be 1,000 times the size of our sun.

PLANETARY NEBULAE

As a small star dies, it begins to collapse in on itself. It then casts a shell of hydrogen gas. Through a telescope, dying stars look like planets; that's why scientists call them **planetary nebulae**.

SUPERNOVAS

When a giant star burns out, it collapses very quickly—in less than a second. It produces a great explosion called a **supernova**, and the resulting gases and dust are scattered throughout the universe. As it dies out, a star may turn into a white dwarf, becoming very small and glowing white, since it's so hot. The **white dwarf** will eventually cool off and become a **black dwarf**. The whole process takes billions and billions of years.

"Beakman's World" (TBS). "Beakman's World" is a wacky science series that explains everything from the structure of the universe to the ingredients found in dirt.

32. When does a human female begin menstruation?

(A) Before she is born
(B) When she reaches puberty
(C) Throughout her life

Babies are born every day. This is the cycle of life; if there were no new babies, the human race would eventually completely die out. Babies are produced through a process called **reproduction**.

WHY CONDOMS?

You hear a lot about them. There are even ads for condoms on TV and radio. The main reason for all the talk about condoms these days is AIDS (p. 275), which you can get by having unprotected sexual intercourse. A condom covers the man's penis with a thin piece of latex (like a balloon) during intercourse so that the sperm does not go into the woman's vagina. Because the man's sperm is not going into the woman, and the woman's bodily fluids are not touching the man's penis, condoms can help prevent AIDS and other sexually transmitted diseases, as well as as helping prevent pregnancy. Condoms are not perfect, however. Condoms may break, or slip off, so they do not provide an absolute guarantee against disease or pregnancy. The only absolute protection is abstinence.

Human reproduction doesn't differ much from any mammal reproduction—the basic mechanics are the same. The human female is born with a certain amount of **eggs**—usually about 300,000. They are stored in her **ovaries**, right next to the **uterus**.

When a girl reaches puberty (p. 281) these eggs begin to ripen, one at a time. About once a month, an egg travels down, out from the ovary, through the **fallopian** tube, to the uterus. If, along the way, it becomes fertilized by a sperm cell, a **fetus** will begin to form. Fed by the mother's system, the fetus develops in the uterus for about nine months until it is ready to be born.

If the egg is not fertilized, it passes through the uterus along with the uterus's lining, called the menses. This process, called **menstruation**, happens about once a month until a woman reaches **menopause**, in her forties or fifties. After menopause, the ovaries no longer release an egg each month, so she cannot have a baby naturally. Science, however, has made it possible even for a woman past menopause to have a baby using an egg donated by another woman.

For his whole life, a man produces **sperm** in his **testes**. Each testis makes about 250,000,000 sperm a day. If they are not released, they get absorbed back into the blood system. The sperm are released through the man's penis during sexual intercourse. When a man gets sexually excited, his penis becomes hard and it can be inserted into a woman's vagina. The sperm is released through a process called ejaculation, and they then head up into the fal-

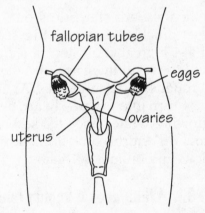

Female reproductive system

lopian tube looking to fertilize an egg. There are only a few days from the time the egg is released in which it can be fertilized. Even if the sperm reaches the egg during that time, it may or may not fertilize the egg.

When a kid's age reaches double digits (p. 158), puberty starts to happen. He may be eleven, she may be sixteen: Puberty begins at a different time for everyone. The primary cause of the changes of puberty is the release of sex hormones. **Estrogen**, the female sex hormone, causes a girl to start menstruating as her eggs begin to ripen and leave the ovaries. It also makes her breasts get bigger and gives her a more rounded, "womanly" shape. She also starts to grow pubic hair around her vagina.

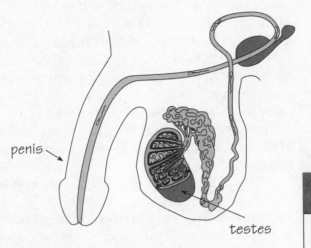

Male reproductive system

definition

puberty
(PYOO ber tee) *noun*
the age or time at which a person's body becomes physically able to produce children.

The principal and the nurse of our school came by my class today to talk about puberty.

Boys begin to produce a hormone called **testosterone** at puberty. Testosterone makes a boy's voice deeper, starts the growth of hair on his face and body, and spurs muscle development and sperm production.

Puberty makes a person physically ready for sexual intercourse and reproduction. Keep in mind, however, that it is years after puberty before people are emotionally ready for the responsibilities (p. 292) sexual intercourse entails. This difference makes adolescence a difficult time. Make sure to ask a parent or an adult you trust for advice if you have questions about sex—don't rely on your friends. There's a lot of misinformation floating around the school yard. If something worries you, find someone you trust—someone older—to give you the information you need.

33. Which of the following is not a computer on-line service?

(A) Prodigy
(B) America On-Line
(C) Windows

You may have heard some of these names when talking about computers (p. 272): America On-Line, eWorld, Prodigy, CompuServe.

All of these are commercial online services. If your computer has a **modem**, a device that allows the computer to hook onto a telephone line and dial to a specific place, then you can go online. You may want to look into the different services to see which one you like. Subscribing to an online service is like subscribing to a network of television shows—much of what each service has is the same, but many items are different.

First, you buy the software to get you started. The software program will dial the service for you and help you to find your way around.

When you dial in, you get a welcome screen that gives you all kinds of options for where to go next. This is The Princeton Review welcome screen. Thousands of high schoolers use this every month to help them figure out where to go to college. There are thousands of these kinds of welcome screens out there to help you find cool information on the things that interest you—sports, music, games, science—everything!

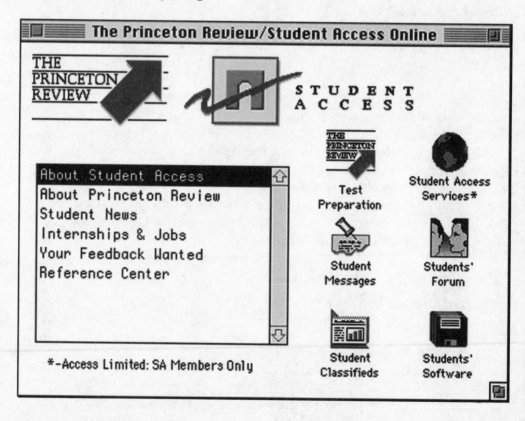

HERE ARE SOME FACTS ABOUT EACH SERVICE

America On-Line (AOL) is the fastest-growing on-line service. It is one of the least expensive and easiest services to use. Directions are simple to follow for everything you need to do. **eWorld** is run by Apple Computer and is also very easy to use. **Prodigy** has the most stuff for kids. It doesn't, however, allow you to send e-mail to people outside of Prodigy. **Compuserve** has the greatest range of service, but it is more expensive and aimed more at business and professional people.

E-mail is short for "electronic mail." If you subscribe to a computer service, you can write to other people using your computer. **Prodigy** is a little different, because it only lets you send e-mail to other Prodigy users. If you look closely, you'll see e-mail addresses all over—news shows, radio stations, and newspapers all give you the option to send your letters by e-mail. The advantage is that there is no stamp, no walking to the mailbox, no envelope necessary. If both you and the person you want to write to have an e-mail address, you can just write your letter and hit send. It goes zipping around the telephone lines and prints out on the screen of the person you sent it to. You can also e-mail people you meet on line and start up an electronic relationship.

The **Internet** is a network of all the other computer networks. It began as a system used by the U.S. government, but now it is mainly a network of universities, companies, and individuals hooking up with each other. Unlike the commercial services, it isn't really run by any one person or place. All of the information on the Internet is not kept in one place, but is located on computers all over the world.

34. Which is responsible for making a compass point north?

(A) Gravity
(B) Magnetism
(C) Electricity

You've probably seen a magnet pull a paper clip or another metal

COOL PLACES TO FIND ONLINE

TV BB

Go to TV BB. You can read what other people have to say about your favorite shows and add your two cents as well. Jerry Seinfeld has been a guest here.

GAMES

CompuServe has a big gaming area and forum including simple stuff like Hangman, or more complicated role-playing games, like CastleQuest. Go to GAMES in the CompuServe menu.

The Prodigy games are found by jumping to the GAME CENTER. Find out about all their games, and vote for your favorite on the POLL. Get tips for Nintendo, Sega, Turbo-Grafix 16 and more in the Apple II Games Forum on AOL—use keyword AGM.

object toward it. Similarly, the earth acts like a giant magnet.

Deep inside of the earth is a core of liquid iron. The electric currents that flow through the core magnetize the iron, creating, in effect, a gigantic magnet as the earth rotates. The magnetic north pole is only a short distance away from the geographic **north pole**—the actual spot around which the earth turns.

The needle in a compass is a small magnet as well. Have you ever tried to touch two magnets to each other? Each magnet has a side that is attracted to the north pole and a side that is attracted to the **south pole**. The side of the magnet inside of a compass that is attracted to the north pole is painted red, and it pivots on a little pin point in the center of the compass so that it will swing around. If you hold it still and straight, the north pole of the magnet in the compass will point to the north pole of the earth. The magnetism of the earth is called **geomagnetism**.

Magnets are used all over. They're used in computers and microwave ovens. They hold the refrigerator door shut. They hold the can onto an electric can opener.

Magnets are used in hospitals for things like X-rays. In another useful procedure called an MRI (Magnetic Resonance Imaging), a patient is put into a huge tube, that is actually a giant magnet. Radio signals are sent to the magnetic field that surrounds the patient, which causes the molecules in the patient's body to move around. A receiver measures the movements and constructs a picture on a computer screen of the images they make. MRIs are a way for a doctor to see what's happening inside

definition

magnetic field
(mag NET ik feeld)
noun, the invisible area around a magnet in which it has its power.

*If you move a paper clip outside of the **magnetic field** of a magnet, it will no longer feel the pull of the magnet.*

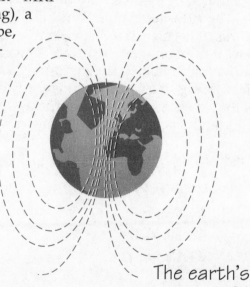

The earth's magnetic fields

of a patient without having to use an X-ray or surgery.

> ### YOU CAN TURN AN ORDINARY PAPER CLIP INTO A MAGNET IF YOU HAVE ANOTHER MAGNET.
>
> *1. Get a bunch of paper clips*
> *2. Get a magnet (the stronger the better)*
> *Hold one paper clip next to another. Do they attract each other? No way. But, if you take a paper clip and rub it along the end of a magnet (in one direction, not back and forth), you will eventually "magnetize" the clip. It will now attract other paper clips.*
> **How it works: all iron, steel, nickel and cobalt have millions of tiny magnets in them. The magnets are facing different ways, so they cancel each other out. By rubbing a piece of metal along a magnet in one direction, you are turning all the magnets around to face one way, magnetizing the metal.*

OPPOSITES ATTRACT

Each magnet has a pole that will point south and a pole that will point north. But if you try to touch the north pole of one magnet to the north pole of another, they will "repel" each other— push each other away. If, however, you touch a north pole to a south pole, they will "attract" each other and pull together. It must be true that opposites attract!

35. What determines things like hair color and height?

(A) Blood type
(B) Brain cells
(C) Genes

Do you ever look in a mirror and wonder how you ended up with the color eyes and type of hair you have? People may tell you that you look like your mother or father, or even your grandmother or grandfather. A fascinating thing called **heredity** is responsible for the way you look, from your hair to your feet. The study of heredity is called **genetics** because genes carry traits from the parent to the child.

Genes are carried around in a **chromosome**. Every single cell in your body—except for the egg cells or the sperm cells—has twenty-three pairs of chromosomes. In those twenty-three pairs is a substance called deoxyribonucleic acid—**DNA**. DNA is the unique mixture that gives you brown hair, dark skin, long legs, green eyes—whatever. It identifies you. You may have heard of DNA testing. When a scientist looks at a sample of blood or skin, she can tell whether it is yours by looking at the DNA to see if it matches your DNA. DNA is a lot like a fingerprint. The combination of genetic material you carry around is different than the genetic material of every other person on the planet (unless you have an identical twin).

We said before that the egg and the sperm cells did not have the full forty-six chromosomes (twenty-three pairs). That's because those cells each carry around half of the set—twenty-three each. When the sperm fertilizes the egg, the two sets join together, and the fetus that starts to form takes its characteristics from the mother's egg and the father's sperm. The sex of the baby is determined by the father's sperm. All female eggs carry a sex chromosome

xx=girls

xy=boys

cool.

labeled x. The sperm, though, carries either an x or a y chromosome. If a sperm carrying an x fertilizes an egg, you end up with a girl. If a sperm carrying a y fertilizes an egg, you end up with a boy.

Scientists are always exploring how people turn out the way they do. Are people just born a certain way? Or does the environment a person grows up in—his family, community, and education, for example—make him who he is? This is called the "nature versus nurture debate." Many scientists feel that "unlocking" the genetic code will help us understand why some people get easily sick, or why some people are violent. According to this thinking, the more you understand about the genetic causes of a certain behavior or illness, the closer you are to solving it.

Many other scientists argue, however, that what happens to you as you grow up is more important than what you are born with. They argue that giving children loving homes, healthy meals, and a good education is the way to solve problems like crime and disease. Which do you think is more important, what genes you are born with or what experiences and opportunities you have? Could it be a combination of both heredity and environment that makes us what we are?

definition

heredity
(huh RED i tee) *noun*, process through which characteristics of people, animals, or plants are passed from parent to child.

*He blamed **heredity** for his baldness.*

WHAT HAVE YOU INHERITED?

The ability to roll your tongue is an inherited trait.

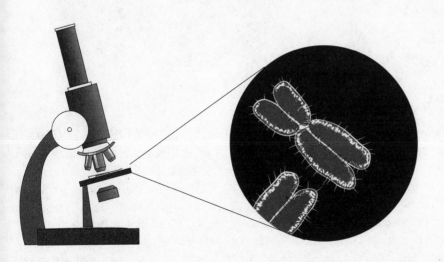

Chromosomes close-up

36. The top layer of the Earth is called the

    (A) Crust

    (B) Mantle

    (C) Core

definition

magma

(MAG muh) *noun,*
liquid or molten rock.

*As **magma** rises from
the heat deep inside the
earth, it cools to form
igneous rock.*

The Earth is made of a core of iron and nickel surrounded by layers of iron, nickel, rock, water and air. Let's take a look at a cross section and move from the inside out.

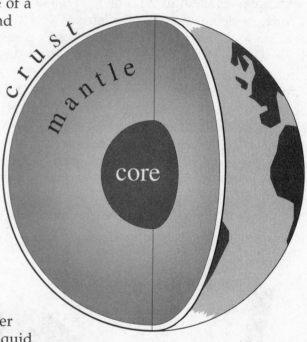

The **inner core** is about 1,700 miles across and very hot—more than 8,000°F. The outer core—made of liquid iron— is a little more than 1,200 miles thick and is 4,000°F.

The **mantle** is the thickest layer—about 1,800 miles deep. Although the bottom of the mantle has temperatures reaching more than 6,000°F, the intense pressure keeps the rock in this layer solid. The **crust** is the top outside layer of the Earth. The hollowed-out parts of the crust are filled with water that make up the oceans (p. 248). The crust reaches a depth of about forty-five miles beneath the continents, but at the bottom of the oceans the crust may be as little as four miles deep. The surface of the Earth's crust is relatively cool, but it gets hot toward the bottom—up to 1,900°F.

The Earth's **atmosphere** is a layer as well. The atmosphere is the layer of air that surrounds the earth. It's about 400 miles thick and shields the earth from many of the damaging rays from the sun. It also protects the earth from extreme temperatures. One of the worries about damaging the atmosphere with pollutants is that it will not be able to perform these functions as well as it always has.

THE EARTH BLOWS OFF A LITTLE STEAM

The heat inside of the earth comes from decaying rocks. The heat is so intense that rocks actually melt. Red hot molten rock, or magma, is sometimes forced to the Earth's surface through cracks in the crust. When the magma erupts to the surface it is called lava. There are about 850 active volcanoes in the world today.

ANSWERS

1. (p.232)	2. A	3. C	4. C	5. B	6. C	7. B
8. B	9. A	10. C	11. (p.247)	12. B	13. C	14. B
15. A	16. C	17. (p.256)	18. A	19. B	20. C	21. (p.262)
22. A	23. B	24. B	25. A	26. B	27. C	28. B
29. C	30. A	31. C	32. B	33. C	34. B	35. C
36. A						

Social Studies

1. What are the people who make up a country called?

(A) Elves

(B) Citizens

(C) Panda Bears

A **country** is like a big family. Being part of a country, like being part of a family, has a lot of benefits. Just as your family's job is to take care of you, it is your country's job to take care of all its **citizens**. A country protects and educates its citizens, helps citizens who are sick and need care, and passes laws to keep order. But, as a citizen, you have certain **responsibilities** as well. Think about your family responsibilities and how they compare to your responsibilities as a citizen of your country.

definition

responsibility

(re SPONS a BIL i tee)
noun, something you
should do, or are
expected to do.

*Every night, it was
John's* **responsibility** *to
take out the trash and
help his dad wash the
dishes.*

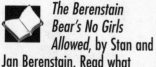

*The Berenstain
Bear's No Girls
Allowed,* by Stan and
Jan Berenstain. Read what
happens when one group of
cubs forms a very exclusive
club.

FAMILY

Follow your family rules.

Keep your home clean.

Get along with your family and friends.

Respect the rights of those in your family.

Learn about your family.

Participate in some family decisions.

COUNTRY

Obey your country's laws.

Keep your environment clean.

Get along with the people around you.

Respect the rights of all people.

Go to school and learn about your country.

VOTE (when you get to be old enough).

There are hundreds and hundreds of countries in the world. Each country has its own rules. It also has its own name for its citizens. People who live in France are called **French** citizens. Citizens of Spain are called **Spaniards**. People who live in the United States are called **Americans**.

Citizens of Japan are called Japanese.

2. Which of these things does your community do for you?

(A) It does your homework.
(B) It walks your dog.
(C) It puts up street signs.

A **community** is a group of people who live in the same area, like a neighborhood, town, or city. These are just some of the benefits a community provides for the people who live in it:

- POLICE PROTECTION
- ROADS
- SNOW AND GARBAGE REMOVAL
- GOLF COURSES
- SCHOOLS
- PARKS

Some of the services you get from your community—like parks and public tennis courts—have to do with having fun. Some of them have to do with keeping you safe. A lot of them are just about cleaning up the mess we make, like getting rid of garbage, cleaning the streets, and recycling. The people in a community help to pay for all of these services with **taxes**. Taxes are the money each family pays each year to the government. (You might have heard grown-ups or **politicians** talk about paying too many taxes.)

One thing your community does is put up stop signs.

definition

community
(ka MEW ni tee) *noun*, a group of people who live in the same area, like a town or a village.

*My **community** has a lot of different people living in it.*

CULTURESCOPE

A COMMUNITY HELPING HAND

Trace your hand in this box. See if you can think of five services your community provides for you and draw a picture of one in each finger. These are all ways the community gives its residents a helping hand.

CLUB KIDS

If you're not in a club, why not start one? It's easy—just pick something you and your friends like doing, like playing soccer or collecting things, and make up a club with a cool name, like the Sensational Soccer Club, or the Cool Card Collectors. Think about your club as if it were a country. What kind of rules are important? What kind of responsibility does the president of the club have? How do you choose a president? What is the best way to decide on rules?

3. Which of these is not a state?

(A) **Texas**

(B) **Chicago**

(C) **Delaware**

Texas and Delaware are **states**. Chicago is a **city** in the state of Illinois. In our country, cities, towns and villages are all parts of states, so states are like big communities made up of smaller ones. Each state is in charge of the cities, towns, and villages that fall within its borders. States in our country set education requirements, decide the age at which people are allowed to drink alcohol, and take care of things that residents of the state share, like highways.

As you can tell by the name, the United States of America is a group of states. The country, or **nation**, governs all the states and takes care of things that affect all the country's citizens equally. The **federal government** of the country makes laws, manages the army, and helps out the states.

THE DIVISION OF GOVERNMENT

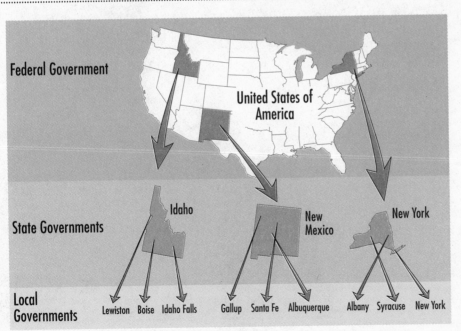

Federal Government

United States of America

State Governments

Idaho

New Mexico

New York

Local Governments

Lewiston Boise Idaho Falls   Gallup Santa Fe Albuquerque   Albany Syracuse New York

definition

government
(GUV urn ment) *noun*, the people who manage or control a city, state, or country, and the system used to control the country.

*In our country, the **government** is run on a local (city, town, or village), state, and federal level.*

The Young People's Atlas of the United States, by James Harrison and Eleanor Van Zandt. More facts about states than you ever knew existed!

4. Who is the President of the United States?

(A) George Bush
(B) Michael Jackson
(C) Bill Clinton

KNOW YOUR PRESIDENTS!

There's a list of all the presidents, their wives, and their vice presidents on p. 347.

The **president** is the boss—the highest elected official in our country. There have been forty-two presidents since **George Washington** (1732-1799) was elected in 1789. Some of them have names you will recognize; others are hardly remembered at all. **Bill Clinton** (1946) is our current president. He is a **Democrat**, and was elected in 1992. **Albert Gore, Jr.** (1948-) is our vice-president. If anything happens to the president, the vice-president takes over.

The president does all kinds of things. He's the commander-in-chief—the head honcho—of our Army, Navy, Air Force, and Marines. He helps pass laws, manage the economy (p. 327), and he represents our country when the leaders of all the different countries get together to talk about things.

Bill Clinton is the 42nd president of the United States.

5. How many months are in a year?

(A) Two

(B) Two Hundred

(C) Twelve

One full **day** passes when the sun has come up, gone down and comes up again. This takes 24 **hours**, which is the amount of time it takes for the Earth (p. 232) to turn around once. There are 7 days in a **week**. A **month** has between 28 and 31 days in it—about 4 to 4 ½ weeks. A **year** is the time it takes for the Earth to go once around the sun. There are 12 months in every year. Can you name them all?

Since months have different numbers of days in them, you need to remember how many days each month has. Some people remember this rhyme:

THIRTY DAYS HATH SEPTEMBER,
APRIL, JUNE AND NOVEMBER;
ALL THE REST HAVE 31,
EXCEPT FOR FEBRUARY, WHICH HAS 28 AND ON A LEAP YEAR 29.

Or, you can make a fist. Starting with January, your knuckles represent months with 31 days and the places in between represent months with 30 days—and February—like this:

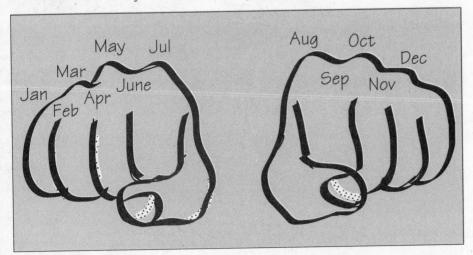

THE DAYS OF THE WEEK

SUNDAY

Monday

TUESDAY

Wednesday

Thursday

FRIDAY

Saturday

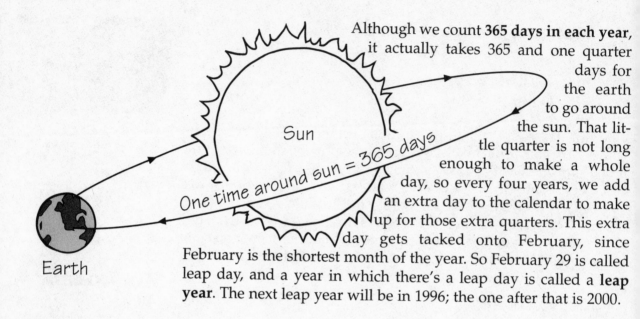

Although we count **365 days in each year**, it actually takes 365 and one quarter days for the earth to go around the sun. That little quarter is not long enough to make a whole day, so every four years, we add an extra day to the calendar to make up for those extra quarters. This extra day gets tacked onto February, since February is the shortest month of the year. So February 29 is called leap day, and a year in which there's a leap day is called a **leap year**. The next leap year will be in 1996; the one after that is 2000.

Sun

One time around sun = 365 days

Earth

Eight Days A Week, by the Beatles. A great song by a band who *didn't* know how many days are in a week. They should have paid more attention in first grade!

THE WHOLE WORLD CELEBRATES NEW YEAR'S DAY

Different countries celebrate New Year's Day by eating different kinds of food. In Japan, they like to eat red snapper on New Year's Day for good luck. In Greece, they bake a cake called a peta with a coin inside. If you get the slice with the coin, you are due special luck in that year. In the United States (especially in the South), black-eyed peas are eaten for good luck on New Year's Day.

Holidays are special days in the year. Some holidays are celebrated only by people in a certain country or a certain state. The **Fourth of July** is only a holiday in the United States, for example. Some holidays are religious, so they are only celebrated by people who practice that religion. Some holidays are on the same date every year, while some fall on different dates from year to year. It would be almost impossible to list every holiday, but check out this list of holidays every kid should know.

6. What is a calendar used for?

(A) To measure time
(B) To measure distance
(C) To measure detergent

The **Gregorian calendar**, the calendar most Americans use every day, dates counting after Jesus Christ's (p. 146) birth. When you say "1987," what you mean is "1987 A.D." A.D. stands for "anno domini," or "the year of our Lord." 1987 A.D. is around 1,987 years after Jesus Christ was born.

What about before that? Here's where it gets confusing. The years before the birth of Christ are given the notation B.C., which stands for "before Christ," as in "956 B.C." Because the years are counted backwards from Christ's birthday, the bigger the number of any year, the more dated. For example, the year 25 B.C. is not as long ago as the year 2,500 B.C.

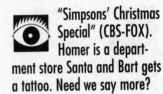

"Simpsons' Christmas Special" (CBS-FOX). Homer is a department store Santa and Bart gets a tattoo. Need we say more?

definition

calendar

(KAL en dur) *noun*, a chart that shows the days, weeks, and months of the year in order.

Mom consulted her calendar to see if she was busy on Saturday.

The Hebrew calendar, according to tradition, begins with Creation—the moment the world began. Jewish (p. 148) tradition holds that that moment came 3,760 years and three months before the birth of Christ. So, if you wanted to translate a year from the Gregorian calendar to the Hebrew calendar, you would add 3,760 to it. For example, the year 1994 in the Gregorian calendar is the year 5,754 in the Hebrew calendar. In the Hebrew calendar the year does not begin in January, either. The Jewish New Year, **Rosh Hashanah**, is in autumn.

The **Chinese calendar** begins measuring time 2,637 years before the birth of Christ. That was the year in which it was invented by Emperor Huang-Ti. The Chinese calendar runs in cycles of sixty years, and in each cycle, every year is assigned a different animal name. 1995 is the year of the pig. 1996 is the year of the rabbit! Because it is based on the moon, like our calendar, it has twelve months, each twenty-nine or thirty days in length.

The **Islamic calendar** begins measuring time on the date that Muhammed (p. 147) left Mecca to go to Medina—622 years after the birth of Christ. Its year is only 354 days long—eleven days shorter than ours. The Islamic calendar is also based on the moon, and has twelve months with twenty-nine or thirty days in each month.

7. Why do we celebrate Thanksgiving?

(A) To remember a feast held by Pilgrims and Indians

(B) To remember a basketball game between Pilgrims and Indians

(C) To remember a dance invented by Pilgrims and Indians

The **Pilgrims** were a group of people who arrived here from Europe in 1620. They originally intended to land in Virginia, but storms blew their ship, the *Mayflower*, north to what is now Massachusetts. There they set up a colony called **Plymouth**. The Pilgrims came here looking for a place to practice their **religion** freely. In England, their native country, they did not have this freedom. When the Pilgrims got to the **New World** (as America was then called by Europeans), there were already people here. Many different tribes of **Native Americans** had been living here for about twelve thousand years. The tribe that lived near Plymouth was called the **Wampanoag**. They spoke a language called **Algonquin**.

The first winter the Pilgrims spent at Plymouth was a very cold and difficult one, and the Indians helped them get through it by giving them corn. Many of the Pilgrims died, but the ones who survived got together with the Wampanoag to celebrate a big feast after the next fall harvest. They gave thanks to God for all they had. A thanksgiving feast at harvest time was a tradition of Algonquin-speaking Indians, so the Europeans were following the lead of Native Americans in setting up this holiday in the fall.

N.C. Wyeth's Pilgrims, text by Robert San Souci. Read about the Pilgrims while looking at beautiful illustrations by one of America's great illustrators.

Mouse on the Mayflower. This video follows the adventures of a daring mouse as he crosses the Atlantic, survives the first brutal winter, and celebrates the first Thanksgiving.

definition

religion

(ree LI jun) *noun*, the belief in a higher power to be worshipped and the following of the rules handed down by that power.

*Sam chose fish for lunch because his **religion** didn't allow him eat meat on Fridays.*

8. **Why are Native Americans called Indians?**

(A) Because they are all from India

(B) Because they are all from Indiana

(C) Because Columbus thought he had arrived in India when he first came to America

In 1492, **Christopher Columbus** (1451-1506) set sail from Spain, using money given to him by Queen Isabella and King Ferdinand. They wanted him to bring back spices, which were considered very valuable. He was trying to find India, but instead he ended up here in America. The problem was that Columbus, like all Europeans at that time, thought that he could go straight to Asia (p. 341) by crossing the Atlantic Ocean (p. 258). When Columbus landed on the shores of America, he called the people he met "Indians" since he thought he was in India!

A Native American family

After Columbus, many more Europeans came to the New World. First, lots of adventurous types came from Spain looking for **gold**. These Spaniards headed for what is now Mexico and South America, where the Aztecs and Incans (p. 333-334) had built beautiful cities filled with gold treasures. The Spaniards fought with these Indians and captured their cities. Millions of South American Indians were killed. They did not have weapons as strong as the Europeans', and many were killed by diseases (p.339) that the Europeans brought with them. The Spaniards settled all throughout the area south of what later became our country. That's why people in Mexico now speak Spanish.

In the north, most of the European settlers were from England. Even though the Indians who already lived here helped the Europeans to survive, the Europeans fought with the Indians to try to take over their lands. There

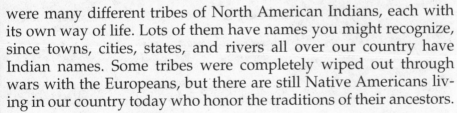

Christopher Columbus

were many different tribes of North American Indians, each with its own way of life. Lots of them have names you might recognize, since towns, cities, states, and rivers all over our country have Indian names. Some tribes were completely wiped out through wars with the Europeans, but there are still Native Americans living in our country today who honor the traditions of their ancestors.

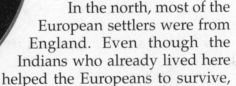

definition

gold (goald)
noun, a very valuable metal used to make coins and jewelry.

The old prospector jumped up and slapped his mule when he found gold. "Now we can retire to Florida!" he giggled as his mule gave him dirty looks.

DISEASES BROUGHT BY EUROPEANS

The Europeans brought many diseases to the Americas against which the Native Americans had no immunity. In Mexico from 1519 to 1600, twenty-six million people died from these diseases, and during the same period in Peru, the population fell from seven million people to under two million.

definition

debt

(det) *noun*, something (usually money) owed by one person to another or others.

*Due to his huge **debt**, Igor decided to get a second job to make some extra money. Being an assistant to a mad scientist just wasn't paying the rent.*

GIVE US YOUR ROBBERS, YOUR THIEVES . . .

To solve the problem of overcrowding in its jails, Britain transported many convicts to Australia. The First Fleet, made up of three ships, arrived in Sydney in 1788, and the convicts on board established the first white colony there.

9. What is a colony?

(A) A field to play baseball on
(B) A type of religious ceremony
(C) A land ruled by a country that is far away

After Columbus's voyage, several European countries sent people to the New World to set up **colonies**, lands that they could rule over from across the ocean. Before our country became a country it was a group of **thirteen colonies** ruled by England. The thirteen colonies later became the original states of the United States of America. Some of the colonies were set up by religious groups like the **Puritans**, who wanted a safe place to practice their religion. Other colonies have different histories. Georgia, for example, was started as a place for poor people who were stuck in jails in England for not being able to pay their **debts**. These people were invited to come to Georgia and start a new life if they promised to work hard and not make trouble.

Eventually, the people who lived in the thirteen colonies decided that they didn't want to be ruled by England any more. They wanted to start their own country, and eventually the United States of America was born.

New Hampshire
Massachusetts
Rhode Island
Connecticut
New York
New Jersey
Pennsylvania
Delaware
Maryland
Virginia
North Carolina
South Carolina
Georgia

10. Where does the President of the United States live?

(A) The Green House

(B) The Red House

(C) The White House

The White House, home of our fearless leader, the president.

definition

residence

(RES i dense) *noun*, the place where someone lives.

*Halle's **residence** is at 212 Maple Street.*

 The Story of the White House, by Kate Waters. All you ever wanted to know about where the president and his family live.

WANT TO TAKE A TOUR OF THE WHITE HOUSE?
....

Write:

The White House
Washington, DC
20500

They'll send you all kinds of information about visiting the White House.

The **White House**, located in Washington, D.C., is the official **residence** of the president. It is among the most popular tourist attractions in the United States, visited by 1.5 million people each year. All types of people from all over the world visit the White House, from kids to kings and queens. It is where the president and **first lady** do their work and live with their family.

The White House has 132 rooms and stands in the middle of an eighteen-acre plot of land. It's address is 1600 Pennsylvania Avenue, Washington, D.C. On a tour of the White House, you get to visit the five rooms on the first floor of the mansion. The State Dining Room can seat as many as 140 guests for dinner. The Red Room is so named because its walls are covered with red silk. The Blue Room is the main greeting area for guests. The Green Room has walls covered with, you guessed it, green silk. The East Room is the largest room in the White House, where guests are often entertained after dinner.

Teddy Roosevelt never backed down from the occasional brawl.

The White House was not always called the White House. Its name was originally the President's House, and then the Executive Mansion. But, since everyone just called it the White House, in 1901, President **Theodore Roosevelt (1858-1919)** authorized the official change of name to the White House.

The White House burned down in 1814 during the War of 1812. The president at the time was **James Madison** (1751-1836), and he and his wife, Dolley, were forced to flee. It wasn't until 1817, when **James Monroe** (1758-1831) was president, that the White House was rebuilt.

2

11. Which form of transportation WON'T get you from the United States to Europe?

(A) Boat
(B) Train
(C) Airplane

Airplane!. This is a great spoof of the serious *Airport* style movies in which there were great airplane disasters. It's funny all the way through the final credits.

How do you get from your home to school every day? Some people walk, some take a bus or a subway, some get a ride in a car. All these ways of getting around are called **transportation**.

Walking is the oldest, easiest, cheapest, healthiest way to get from one place to another. But, of course, you can't always walk everywhere you go. You might be able to easily walk from your house to school or to your friend's house. It wouldn't be so easy to walk to another city, or to another state. It would be impossible to walk from the United States to **Europe**. There's that big ocean (p. 258) in the way.

When you don't feel like walking, or you want to get somewhere fast, or just feel like taking a ride, you have other transportation choices—biking, rollerblading, and skateboarding are three of them. Before cars, people used animals and carts for thousands of years to get from place to place.

Trains changed the world when they were first developed about 150 years ago. For the first time, people and cargo could move at great speed over long distances. Ever since, trains have been a popular method of transportation. Some people love riding on trains so much that they take trains instead of planes, buses, or cars whenever possible. One good thing about taking a train instead of a plane is that you can enjoy the scenery as the train passes by.

If you want to travel across the ocean, however, you'll need to take either a boat or an airplane. **Boats** have been around for a very long time. The first boat probably was a log that some adventurous person jumped on as it floated down a river. Today, boats come in all shapes and sizes, from small canoes to huge aircraft carriers and ships. In cities that are surrounded by water, many people use boats to get to and from work or school. These boats, called **ferries**,

definition

transportation
(tran spor TAY shun)
noun, a way to get from one place to another.

*Meredith's favorite mode of **transportation** is the train because she loves to watch the world go by slowly.*

FERRYBOATS

The Staten Island Ferry in New York carries 49,000 people every day! That's over seventeen million people every year!

Although cars are now the most popular form of transportation, they are fairly new. Cars have only been around for about a hundred years.

TRANSPORTATION TIMELINE

7,000 BC
basically, you walk or you stay home.

5,000 BC
donkeys and oxen carry all the goods, but you still have to hoof it.

3,500 BC
in Mesopotamia, the first wheeled vehicles come on the scene.

1,500 BC
deep-sea sailing ships begin to explore the world.

1800s
steam-powered vehicles arrive; trains are a big hit, and the ships move faster than ever before

1880s
The first cars are built.

1903
Orville and Wilbur Wright fly the first plane at Kitty Hawk, North Carolina.

1957
The Soviet Union sends the first satellite, Sputnik, into space (rockets soon follow).

1976
The Concorde, the first supersonic airplane, starts flying. It flies at 1,550 mph, and you can now cross the Atlantic to Europe in an increasingly short time–fewer than three hours.

1981
The first space shuttle, a reusable, crewed spacecraft, was launched by the U.S. on April 12, 1981. The shuttle was developed to reduce the cost of space exploration.

are so big you can drive your car right onto them. Another type of big boat is a cruise ship, which people go on for a vacation. They have pools and gymnasiums and dance floors right on them, and passengers sleep in little rooms called cabins.

Since 1783, when Pilatre de Rozier and the Marquis d'Arlandes made their first flight in a **balloon**, people have been fascinated with air travel. In 1903, when the **Wright brothers** made their famous airplane flight, a new way to travel long distances was born. There's no faster way to get from one place to another. **Airplanes** come in all sizes, from tiny planes with room only for the pilot and co-pilot, to huge 747s that carry more than 400 passengers. Another type of aircraft is the **helicopter**, which has a large propeller on top of it. Helicopters are different from planes because they can move in any direction in the air, and they can even stay completely still while hanging in the air.

This is the Kittyhawk, the first airplane (that worked).

12. Where are the symbols on a map explained?
   (A) A dictionary
   (B) A legend
   (C) A mountain

Scale

0   miles   100   200

Legend
★ state capital
● cities
♣ state parks
⚓ campgrounds

There are many different kinds of **maps**. You might find a folded-up map in the glove compartment of a car—that's a **road map**. An **atlas** is a big book of maps, usually from all over the world. If you need to find your way to a place you've never been, a map can help you—but only if you know how to read it!

The **legend** is the part of the map in which all the symbols on the map are explained. As you get better at map reading, you'll find that the symbols on most maps are pretty much the same.

There are symbols to tell you what kind of road you are on that look like this:

definition

interstate

(IN ter stayt) *adj.*, something that goes between two or more states.

Teresa's family took the interstate highway from Ohio to Illinois, where Teresa's grandmother lived.

The numbers on these signs tell you which highway or toll road you are on. The numbers on the roads themselves tell you how far it is from one place to another. These are some other symbols found on maps:

- - - - - - - States usually have their borders defined by dotted or solid colored lines.

● Cities may be represented by dots that vary in size, depending on how large the city is.

★ The state capital is usually identified by a star.

🌲 Large parks are large green areas on maps. Smaller parks are marked with a tree.

🌲 Campgrounds are marked with little pine trees or picnic tables.

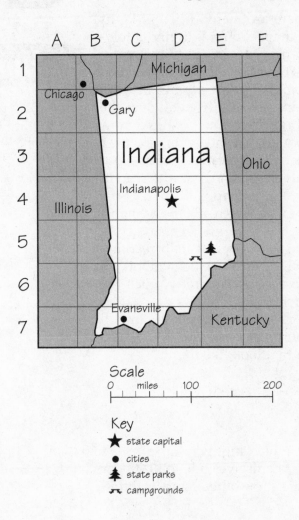

Scale

0   miles   100   200

Key
★ state capital
● cities
🌲 state parks
🌲 campgrounds

The scale on the map tells you how much space on the map is equal to how many miles in the real world. On a typical scale, one inch on the map represents 100 miles of travel.

Sometimes what appears to be a very small distance can be hundreds of miles, so don't be fooled. Always check the scale before you figure out directions. Most books of maps have **indexes** in the back that tell you where to find a particular place by identifying its **coordinates**. If you look up Indiana, for example, it may say 36 D-4. That means to look on page 36, in the area of the map where D and 4 meet.

Coordinates can be a fast way to find what you're looking for.

13. Circle the two regions of the United States that fought in the Civil War.

A **civil war** is a war fought between two groups of citizens (p. 291) that live in the same country. The United States had a civil war that began in 1861—not even a century after the country had begun. The war began because the northern and southern states disagreed about the practice of **slavery**, in which certain people are considered the property of other people. Southern slaveholders forced slaves to work on large farms called plantations and as servants in homes. Slaves were not paid for their work and were usually given only the most basic food, clothing, and houses. Under slavery, families were often broken apart when one member of a family was sold to a new owner and had to move far away.

The first slaves in the United States were Africans kidnapped from their homes and brought here in chains. The children, grandchildren, and great-grandchildren of these African people were born here as slaves.

A political cartoon depicting Abe Lincoln and Jefferson Davis "fighting."

GO UNDERGROUND

Before the Civil War, slaves who attempted to escape to freedom often traveled the Underground Railroad. The Underground Railroad was a network of people stretching from the southern slave states to the northern states and Canada. These people hid the fleeing slaves, sometimes in secret rooms of their houses, provided transportation, and did everything they could to get the slaves to safety in the North.

The Ghost Wore Gray, by Bruce Colville. Nina and Chris are haunted by a ghost form the Civil War. What is he trying to tell them?

definition

abolish

(uh BAHL ish) *verb*, to get rid of completely; to put an end to.

*Our teacher **abolished** all gum chewing in our classroom this year.*

Ulysses S. Grant

Since all of the slaves were black people, and the rest of the Southerners were white, it was hard for slaves to escape because they could be easily spotted. Many laws were written in the South to make it impossible for black people to win freedom from slavery. For example, it was illegal to teach a slave how to read and write. The less a slave knew, the easier it was to keep him on the plantation. The only way a slave could gain freedom was to escape the slaveholder and run away to the North.

In the North, slavery had been made illegal, and many Northerners wanted to end slavery in the entire country. In 1861, President **Abraham Lincoln** (1809-1865) decided that he wanted to abolish slavery. The southern states banded together and withdrew from the United States to form their own union called the **Confederacy**. **Jefferson Davis** (1808-1889) was president of the Confederacy, and **Robert E. Lee** (1807-1870) led the Confederate troops.

What followed was the worst war fought in America. It lasted four years, and when it ended in 1865, 600,000 Americans had been killed. The **North**, led by **General Ulysses S. Grant** (1822-1885) declared victory, and slavery was **abolished** in the United States. The **South** was devastated by the war, and the region took many years to rebuild.

Robert E. Lee

14. Who gave the famous speech that begins, "I have a dream . . ."

(A) Ronald Reagan
(B) Richard Nixon
(C) Martin Luther King, Jr.

Martin Luther King, Jr. (1929-1968) was born in Atlanta, Georgia. He became a Baptist minister in 1954, and in 1963 led 250,000 people in a march to Washington D.C., where he delivered his famous "I Have a Dream" speech:

Martin Luther King , Jr.

I HAVE A DREAM THAT ONE DAY THIS NATION WILL RISE UP AND LIVE OUT THE TRUE MEANING OF ITS CREED: "WE HOLD THESE TRUTHS TO BE SELF-EVIDENT; THAT ALL MEN ARE CREATED EQUAL." I HAVE A DREAM THAT ONE DAY ON THE RED HILLS OF GEORGIA THE SONS OF FORMER SLAVES AND THE SONS OF FORMER SLAVE OWNERS WILL BE ABLE TO SIT DOWN TOGETHER AT THE TABLE OF BROTHERHOOD.

THE NAACP

Discrimination is still a problem for many people of color. Often it is hard for minorities in this country to find jobs, houses, and communities that will accept them. If you want to help in the fight against discrimination, write:

NAACP
260 Fifth Avenue
Sixth Floor
New York, NY 10001

"Happy Birthday," by Stevie Wonder. A tribute to Martin Luther King, Jr., this song was part of the campaign to make a federal holiday out of King's birthday.

Martin Luther King, Jr. tried to make people understand that it is wrong to treat people differently because of the color of their skin. When he was growing up in the South, the law stated that, even though slavery had ended, blacks and whites had to be separated when they went to school, when they rode on the bus, in restaurants—even at water fountains.

CIVIL RIGHTS TIMELINE

1863
Emancipation Proclamation issued by Abraham Lincoln freeing the slaves.

1955
Rosa Parks, a seamstress at a department store, is arrested for refusing to give up her seat on a Montgomery bus to a white person.

1955–56
Montgomery Bus Boycott takes place.

1963
Martin Luther King, Jr. leads a huge march on Washington D.C. where he delivers his "I have a dream" speech.

1965
Selma-Montgomery March led by Rev. King.

1964–65
Civil Rights Act passed, outlawing racial discrimination in the United States.

This was called **segregation**. Dr. King was a leader of the **Civil Rights movement** which helped change laws that kept African-Americans from having the same freedom and opportunities that whites did. He organized peaceful protests, trying to persuade the country to change things through words and ideas rather than guns and fists. One of the most famous nonviolent methods of the Civil Rights movement was a **boycott** of the buses in Montgomery, Alabama. The Montgomery boycott began after **Rosa Parks,** an African-American woman, was arrested for not giving up her seat on the bus to a white person. For a full year, the black people of Montgomery did not ride the buses, making the city lose a lot of money in fares. In 1964, more than 100 years after the slaves were freed, segregation was made illegal in the U.S. Tragically, Dr. King was **assassinated** in 1968, but not before he had won the Nobel Peace Prize and changed the way many people thought about how black and white people should get along.

Rosa Parks, freedom fighter.

Martin Luther King Jr. and thousands of protesters march on Washington in 1963.

15. Who wrote the Declaration of Independence?

(A) George Washington
(B) Thomas Jefferson
(C) Bill Clinton

3

In 1774, when the United States was still just thirteen colonies ruled by England, a group of men from each of the thirteen original colonies joined together to form the **Continental Congress**. Their purpose was to protest against British rule. Many of the names of people in the Continental Congress will sound familiar to you, like George Washington, Thomas Jefferson, Ben Franklin, John Adams, and John Hancock.

At first, the Continental Congress wanted to work with England, but by 1775, the American Revolutionary War had begun. In January of 1776, a booklet called *Common Sense*, written by

 1776. A musical about the first American Congress's struggle with independence. (It's a lot more fun than it sounds.)

Thomas Paine (1737-1809) appeared in the colonies. This little book offered strong reasons why the colonists should seek independence from Britain. It was widely read, not only by the members of the Continental Congress, but by many ordinary colonists, and the idea of **independence** started catching on all over.

A committee was formed to write a document stating that America was free from England from then on. **Ben Franklin** (1706-1790) and **John Adams** (1735-1826) were on the committee, but it was Thomas Jefferson who wrote the first draft of the **Declaration of Independence**. The Congress made changes to his draft. The most famous of these changes is a section they removed in which Jefferson had argued forcefully against the King of England for permitting slavery. But, when Jefferson brought this before the Congressmen, some of whom were weathly slaveowners, they made him delete the section that said King George III had "waged a cruel war against human nature itself, violating its most sacred rights of life and liberty in the persons of a distant people who never offended him, captivating and carrying them into slavery in another hemisphere, or to incur miserable death in their transportation [there]."

Yet, even without this section, the Declaration of Independence turned out to be a document people could use to fight for freedom. Those who have fought for the rights of women, African-Americans, and all oppressed people have used the words of the Declaration of Independence.

The signatures on the Declaration of Independence.

WE HOLD THESE TRUTHS TO BE SELF-EVIDENT, THAT ALL MEN ARE CREATED EQUAL, THAT THEY ARE ENDOWED BY THEIR CREATOR WITH CERTAIN INALIENABLE RIGHTS, THAT AMONG THESE ARE LIFE, LIBERTY AND THE PURSUIT OF HAPPINESS.

All the members of the Continental Congress signed, to show their willingness to stand together. The most famous signature was that of **John Hancock**, in his beautiful, elaborate handwriting.

16. What type of government does the United States have?

(A) Monarchy

(B) Democracy

(C) Autocracy

A **democracy** is a form of government in which the people make all the rules and decisions. The United States uses a **representative democracy.** That means that we vote for people—representatives —who make the laws and decide how to spend the money. In a **direct democracy**, all the people would have to vote on every decision—an almost impossible system for a country as large as the United States. It is, however, up to citizens to speak or write to their elected repre- sentatives and let them know their opinions about the issues the representatives must decide on.

There are three branches to our government: executive branch, legislative branch, and judicial branch. The president (p. 296) is head of

The U.S. Congress in session.

The nine U.S. Supreme Court Justices.

the **Executive branch** of government. He is in charge of the army, appoints judges, carries out laws, and deals with foreign countries. He appoints people to help him, like the Secretary of the Treasury, who is in charge of money, and the Secretary of State, who is responsible for our relations with other countries. Some of the president's appointments must be approved by Congress.

LADIES AND GENTLEMEN, THE SUPREMES!

The Supreme Court is the highest court in the U.S. Since 1869 it has been made up of a Chief Justice and eight Associate Justices. Lifetime appointments to the court are made by the president, with the advice and consent of the senate. Justices can only lose their place on the Court for misconduct. The Supreme Court hears appeals from the Court of Appeals and from the state supreme courts. It also settles conflicts between the various branches of the federal government.

The **U.S. Congress** is our country's **Legislative branch**. It consists of two "houses," the **Senate** and the **House of Representatives**. Two senators are elected from each state (100 in all); Senators are elected for six-year terms. The House of Representatives is made up of representatives from each state according to the size of its population. This means that larger states send more representatives to the House. In all, there are 435 representatives.

The Congress passes laws, can

declare war on a foreign country, and works on the federal budget—the master plan for how our tax money will be spent each year.

The **Judicial branch** interprets the U.S. Constitution. This means that the judicial branch decides whether the laws that are passed go against the principles written in the Constitution. The judicial branch judges whether Congress or the President do anything unconstitutional, as well.

Our government is set up according to a system called "checks and balances." That simply means that no one part of the government has absolute power to do anything. Each of the three branches must work with the other two. For example, the president is in charge of the army, but only Congress can declare war. And any act the Congress passes can be **vetoed**—rejected—by the president. Every power possessed by every branch has a "safeguard"—a way for someone to challenge it if they think it is wrong. The good thing about our government is that no one has complete authority or power.

definition

veto

(VEE toh) *verb,* to reject a law or to stop it from happening.

*The president has the right to **veto** any law proposed by Congress in the United States.*

17. Which president left office in a scandal called Watergate?

(A) Richard Nixon

(B) Andrew Jackson

(C) James Polk

If you drive around Washington, D.C., you'll probably pass by the **Watergate** Apartment and Office Complex, where the presidency of **Richard Nixon** (1913-1994) began to unravel. The story of what happened at Watergate in 1972 is one of the strangest chapters in American history. President Nixon, a Republican, was running for a second term against George McGovern, a Democrat. On June 17th, five men were arrested at the Watergate office of the Democratic National Committee for planting "bugs"—secret listening devices—in the Democratic headquarters. They also stole papers that revealed the Democrats' strategy for the election. This botched plan was not only illegal but also ridiculous, since Nixon was way ahead in the **polls**—he had practically won the election already. Even though the burglars were part of the Committee to Re-elect the President, no one could pin it all on Nixon or the White House, and

IF YOU HAD TO VOTE FOR PRESIDENT TODAY

Public opinion polls are conducted before elections to try to predict which party will win. Most polls take random samples of around 1,000 voters, which gives results that should be accurate about 95 percent of the time. Opinion polls have been criticized because some people think they may influence, rather than predict, the outcome of an election. For example, on election day, people may change their votes in order to be on the "winning" side, or they may feel they needn't bother voting because their party is predicted to win.

Richard Nixon

Nixon won the election in a landslide that November.

By February of the next year, rumors started to spread that Nixon and his staff were up to no good. The Senate formed a committee to study what had happened during the campaign. Eventually, a whole cover-up emerged. Some of the burglars who were in jail for the break-in admitted that they were given money to keep quiet about who was really behind the Watergate burglary. People in the Nixon administration began to resign, some admitting that they had destroyed evidence about the break-in. When it was revealed in testimony that Nixon had been secretly recording all conversations in the Oval Office of the White House (p. 305), it became clear that Nixon was involved in the scandal. At the same time, Nixon's vice president, **Spiro Agnew** (1918-), resigned after getting caught for not paying taxes years before. Refusing to hand in the Oval Office tapes, Nixon fired the lawyer who was investigating the case, **Archibald Cox**. Suspicions grew about Nixon's behavior in all of this, and word got out that the Senate wanted to **impeach** him. Nixon then handed over the tapes, but parts had been erased, arousing even more suspicions. Finally, Nixon resigned from office on August 9, 1973, just in time to avoid certain impeachment and possible jail time. **Gerald Ford** (1913-), who had taken over for

Spiro Agnew, became president when Nixon resigned. Ford **pardoned** Nixon, so that Nixon could not be charged with a crime and put on trial. Many of the Nixon staff members, however, ended up in jail. Nixon went on to a quiet life, writing a number of books and maintaining his innocence until his death in 1994. He was the first president in American history to resign from office.

The Watergate Hotel, where it all happened.

 All the President's Men. This movie about the two reporters who uncovered the Watergate scandal may be a little difficult for some, but if you are interested in learning what really happened, this is a good place to start.

definition

pardon
(PAR dun) *verb*, to release from punishment, to forgive.

Jackie **pardoned** *her brother for destroying her homework, even though her lessons were due that morning.*

18. Which of the following was the chief immigration station of the United States in the early 1900s?

(A) The Statue of Liberty
(B) Ellis Island
(C) The Empire State Building

Engraved on a bronze plaque on the base of the Statue of Liberty is a poem by **Emma Lazarus** (1849-1887). It reads, in part:

FAMOUS IMMIGRANTS TO THE UNITED STATES

Alexander Graham Bell
Albert Einstein
Hakeem Olajuwon
Alfred Hitchcock
John J. Audubon
Martina Navratilova
Henry Kissinger
Arnold Schwarzenegger

definition

alien

(AY lee un) *adj.* a person who is a citizen of a country other than the one in which she is living.

*Velma's father is an **alien** and her mother is a U.S. citizen*

GIVE ME YOUR TIRED, YOUR POOR, YOUR HUDDLED MASSES YEARNING TO BREATHE FREE, THE WRETCHED REFUSE OF YOUR TEEMING SHORE. SEND THESE, THE HOMELESS, TEMPEST-TOSSED TO ME. I LIFT MY LAMP BESIDE THE GOLDEN DOOR!

What did Emma Lazarus mean by "the golden door?" For many immigrants, the United States offered the chance for a decent life they could not find in their original countries. In the 1800s, religious persecution, famine, and poverty forced many Europeans from their homes. The "great potato famine" in Ireland, for example, caused many Irish to leave their country. Immigrants from all over were drawn to a land in which they would be free to live where and how they pleased, and to earn enough money to support their families. Ships brought millions of immigrants from Europe—and some from Asia and Africa—to the port of New York City. There, the **Statue of Liberty** welcomed them to their new lives.

After their long voyage, immigrants disembarked on **Ellis Island**, which sits in the harbor of New York City. Ellis Island was for them a "golden door." There, more than 12 million immigrants

The Statue of Liberty

were examined for diseases, registered, and processed. For some, the dream ended right there. Many immigrants were turned away because they had contagious diseases. For those who made it through, the process could be grueling. Some immigrants lost their original names when immigration officers simply spelled the foreign names however they understood them.

ELLIS ISLAND

Ellis Island's use as a large-scale immigration station ended in 1924. The island stayed open for a number of years as a detention center for illegal aliens before being closed down completely in 1954. Recently, Ellis Island was restored and reopened as a museum and monument to the millions of immigrants who passed through. For information on visiting Ellis Island, write:

Statue of Liberty National
   Monument
National Park Service
U.S. Dept. of the Interior
Liberty Island
New York, NY 10004

Immigrants arriving at Ellis Island.

Almost 22 million immigrants came to the United States from 1890 to 1930—more than all the people who had come here since colonial times. Prejudice against immigrants contributed to the mounting pressure to limit the number of immigrants each year, so limits were put in place in the 1920s. These limits, or quotas, along with the Great Depression (p. 326) of the thirties, reduced immigration a great deal.

Today, there are still quotas on immigration. The number of immigrants admitted to the U.S. has changed throughout the years, as has the process by which aliens become citizens. A person who wants to come to the U.S. to live must first be issued a **visa**—a special permit allowing them to live in this country. To become a citizen, the person must live here for five years in a row, have some knowledge of U.S. history, and have basic reading and writing skills. After meeting these requirements he swears allegiance to the United States in a naturalization ceremony and becomes a citizen of the United States with the same rights and responsibilities as anyone born here.

Our country has traditionally been a place that welcomed those who had problems in their own lands. What has made the United States unique is the wide variety of people and cultures that make

up our country. Except for Native Americans, everyone you will ever meet in the United States can trace his or her family back to somewhere else.

19. Who was the main enemy of the United States in World War I?

(A) England
(B) Canada
(C) Germany

The Great War, or **World War I** as it later came to be known, began in Europe in 1914. The United States did not enter the war until 1917. By 1919 the American side, called the **Allies**, had defeated the German side, called the **Central Powers**, and the **Treaty of Versailles** was signed to end the war.

TRENCH WARFARE

Trench Warfare came into use in 1914 by the European forces during World War I. First used at the Battle of the Marne, trench warfare involved each side digging a huge trench, where the soldiers stayed, trapped, unable to move without getting shot by opposing snipers. What were they thinking?

At first, the quarrel was strictly between the European powers. Russia was angry at Germany and Germany's **ally**, Austria-Hungary, for grabbing more and more land close to the Russian border. Germany and Russia declared war on each other, and France and England jumped in to defend their ally, Russia. France and England had grudges against Germany and Austria-Hungary anyway. They felt that Germany had been trying to build up too much power, and that the Germans and their friends had been talking tough a little too often. Some people say that a war in Europe was inevitable at that time, since all of these nations were growing stronger—and more suspicious of each other's power.

The U.S. was drawn into the war after a German submarine sank the British passenger ship **Lusitania** in 1915. The Lusitania was travelling from New York to England, and on board were many Americans. One hundred twenty-eight Americans died when the ship, almost split in half by the German torpedo, went down in less than twenty minutes. But as furious as they were, the Americans didn't respond right away. It took another aggressive act by Germany to get the U.S. to fight in a brutal war all the way across the Atlantic. This time, the Germans sent a telegram to the government of Mexico offering to help the Mexicans regain territory they had previously lost to the U.S. (an area that is now the states of Texas, Arizona, and New Mexico) in return for Mexican support. The telegram was intercepted by some British spies, and soon after that President **Woodrow Wilson** (1856-1924) asked the American people to join the war against Germany in order to "make the world safe for democracy."

It's no wonder the Americans waited so long before entering World War I. It was the bloodiest, most destructive war in history, thanks to new weapons like the machine gun, which was used to mow down hundreds of soldiers very quickly. More than ten million lives were lost. Once we did agree to fight, the American troops made a big difference in the course of the war. After four years of slow, brutal warfare, the Germans gave up about a year and a half after the American soldiers arrived in Europe.

---

definition

ally
(AL eye) *noun*, a person, group, or country joined with others for a common goal.

*Annette knew she had an **ally** in me, because we both wanted gym class to end.*

A LEAGUE OF THEIR OWN

As well as ending the war, the Treaty of Versailles formed the League of Nations, a group of representatives from many countries around the world. The goal of the League of Nations was to talk over disagreements between countries before a war started. Unfortunately, the U.S. did not sign the treaty—even though the League of Nations was President Wilson's idea—and it broke up in 1946.

20. What was the Great Depression?

(A) A time of crisis and poverty for many Americans during the 1930s
(B) Part of the Grand Canyon formed in this century
(C) A psychological slump America experienced in the 1970s

After all the suffering and worry of World War I, the U.S. let out a big sigh of relief in the 1920s, a fast-paced time of excitement and celebration. People were hopeful, and they borrowed and spent lots of money—too much money for the country's good. In the 1930s, many people and companies went broke, and suddenly the U.S. was plunged into a time of hardship called the **Great Depression**. Millions of Americans were fired from their jobs, and families went hungry. Many people were kicked out of their homes when they could no longer afford them, and were forced to live in shacks made out of pieces of wood and metal that they found.

HOOVERVILLES

During the Depression from 1929 to 1940, Hoovervilles sprang up around all the large U.S. cities. Herbert Hoover, who was president at the beginning of the Depression, opposed direct government aid for the unemployed, and his policies were blamed for the plight of millions. It is no wonder then that the shantytowns the unemployed and destitute built to house themselves were named after him.

Franklin Delano Roosevelt

It wasn't until a new President named **Franklin Delano Roosevelt** (1882-1945) was elected that the Great Depression came to an end. Roosevelt put into place dozens of programs designed to get the country's **economy** moving again and put Americans back to work. We'll probably never know if Roosevelt's plan, which he called the **New Deal**, put an end to the Depression all by itself, but the New Deal made important changes in the way our country is run. Probably the biggest change was the invention of **Social Security**, which makes sure that when Americans lose their jobs, become too sick to work, or retire, they have some money to live on.

definition

economy
(ee KAHN uh mee) *noun*, the management of earning and spending money.

When the economy turned sour, Fred's mom lost her job at the vacuum cleaner factory.

21. **Who was the leader of Germany during World War II?**

(A) Adolf Hitler

(B) Harry Truman

(C) Winston Churchill

Losing World War I was a big blow to the people of Germany, and before long a politician arrived on the scene who promised Germans he would bring their nation a new period of power and glory. His name was **Adolf Hitler** (1889-1945) and his outrageous, hateful policies eventually led the world into another all-encompassing war, **World War II**, which lasted from 1939 to 1945. This time, Germany was allied with Italy and Japan. These three nations

The Horrors of Hitler

Adolf Hitler was the leader (Führer) of the Nazi Party in Germany from 1921 until his death in 1945. In 1934 he became head of state and declared his party the only legal one. In 1939 Hitler's army invaded Poland, marking the beginning of WWII, which lasted six years. In July 1944 high-ranking German generals plotted to assassinate Hitler by bombing a staff meeting—Hitler narrowly escaped death. In April the following year, with Berlin now largely occupied by the Soviets, Hitler married his mistress, Eva Braun, and the following day they committed suicide.

Adolph Hitler

were called the **Axis Powers**. The other side, again known as the Allies, was made up of Great Britain, France, Russia (then called the USSR), China, and the United States. The Allies eventually won this war too, but not before about fifty-five million lives were lost.

Hitler rose to power in Germany by stirring up hatred against Europeans who were not German, and above all against Jews (p. 148), whom he made a **scapegoat** for all of Germany's problems. With the German people rallying around Hitler's message of German superiority, the powerful German army began to invade other European countries in 1938, and kept up a march intended to conquer all of Europe—and eventually the whole world. Britain and France decided that Hitler had to be stopped and declared war. While battles raged across Europe, Hitler put into action a terrifying plan to systematically murder all the Jews of Europe. This plan, called the **Holocaust**, eventually resulted in the deaths of over six million Jews, along with many others whom Hitler decided should be put to death. Jews and "undesirables" were taken from their homes and brought to **concentration camps**, where mass killings took place.

At the beginning of World War II, America did not enter the fighting, but helped the Allies by sending them supplies. Most Americans were hesitant to fight another war, even though our friends in Europe seemed to be in great danger. But in 1941, Japan,

Auschwitz

AUSCHWITZ WAS THE SITE OF ONE OF THE MOST NOTORIOUS CONCENTRATION CAMPS BUILT BY THE NAZIS DURING WWII. THE CAMP INCLUDED FOUR GAS CHAMBERS, EACH ABLE TO HOLD 6,000 PEOPLE, WHICH WERE USED TO EXTERMINATE JEWS AND OTHER POLITICAL AND SOCIAL MINORITIES.

To Be or Not to Be, starring Jack Benny. This is an unbelievably funny film about how a bunch of actors in Poland trick the Nazis. Also remade in 1983 by Mel Brooks.

Germany's ally in Asia, bombed American ships stationed at **Pearl Harbor**, in the state of Hawaii. In response, President Roosevelt asked Congress to declare war on Japan, and the U.S. entered the war.

It wasn't until 1944 that the tide of the war began to turn decisively toward the Allies. Thousands of Allied troops stormed the beaches of **Normandy**, France, and fought fiercely to drive back the German army into Germany. By 1945, the Allies had invaded Germany. Crushed by the prospect of defeat, Adolf Hitler killed himself, and Germany surrendered.

But Japan had yet to give up, and on August 6, 1945, the United States

JAPANESE INTERNMENT CAMPS

AFTER JAPAN ATTACKED PEARL HARBOR, MANY AMERICAN CITIZENS OF JAPANESE ANCESTRY WERE FORCED FROM THEIR HOMES AND JOBS BY THE U.S. GOVERNMENT AND PLACED IN INTERNMENT CAMPS, SOME FOR THE DURATION OF THE WAR. THESE JAPANESE AMERICANS HAD DONE NOTHING WRONG, BUT THE GOVERNMENT SUSPECTED THEM OF AIDING JAPAN. THE U.S. GOVERNMENT PLACED NO SUCH RESTRICTIONS ON GERMAN AMERICANS OR ITALIAN AMERICANS, THOUGH WE WERE AT WAR WITH THOSE COUNTRIES AS WELL.

Buck Privates. Abbott and Costello enlist. A great movie with great music.

The Diary of Anne Frank, by Anne Frank. In a remarkable first-hand account, Anne Frank a young German Jewish girl in hiding, reveals the trials and suffering of those persecuted by the Nazis.

definition

scapegoat

(SKAPE goat) *noun*, one who takes the blame for others

Even though he didn't steal the teacher's ruler, Reginald was made the scapegoat because he was the one who sat nearest to her desk.

made a decision that would change the course of history. President **Harry Truman** (1884-1972) decided to save the lives of thousands of American soldiers who would have had to invade Japan. Instead of attacking Japan using troops, the U.S. chose to use a terrible new weapon called the **atomic bomb**. The atomic bomb is different from other weapons of war because it spreads death and destruction over a very large area. It cannot be aimed solely at troops

A child in the rubble of Hiroshima.

or military targets, so ordinary people—including children—are killed. Also, while the atomic bomb kills thousands of people in a single flash of heat and light, thousands more people die slow, painful deaths afterwards from the effects of burns and **radiation** (which is like a type of poison). The first atomic bomb was dropped on the city of **Hiroshima**, and eighty thousand people died. Japan still did not give up, so the U. S. dropped another atomic bomb on **Nagasaki**, and the Japanese government surrendered. World War II ended after six years of fighting.

22. Who is the leader of the United Nations?

(A) Bill Clinton

(B) Boutros Boutros-Ghali

(C) Frank Sinatra

After World War II, the Allied powers got together to set up an organization that would bring together all the nations of the world. The Allies hoped that the **United Nations** would help support peace by giving countries a place to discuss their differences without resorting to war. The U.N. also helps countries after disasters like earthquakes or famines, and helps poor countries develop. U.N. member countries pay **dues** according to what they can afford, with some richer countries voluntarily giving more. The leader of the U.N., called the Secretary-General, is chosen by the General Assembly. The current Secretary-General is **Boutros Boutros-Ghali**, an Egyptian. Even though the U.N. has not been very successful in keeping peace, it is still an important and influential world organization.

There are many special programs and agencies run by the U.N., such as the **United Nations International Children's Fund (UNICEF)**, established in 1953. UNICEF sees to the needs of children throughout the world. Another agency, the **United Nations Environment Program (UNEP)**, established in 1972, keeps an eye on the state of the world's environment and promotes environmentally safe development.

definition

dues

(dooz) *noun*, a payment or obligation.

*Bronwyn forgot to pay her **dues** three weeks in a row, so the sailing club had to ask her to leave.*

Boutros Boutros-Ghali

THE BEGINNING OF THE CHARTER OF THE UNITED NATIONS

WE THE PEOPLES OF THE UNITED NATIONS DETERMINED to save succeeding generations from the scourge of war, which twice in our lifetime has brought untold sorrow to mankind, and to reaffirm faith in fundamental human rights, in the dignity and worth of the human person, in the equal rights of men and women and of nations large and small, and to establish conditions under which justice and respect for the obligations arising from treaties and other sources of international law can be maintained, and to promote social progress and better standards of life in larger freedom . . .

23. Which document begins "We, the People"?

(A) The Constitution
(B) The Gettysburg Address
(C) The Declaration of Independence

In 1783, after our country won independence from Great Britain, the thirteen original states pretty much did their own thing for four years. In 1787, **George Washington**, with a group of other men (such as **Thomas Jefferson** and **John Adams**) known as "the Founding Fathers," decided to create a government that would be in charge of all the states. They went about writing the **Constitution**. Here's how it begins (pay no attention to the bad spelling—people spelled weird back then):

> WE, THE PEOPLE OF THE UNITED STATES, IN ORDER TO FORM A MORE PERFECT UNION, ESTABLISH JUSTICE, INSURE DOMESTIC TRANQUILITY, PROVIDE FOR THE COMMON DEFENCE, PROMOTE THE GENERAL WELFARE, AND SECURE THE BLESSINGS OF LIBERTY TO OURSELVES AND OUR POSTERITY, DO ORDAIN AND ESTABLISH THIS CONSTITUTION FOR THE UNITED STATES OF AMERICA.

definition

ratify
(RAT i fy) *verb* to accept in an official way.

*The U.S. Constitution was **ratified** by all thirteen original states.*

The Constitution, **ratified** in 1788, is the basis of our laws and our government. The writers of the Constitution came up with the idea for the three branches (p. 317) of our government, and they set out our basic rights, such as the right to practice any religion we choose, and the right to speak out even if we don't like the actions of our government. But there are often differences of opinion about what is or is not constitutional. The Constitution was written over 200 years ago; the writers couldn't possibly have known about all the changes that have come since then. This is why the Constitution is called a "living document"—it must be constantly reinterpreted as our country moves into the future and new problems arise. Shortly after the Constitution was **ratified**, twelve **amendments**—additions to the Constitution—were considered. In 1791, ten of them were ratified. Called the **Bill of Rights**, these amendments guaranteed, among other things, the freedom of religion, speech, press, and the right to a speedy trial.

24. In which present country did the Aztec civilization flourish?

(A) Mexico

(B) The United States

(C) Cuba

The **Aztecs** were a group of Native Americans who lived more than 700 years ago in what is now Mexico. Aztec civilization was highly advanced. The temples, causeways, and canals they built were very complex and well-planned. The Aztecs also added to their wealth by collecting payments from tribes they had conquered.

Many of the pyramids from this time period still stand.

The Aztec capital, **Tenochtitlan,** was built on the site of present-day **Mexico City**. The Aztecs are famous for their pyramids and temples at which they offered up constant human sacrifices to please their gods. Up to 1,000 people a week were killed as offerings to their main god Huitzilopochtli (Hummingbird Wizard). Many of these offerings were the captured soldiers of nearby enemies, but often the Aztec priests used their own people. In 1519, the Spanish conquistador **Hernán Cortes** (1485-1547) landed with a

definition

excavate
(ECKS cuh vayt) *verb*, to dig out.

*Marcos **excavated** the covered-up cave, after finding an old pirate's map promising secret treasure.*

"Time-Life's Lost Civilization" (NBC). This ten-part documentary series looks at lost civilizations from the Aztecs to the Kingdoms of the Nile.

SACRIFICE CITY

During human sacrifices, the Aztec priests sometimes cut out a person's heart and offered it up to the gods, throwing the victim's body off the wall of the temple to the ground. The Aztecs believed their civilization would end unless they gave constant sacrifices to the gods.

definition

conquer

(KAHN ker) *verb*, to defeat; to take control of.

*Valerie and several of her friends **conquered** my fort with a flurry of snowballs.*

COLOR WORDS

The Incans could neither read nor write. They recorded everything on a series of strings called a quipu. The color of the string, the knots on it, and the number of strings used conveyed information.

large army of well-equipped soldiers. He destroyed Tenochtitlan and killed the last Aztec ruler, Montezuma II.

The **Incan** civilization was also made up of Native Americans, but they lived in South America. By the 1500s, the Incas were more than 10 million strong, covering a territory of more than 2,000 miles along the coast of South America.

The Incas were expert farmers, weavers, and goldsmiths who

The Incan city Machu Picchu

produced some of the great treasures of South America. **Machu Picchu**, a huge fortress city built by the Incas, is carved into the side of a mountain. The chief Inca was worshipped as a god by his subjects. When chief Huayna Capac died, a battle began over who would take his place. When the Spanish arrived soon after, they had no problem conquering a nation that was already in turmoil, bringing about the end of the great Incan culture.

25. Hieroglyphics are

(A) a group of ancient Egyptian rulers

(B) ancient burial tombs

(C) an ancient form of writing

About 5,000 years ago, in ancient Egypt, a system of writing was started that used symbols. These **hieroglyphics** were used to write the Egyptian language for more than 3500 years, until about 400 A.D. By that time, Egypt had been under the control of the Roman Empire for a while. Eventually, Egyptians used a combination of the Greek alphabet and their own. This language is called **Coptic**. Coptic disappeared over time and the language of Egypt became Arabic. Arabic is spoken in Egypt today.

That's what happens over the course of centuries: ancient languages die out gradually, and one day people find themselves looking at strange symbols wondering what they could possibly mean. For more than 1,000 years, people came and studied the hieroglyphs on the walls of ancient temples and in the tombs of Egypt. They made up what they thought were translations of this mysterious language. Most scientists believed that the pictures of birds, plants, and animals stood for other things.

Then, in 1799, the **Rosetta Stone** was found by the army of French dictator

Hieroglyphics

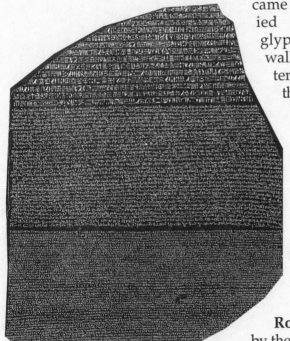

The Rosetta Stone

The Metropolitan Museum of Art's Fun with Hieroglyphs, by Catharine Roehrig. This great book includes rubber stamps so you can create your own messages.

NILE BY A MILE (OR TWO)

The Nile River is the longest river in the world at 4,160 miles long. The Amazon River is second. The Mississippi is third.

Napolean Bonaparte (1769-1821) as they were attacking Egypt. This huge piece of stone, which can be dated to exactly March 27, 195, is divided into three sections of writing. The top section is written in hieroglyphs. The middle is written in a script called Demotic—a late form of the Egyptian language. The bottom section is written in ancient Greek. Since ancient Greek was a known language, it was possible to translate the Demotic and Hieroglyphic parts of the stone. Scholars found out that hieroglyphic symbols stood for sounds, rather than merely representing the things they were pictures of.

There's lots more to the culture of ancient Egypt than hieroglyphics. The **Nile River**, which runs through Egypt, made the land very fertile. Most Egyptians were farmers, tilling the rich Egyptian soil. Egyptian doctors made great advances in medicine—even performing some basic dentistry.

Ancient Egyptians believed in an afterlife. They thought people lived forever if their bodies were preserved. They perfected techniques of **embalming** the body so that it would not rot. These **mummies** were stored in coffins decorated with portraits of the dead person and hieroglyphics to ward off evil. The **pyramids** of Egypt are giant royal tombs filled with jewelry, riches, and food for

The Great Pyramids

King Tut, the boy king.

the dead **pharoahs**. But these tombs were often robbed, so later pharoahs were buried in the Valley of the Kings, where they lay in unmarked tombs, guarded day and night.

King Tutankahmen, or **King Tut**, is the most famous pharaoh in our time, because his tomb, excavated in 1922, was virtually untouched by the grave robbers that looted almost all of the other pharoahs' tombs. A solid gold coffin, many works of art, and Tut's famous gold mask were among the treasures found in the tomb. Egyptians worshipped pharaohs like Tut, whom they believed to be descendants of Re, the sun god. The Egyptians also believed all of their land belonged to the pharaohs.

26. Which of these three cities was a city-state of Ancient Greece?

(A) Rome
(B) London
(C) Athens

Many aspects of our culture today can be traced back about 2,500 years to ancient Greece. Lots of words in the English language have roots in ancient Greek—the word "democracy" for example. Ancient Greece was made up of independent, self-governing cities, known as **city-states**. The two most important were Athens and Sparta.

The most influential playwrights, artists, and thinkers of ancient Greece lived in **Athens**. **Socrates** (c. 469-399 B.C.), an Athenian, was perhaps the most famous Greek philosopher. He asked important questions about how we should live, and he taught his philosophy by asking his students a series of questions in order to prod them to reach their own conclusions. This method

The Parthenon

definition

philosophy
(fil AH suh fee) *noun*, the study of the meaning of life and how life works.

Kathy had always dreamed of studying philosophy when she got to colleege.

of teaching is called the **Socratic Method**. Interestingly, Socrates never wrote a book; it was up to one of his followers, **Plato** (c. 428-347 B.C.), to record the story of Socrates' life and set forth his philosophy. Another great philosopher from ancient Greece was **Aristotle** (384-322 B.C.). Aristotle emphasized reason and moderation as the best way to live a happy life. He also wrote a lot about what makes a good government, and he came up with theories about what makes works of art and literature beautiful.

Drama as we know it also started in Athens. Playwrights such as **Sophocles** (495-406 B.C.) and **Aristophanes** (c. 448-380 B.C.) wrote tragedies and comedies that are still often performed today. Prizes were given to the best actor and playwright.

Pericles (c. 490-429 B.C.), the beloved leader of Athens during the city's most pros-

Socrates was forced by authorities to kill himself by drinking a glass of hemlock because they didn't agree with his teachings. This is a painting of that fateful day.

perous period, led a movement to build up and beautify Athens. Under Pericles' rule the **Parthenon**, the most perfect example of ancient Greek architecture, was built. Athens was also famous for its thriving marketplace—a huge, open place where people from all over the world came to buy and sell their goods—called the **agora**.

Sparta was a war-loving city-state. Men in Sparta trained rigorously for lives devoted to military service. Training began at the age of seven, and Spartans remained soldiers until they were sixty. The Spartan army gained a reputation throughout the world as a fierce, determined, and disciplined force. The women of Sparta were physically strong, too—they wrestled and ran for fitness.

In about 300 B.C., Philip of Macedonia conquered all of the Greek city-states and brought them together into one league. Philip did not survive long after his victory, but his son Alexander, known as **Alexander the Great** (356-323 B.C.) took over and spread much of Greek civilization throughout the Middle East and North Africa.

27. Which of the following countries is the most populated?

(A) China
(B) United States
(C) Russia

Throughout history, the population of the world has risen and fallen. Often tragedies wipe out large numbers of people in a short time. The **bubonic plague**, a killer disease also known as the **Black Death**, spread through Europe in the 1300s, killing about a third of the population of that continent. Famines have resulted in the deaths of huge portions of some populations. In fact, up until about 800 A.D., these catastrophes, along with shorter life expectancies, kept the population of the world down below 200 million. World population has risen most dramatically in the last 100 years. New technology, advances in hygiene, new drugs, pesticides—these things help to keep people alive, prevent diseases that shorten lives, and stop disastrous events like plagues and famines. The population of the world is now well over 5 billion, and many scientists predict that it will be over 6 billion by the year 2000. The world population is growing at a rate of about 180 people per minute.

The Information Please Kid's Almanac, by Alice Siegel and Margo McLoone Basta. If you want even more statistics and information about the world around you, this is a great book.

6

28. What is the only country that forms a continent as well?

(A) Africa

(B) Australia

(C) America

PEOPLE PILE

The most densely populated area in the world is the Portugese province of Macau, on the coast of China. There are about 81,000 people living in each square mile.

Bangladesh is the most densely populated country, with an average of over 2,000 people living in each square mile.

Most of the earth is covered by water (p. 248). The land of the earth is almost all concentrated in seven major pieces, called the **continents**. The continents pretty much fall within one half of the globe, with the Pacific Ocean taking up the other half.

Asia contains more than 17 million square miles and is the largest of all the continents. The countries of India, China, and Japan are part of Asia. The continent of **Europe** is home to the countries of

A busy Chinese street

definition

population

(pop yoo LAY shun) *noun*, the number of people or animals living in a certain area

*The whale **population** was so reduced by hunting that Mike's dad spoke before Congress in support of a law that limited whale hunting.*

POPULATON EXPLOSIONS		
CHINA	OVER	1,100,000,000
INDIA	OVER	840,000,000
USA	OVER	250,000,000
INDONESIA	OVER	187,000,000
BRAZIL	OVER	150,000,000
JAPAN	OVER	123,000,000
PAKISTAN	OVER	110,000,000
BANGLADESH	OVER	108,000,000
NIGERIA	OVER	88,000,000

SO LONELY

The most sparsely populated area is Antarctica, which has only about 2,000 people on the whole continent—all scientists there to perform experiments.

The Australian continent is full of Kangaroos.

England, France, Italy, and Spain. South of Europe is the continent of **Africa**. Nigeria, Chad, Rwanda, and Egypt are all in Africa. The United States, Canada, and Mexico are on the continent of **North America**. The continent of **South America** includes the countries of Brazil, Peru and Argentina. **Australia** is the only country that fills up its own continent. **Antarctica** is a continent; the arctic is not. The North Pole is covered by ice, not land.

It's pretty well accepted that the seven continents were once one big land mass, which scientists call **Pangaea**. About 200 million years ago, this giant mass began to break apart, gradually moving across large areas of water. This is called **continental drift**. Each continent is on a separate plate of rock that extends about sixty miles into the earth's mantle (p. 288). These plates don't just sit still. They move a tiny bit—about one inch every year. The Atlantic Ocean gets a little bigger every year as Europe and Asia drift away from the Americas.

CONTINENTAL DRIFT

In 1912, Alfred Wegener, a German scientist, first came up with the theory that the continents drifted. Looking at a map of the world, he speculated that the continents had once fit together like a huge jigsaw puzzle.

THE SEVEN CONTINENTS

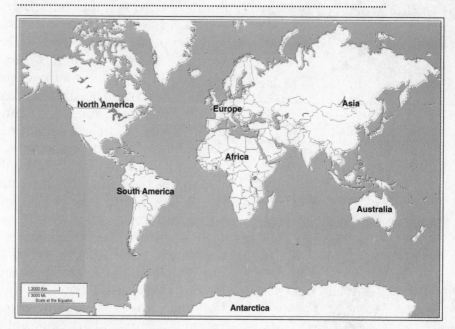

29. Who was the first woman appointed to the United States Supreme Court?

(A) Kathy Lee Gifford

(B) Sandra Day O'Connor

(C) Susan B. Anthony

In the United States, women have been fighting for equality for many years. When our country began, women had very few rights. They couldn't vote and they couldn't own property—in fact, they were considered the property of their fathers, or, if they were married, their husbands.

In the middle of the 1800s, women began to group together to fight for their rights. They wanted the same rights that men had: the right to vote, the right to an education, the right to work, the right to own property, among others. Eventually, they focused on winning the right to vote, called **suffrage**. In the early 1900s, these women became known as **suffragettes**. The term was meant to be

Suffragettes protesting the unequal treatment of women.

insulting, but the suffragettes wore the name proudly. They often went to jail in the fight for the vote. By the 1920s, victory was theirs—women over the age of thirty were given the right to vote by the ninteenth Amendment to the Constitution (today women can vote at eighteen).

definition

suffrage
(SUF rij) *noun*, the right to vote.

In a democracy, suffrage is very important, because the only way to change government is to vote.

The 1960s saw a new fight for women's rights: the **Women's Liberation Movement**. This time, women fought to be given equal pay for doing the same work men did, and for better support for children and families. They also sought to raise people's awareness of violence against women. Today, women like **Sandra Day O'Connor** and **Ruth Bader Ginsburg**, Supreme Court Justices, and Attorney General of the United States **Janet Reno**, help to show everyone that women can hold positions of great importance in our country's government.

"Is This All?"

Betty Friedan (1921-) wrote a book called The Feminine Mystique, published in 1963, which was about the dissatisfaction of women who were expected to stay home while men were out in the world working. "Is this all?" was the question she put into words for many women. The Feminine Mystique provided a push for the women's movement of the 60s, and Friedan became the first president of NOW (the National Organization of Women).

Susan B. Anthony (1820-1906) of the United States was one of the leaders of the Suffragette movement. She started a newspaper for the feminist movement called *Revolution*.

RIVETING ROSIE

Rosie the Riveter was not a real person, but she represented the women who went to work in the factories during World War II, taking the place of the men who were at war. Rosie the Riveter symbolized the idea that women could do more than just cook and clean.

6

30. Where did the U.S. fight a war during the 1960s and 1970s?

(A) Bulgaria

(B) Vietnam

(C) Korea

definition

totalitarian
(toe tal i TARE ee un)
adj. permitting no rival loyalties or parties.

*Carmen fled the **totalitarian** regime of her native land and moved to Canada.*

The U.S. fought two big wars in Asia (p. 340) after World War II. The first, the **Korean War**, took place between 1950 and 1953. The second, the **Vietnam War**, was the longest war in U.S. history, lasting from the early 1960s until 1973. Both of these wars were fought because the U.S. was concerned about the rise of **communist** governments, which set up systems of **totalitarian** rule, and took away many freedoms and rights of that country's citizens. The biggest communist countries were the Union of Soviet Socialist Republics (made up of Russia and some other smaller states) and China. In Korea, Communists who ruled North Korea tried to take over non-Communist South Korea, and the U.S. fought successfully with the South Koreans to drive the North Koreans back.

The Vietnam War was a more complicated and frustrating war for the U.S. Like Korea, Vietnam was divided into a communist

American Troops in Vietnam

North and a non-communist South, and the U.S. became worried when the North made moves against the South. President **Lyndon B. Johnson** (1908-1973) felt that if Vietnam fell to the communists, many more Asian countries would soon follow. In 1965, after the bombing of North Vietnam did not cause the Communists to surrender, the U.S. started sending more and more American troops to Vietnam. But year after year, the war did not seem to be turning in the U.S.'s favor. The North Vietnamese were fighting on their home turf, for their own country, and they fought fiercely. American troops were at a disadvantage.

Back in the U.S., Americans were frustrated and angry. Thousands of Americans were being killed in a small, faraway country. Many Americans, especially college students who saw their friends drafted and killed, felt that no cause, and certainly not keeping communists out of Vietnam, could justify all the killing

THE VIETNAM WAR MEMORIAL

There is a monument in Washington D.C. to the 56,555 U.S. soldiers who were killed in Vietnam on which each soldier's name is engraved. The monument helps us remember how horrifying the Vietnam war was.

KARL MARX & COMMUNISM

Karl Marx (1818-1883) was a German philosopher, economist, and social theorist. He wrote a number of works, most notably Das Kapital (1867-95), which became the fundamental text of Marxist economics. Marx's works focus on the struggle between the classes and on the importance of economic factors in politics. His theories have influenced later thinkers and political activists.

A supporter of the Peace Movement.

🎵 "Where have all the Flowers Gone," by Pete Seeger. This is a beautiful anti-war song—one of many from the Vietnam era.

and brutality. Protests were organized regularly to convince the U.S. government to bring the troops home and let Vietnam fight its own civil war. The **Peace Movement**, as it was called, felt that government money should be spent not for war but for helping people at home. Finally, in 1973, the last American troops came home, without having defeated the North Vietnamese. By the end of the war, almost 57 thousand Americans had died in Vietnam.

ANSWERS

1. B	2. C	3. B	4. C	5. C	6. A	7. A	8. C	9. C	10. C
11. B	12. B	13. North, South	14. C	15. B	16. B	17. A	18. B	19. C
20. A	21. A	22. B	23. A	24. A	25. C	26. C	27. A	28. B	29. B
30. B

The Presidents

PRESIDENT (YEARS IN OFFICE)	FIRST LADY	VICE PRESIDENT
 **GEORGE WASHINGTON** (1793-1797) WASHINGTON WAS THE FIRST PRESIDENT AND LEADER OF THE AMERICAN REVOLUTIONARY WAR TROOPS.	MARTHA WASHINGTON	JOHN ADAMS
JOHN ADAMS (1797-1801) JOHN ADAMS FOUGHT AGAINST RULE BY THE BRITISH.	ABIGAIL ADAMS	THOMAS JEFFERSON
THOMAS JEFFERSON (1801-1809) JEFFERSON WROTE THE DECLARATION OF INDEPENDENCE AND REFUSED TO LIVE IN A PALACE.	MARTHA JEFFERSON	AARON BURR GEORGE CLINTON

PRESIDENT (YEARS IN OFFICE)	FIRST LADY	VICE PRESIDENT
JAMES MADISON (1809-1817) MADISON WAS THE MAIN WRITER OF THE U.S. CONSTITUTION	DOLLIE MADISON	GEORGE CLINTON ELBRIDGE GERRY
JAMES MONROE (1817-1825) MONROE WAS THE LAST PRESIDENT TO HAVE BEEN INVOLVED IN THE REVOLUTIONARY WAR.	ELIZABETH MONROE	DANIEL D. TOMPKINS
JOHN QUINCY ADAMS (1825-1829) HE WAS JOHN ADAMS' SECOND SON.	LOUISA ADAMS	JOHN C. CALHOUN
ANDREW JACKSON (1829-1837) PEOPLE SAID HE WAS AS TOUGH AS HICKORY WOOD.	RACHEL JACKSON	JOHN C. CALHOUN MARTIN VAN BUREN
MARTIN VAN BUREN (1837-1841) VAN BUREN WAS KNOWN FOR GETTING WHATEVER HE WANTED.	HANNAH VAN BUREN	RICHARD M. JOHNSON
WILLIAM HENRY HARRISON (1841) HE LED HIS ARMY TO VICTORY OVER THE SHAWNEE INDIANS IN THE BATTLE OF TIPPECANOE.	ANNA HARRISON	JOHN TYLER

PRESIDENT (YEARS IN OFFICE)	FIRST LADY	VICE PRESIDENT
JOHN TYLER (1841-1845) HE WAS THE FIRST VICE PRESIDENT TO TAKE OVER AS PRESIDENT AFTER THE DEATH OF THE PRESIDENT IN OFFICE.	LETITIA TYLER JULIA TYLER	NONE
JAMES KNOX POLK (1845-1849) WHEN HE WAS ELECTED, MANY PEOPLE DIDN'T EVEN KNOW WHO HE WAS!	SARAH POLK	GEORGE M. DALLAS
ZACHARY TAYLOR (1849-1850) HE WAS A COMMANDING SOLDIER AND ALWAYS READY FOR BATTLE.	MARGARET TAYLOR	MILLARD FILLMORE
MILLARD FILLMORE (1850-1853) HE BECAME PRESIDENT UPON THE DEATH OF PRES. TAYLOR.	ABIGAIL FILLMORE	NONE
FRANKLIN PIERCE (1853-1857) PIERCE WAS UNABLE TO HALT THE GROWING TENSIONS BETWEEN NORTH AND SOUTH.	JANE PIERCE	WILLIAM R. KING
JAMES BUCHANAN (1857-1861) ELECTED AT SIXTY-FIVE YEARS OLD, HE WAS CONSIDERED PRETTY OLD TO BE PRESIDENT.	NONE	JOHN C. BRECKINRIDGE

PRESIDENT (YEARS IN OFFICE)	FIRST LADY	VICE PRESIDENT
ABRAHAM LINCOLN (1861-1865) LINCOLN FREED THE SLAVES BY SIGNING THE EMANCIPATION PROCLAMATION.	MARY TODD LINCOLN	HANNIBAL HAMLIN ANDREW JOHNSON
ANDREW JOHNSON (1865-1869) HE BEGAN AS A TAILOR AND WAS TAUGHT TO READ AND WRITE BY HIS WIFE, ELIZA.	ELIZA JOHNSON	NONE
ULYSSES S. GRANT (1869-1877) GRANT SERVED TWO TERMS AS PRESIDENT AFTER LEADING THE UNION FORCES IN THE CIVIL WAR.	JULIA DENT GRANT	SCHUYLER COLFAX HENRY WILSON
RUTHERFORD B. HAYES (1877-1881) HE LOST THE POPULAR VOTE, BUT WON BY ELECTORAL VOTES.	LUCY HAYES	WILLIAM A. WHEELER
JAMES A. GARFIELD (1881) GARFIELD ONLY SERVED FOUR MONTHS IN OFFICE BEFORE BEING ASSASSINATED.	LUCRETIA GARFIELD	CHESTER A. ARTHUR
CHESTER A. ARTHUR (1881-1885) ARTHUR SERVED THE REMAINDER OF GARFIELD'S TERM.	ELLEN ARTHUR	NONE

PRESIDENT (YEARS IN OFFICE)	FIRST LADY	VICE PRESIDENT
GROVER CLEVELAND (1885-1889 & 1893-1897) THE ONLY PRESIDENT TO SERVE NON-CONSECUTIVE TERMS.	FRANCES CLEVELAND	ADLAI STEVENSON
BENJAMIN HARRISON (1889-1893) HE WAS GRANDSON OF WILLIAM HENRY HARRISON, OUR NINTH PRESIDENT.	CAROLINE HARRISON	LEVI P. MORTON
WILLIAM MCKINLEY (1897-1901) MCKINLEY WAS RESPONSIBLE FOR INVOLVING THE U.S. IN THE SPANISH-AMEERICAN WAR.	IDA MCKINLEY	GARRET A. HOBART THEODORE ROOSEVELT
THEODORE ROOSEVELT (1901-1909) HE COMMANDED A FAMOUS GROUP IN THE SPANISH-AMERICAN WAR CALLED THE ROUGH RIDERS.	ALICE ROOSEVELT EDITH ROOSEVELT	CHARLES W. FAIRBANKS
WILLIAM HOWARD TAFT (1909-1913) HE WEIGHED OVER 300 POUNDS!	HELEN TAFT	JAMES S. SHERMAN
WOODROW WILSON (1913-1921) HE LED OUR COUNTRY THROUGH WORLD WAR I.	ELLEN WILSON EDITH WILSON	THOMAS R. MARSHALL

CULTURESCOPE

President (Years in office)	First Lady	Vice President
Warren G. Harding (1921-1923) Harding died in office of natural causes.	Florence Harding	Calvin Coolidge
Calvin Coolidge (1923-1929) He was a quiet man, so quiet they called him silent Cal.	Grace Coolidge	Charles G. Dawes
Herbert Hoover (1929-1933) Hoover failed to adequately deal with the Great Depression.	Lou Hoover	Charles Curtis
Franklin Delano Roosevelt (1933-1945) Our longest serving president, FDR was among the most popular.	Eleanor Roosevelt	John Garner Henry A. Wallace Harry S. Truman
Harry Truman (1945-1953) Truman took over when FDR died and saw the U.S. through the end of WWII.	Bess Truman	Alben W. Barkley
Dwight D. Eisenhower (1953-1961) Eisenhower was a WWII hero. His nickname was "Ike."	Mamie Eisenhower	Richard M. Nixon

PRESIDENT (YEARS IN OFFICE)	FIRST LADY	VICE PRESIDENT
JOHN F. KENNEDY (1961-1963) KENNEDY WAS ASSASINATED BY LEE HARVEY OSWALD.	JACQUELINE KENNEDY	LYNDON B. JOHNSON
LYNDON BAINES JOHNSON (1963-1969) HE WAS THE FIRST PRESIDENT TO REFUSE TO RUN FOR A SECOND TERM.	"LADY BIRD" JOHNSON	HUBERT H. HUMPHREY
RICHARD M. NIXON (1969-1974) NIXON WAS THE FIRST PRESIDENT TO RESIGN FROM OFFICE.	PAT NIXON	SPIRO AGNEW GERALD FORD
GERALD FORD (1974-1977) FORD TOOK OVER AFTER NIXON AND HAD A REPUTATION FOR BEING CLUMSY.	BETTY FORD	NELSON ROCKEFELLER
JAMES EARL CARTER (1977-1981) CARTER WAS A PEANUT FARMER BEFORE HE ENTERED POLITICS.	ROSALYNN CARTER	WALTER F. MONDALE

President (Years in office)	First Lady	Vice President
RONALD REAGAN (1981-1989) HE WAS A FORMER ACTOR WHO BECAME A POPULAR PRESIDENT.	NANCY REAGAN	GEORGE BUSH
GEORGE BUSH (1989-1993) VERY POPULAR EARLY IN HIS PRESIDENCY, BUSH WAS NOT REELECTED.	BARBARA BUSH	DAN QUAYLE
WILLIAM J. CLINTON (1993-) HIS WIFE HILLARY PLAYS A LARGE ROLE IN THE GOVERNMENT.	HILLARY RODHAM CLINTON	ALBERT GORE, JR.

States and Capitals

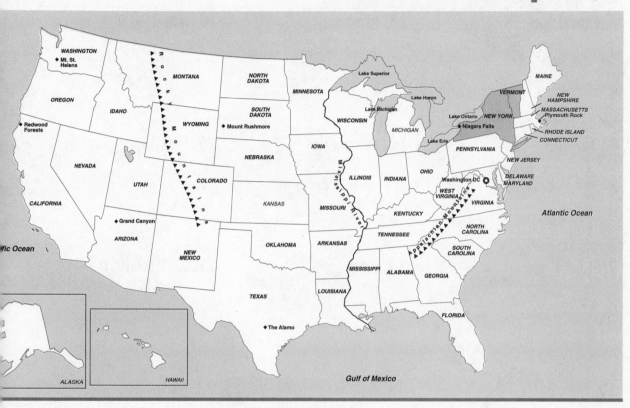

THE FIFTY STATES AND THEIR CAPITALS

1. ALABAMA
Montgomery

2. ALASKA
Juneau

3. ARIZONA
Phoenix

4. ARKANSAS
Little Rock

5. CALIFORNIA
Sacramento

6. COLORADO
Denver

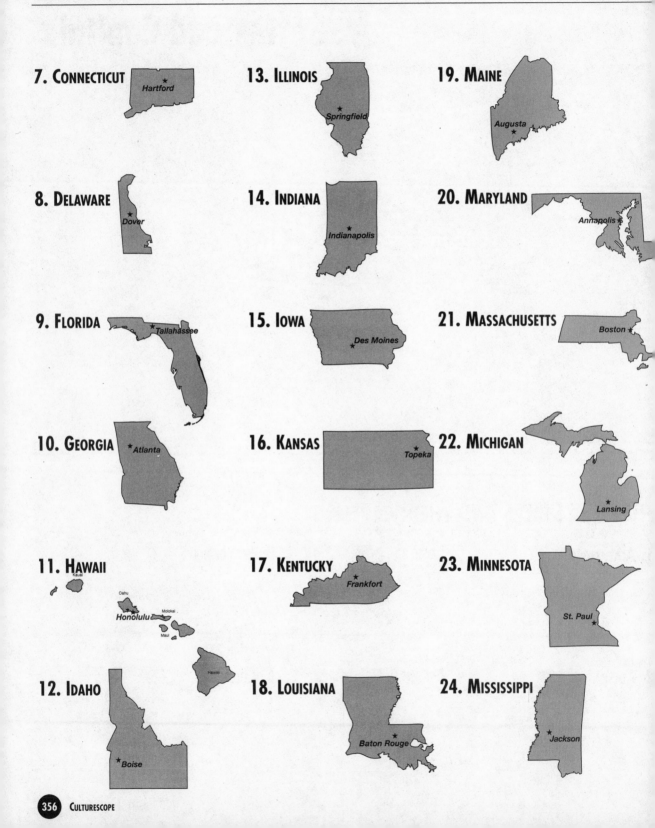

7. Connecticut Hartford

13. Illinois Springfield

19. Maine Augusta

8. Delaware Dover

14. Indiana Indianapolis

20. Maryland Annapolis

9. Florida Tallahassee

15. Iowa Des Moines

21. Massachusetts Boston

10. Georgia Atlanta

16. Kansas Topeka

22. Michigan Lansing

11. Hawaii Kauai, Oahu, Molokai, Honolulu, Maui, Hawaii

17. Kentucky Frankfort

23. Minnesota St. Paul

12. Idaho Boise

18. Louisiana Baton Rouge

24. Mississippi Jackson

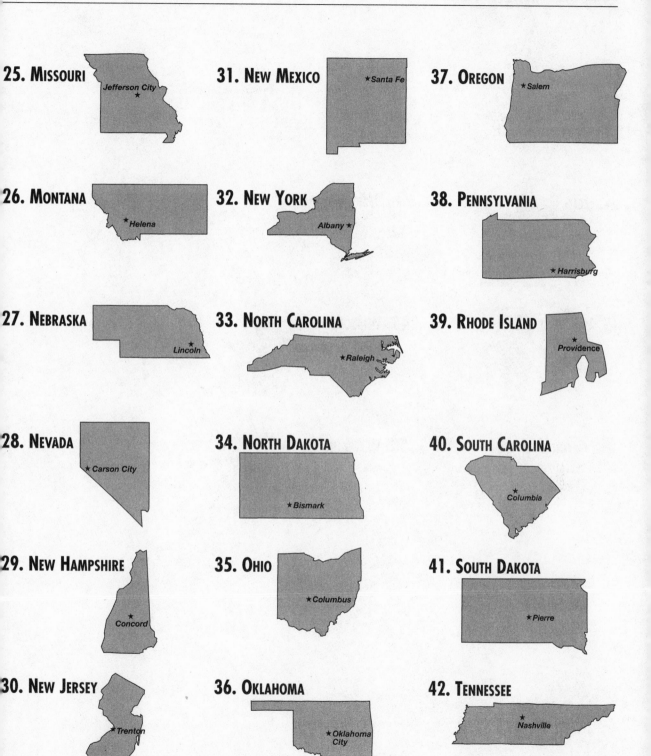

25. MISSOURI
Jefferson City ★

26. MONTANA
★ Helena

27. NEBRASKA
Lincoln ★

28. NEVADA
★ Carson City

29. NEW HAMPSHIRE
★ Concord

30. NEW JERSEY
★ Trenton

31. NEW MEXICO
★ Santa Fe

32. NEW YORK
Albany ★

33. NORTH CAROLINA
★ Raleigh

34. NORTH DAKOTA
★ Bismark

35. OHIO
★ Columbus

36. OKLAHOMA
★ Oklahoma City

37. OREGON
★ Salem

38. PENNSYLVANIA
★ Harrisburg

39. RHODE ISLAND
★ Providence

40. SOUTH CAROLINA
★ Columbia

41. SOUTH DAKOTA
★ Pierre

42. TENNESSEE
★ Nashville

43. TEXAS

★ Austin

44. UTAH

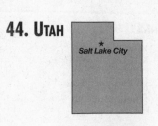

★
Salt Lake City

45. VERMONT

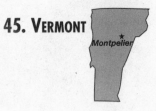

★
Montpelier

46. VIRGINIA

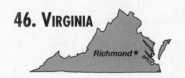

Richmond ★

47. WASHINGTON

★ Olympia

48. WEST VIRGINIA

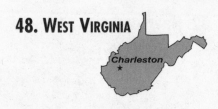

Charleston
★

49. WISCONSIN

Madison
★

50. WYOMING

Cheyenne
★

The Reading Lists (and More!)

THE FIRST GRADE READING LIST

You may or may not be reading in first grade. Everyone begins reading at his or her own pace. The important thing is to enjoy a good story whether you're reading or listening. Try these books to get a good head start.

The Jolly Postman, by Janet & Allan Ahlberg
Read the letters that the postman delivers—including some fun surprises.

Digging Up Dinosaurs, by Aliki
Are you a dino-maniac? This book will give you lots of great facts.

Miss Nelson (series), by Harry Allard and James Marshall
Miss Nelson's class is always fun to read about.

The Paper Crane, by Molly Bang
This is a famous Japanese folk tale about a mysterious paper crane.

Madeline, by Ludwig Bemelmans
Everyone should know this famous French girl.

Mike Mulligan and His Steam Shovel, by Virginia Lee Burton
A classic, we'll say no more.

Strega Nona, by Tomie de Paola
Tomie de Paola retells a funny Italian story.

The Magic School Bus (series), by Joanna Cole, Bruce Degen, illus.
Ms. Frizzle is a wonderful, funny teacher who takes her class on a series of unbelievable adventures.

Corduroy, by Don Freeman
Meet Corduroy, a little bear with a button missing.

A Story A Story, by Gail Haley
Meet Anansi, a famous African spider who weaves a wonderful story.

Danny and the Dinosaur, by Syd Hoff
A wonderful "beginning to read" story.

The Monkey and the Crocodile: Jakata Tales
These are beautiful stories from India.

Whistle for Willie, by Ezra Jack Keats
Anything by Ezra Jack Keats is a good choice.

The Story of Ferdinand, by Munro Leaf
Ferdinand the bull is the world's most famous peace lover.

George and Martha, by James Marshall
George and Martha are best friends who learn what it really means to be a friend.

Amelia Bedelia (series), by Peggy Parish
Amelia Bedelia gets everything wrong. You won't believe it.

Where the Wild Things Are, by Maurice Sendak
Everyone should know about Max, and what happened when he
wore his wolf suit.

The Cat in the Hat, by Dr. Seuss
All Dr. Seuss books are great for beginning readers.

Curious George, by H.A. Rey
Who is the man in the yellow hat? Find out.

Ira Sleeps Over, by Bernard Waber
Read *Lyle, Lyle, Crocodile* after you finish this great book.

THE SECOND GRADE READING LIST

Now that you're in second grade, you probably enjoy reading on
your own, as well as having books read to you. You're not too old
to enjoy a good story time. Here are twenty books to try in second
grade, and they're just as good if you read them yourself or if someone reads them to you.

Arthur (series), by Mark Brown
Arthur and his friends are the main characters in this whole series
of books.

The Girl Who Loved Wild Horses, by Paul Goble
A good "starting to read" book.

Hershel and the Hanukkah Goblins, by Eric Kimmel
A fun way to learn about the Hanukkah story.

Frog and Toad (series), by Arnold Lobel
Frog and Toad are good friends. This series is a good easy reader.

Tikki Tikki Tembo, by Arlene Mosel
This tells the funny story of how the Chinese people changed their
names.

In all his young life Sylvester had never had a wish gratified so quickly. It struck him that magic must be at work, and he guessed that the magic must be in the remarkable-looking red pebble. (Where indeed it was.) To make a test, he put the pebble on the ground and said, 'I wish it would rain again.' Nothing happened. But when he said the same thing holding the pebble in his hoof, the sky turned black, there was lightning and a clap of thunder, and the rain came shooting own.

The Keeping Quilt, by Patricia Polacco
A beautiful story about tradition and coming to a new country. Also check out *Just Plain Fancy*, *Meteor!*, and *Renchenka's Eggs*, by the same author.

The Wingdingdilly, by Bill Peet
Bill Peet is one of the most popular children's authors of all time. After reading this, try *Chester, The Worldly Pig*, *Cowardly Clyde* and anything else by Bill Peet.

Tar Beach, by Faith Ringgold
Tar Beach is what these children call their roof, where they dream about flying. A great story about city life.

In a Dark, Dark Room, by Alvin Schwartz
Some scary stories.

Sylvester and the Magic Pebble, by William Steig
What happens when Sylvester finds a magic pebble.

Jumanji, by Chris Van Allsburg
A very weird game—you may never look at Monopoly the same way again.

Stories for Children, by Oscar Wilde
This famous Irish author's fairy tales for children.

Morris and Boris, by Bernard Wiseman.
Great practice reading books.

The Third Grade Reading List

Third grade is a time when you're reading chapter books full force, but you still want to read a picture book occasionally. Comic books are lots of fun and a nice way to relax after your regular reading.

The Wind In the Willows, by Kenneth Grahame
Find out about Mr. Toad and that wild ride.

Freckle Juice, by Judy Blume
Judy Blume is an "absolute must" author to get to know in third grade.

Paddington Bear (serie), by Michael Bond
Paddington Bear gets into a whole lot of adventures. Try one of the series.

Ramona (series), *Henry Huggins* (series), by Beverly Cleary
Everyone know Ramona, Henry and Ribsy.

Charlie and the Chocolate Factory, and *James and the Giant Peach*, by Roald Dahl
Charlie gets into quite an adventure with Willy Wonka. James has two mean aunts, and finds a big peach one day.

Pecos Bill and Paul Bunyan, by Steven Kellogg
Learn about America's most famous folk heros with Steven Kellogg's wonderfully illustrated books.

Encyclopedia Brown (series), by Donald Sobol
Encyclopedia Brown solves every mystery.

Amos and Boris, by William Steig
Any book by William Steig is a wonderful choice.

Little House on the Prairie (series), by Laura Ingalls Wilder
Find out about life in the west with this series of true stories by Laura Ingalls Wilder.

The Trumpet of the Swan, by E.B. White
For many people, this is the best E.B. White book.

FROM *JAMES AND THE GIANT PEACH* BY ROALD DAHL

James decided that this was most certainly not a time to be disagreeable, so he crossed the room to where the Centipede was sitting and knelt down beside him.

"Thank you so much," the Centipede said. "You are very kind."

"You have a lot of boots," James murmured.

"I have a lot of legs," the Centipede answered proudly. "And a lot of feet. One hundred, to be exact."

"There he goes again!" the Earthworm cried, speaking for the first time. "He simply cannot stop telling lies about his legs! He doesn't have anything like a hundred of them! He's only got forty-two! The trouble is that most people don't bother to count them. They just take his word. Any anyway, there is nothing marvelous, you know, Centipede, about having a lot of legs."

"Poor fellow," the Centipede said, whispering in James's ear. "He's blind. He can't see how splendid I look."

ARE YOU A READER? HOW MANY OF THE FOLLOWING CAN YOU SAY "YES" TO?

....

____ *I read something every day.*

____ *I have a library card.*

____ *I go to the library and take books out.*

____ *I like to play word games.*

____ *I like to get books as presents.*

____ *I try to write in my journal on a regular basis.*

____ *I like to read magazines.*

____ *I like to have someone read stories to me.*

If you can say "yes" to at least five of the above, you're a top reader.

The Indian in the Cupboard, by Lynn Reid Banks
How would you take care of a little toy Indian that came to life?

The Autobiography of Bill Peet, by Bill Peet
A wonderful life story by the author of many great children's books, like *The Wingdingdilly* and *Chester, The Worldly Pig*. Bill Peet was also an animator for Disney. You'll recognize his drawings and find out who the animals in his stories really represent.

The Adventures of Tintin, by Herge
A series of comic books that chronicle the worldly adventures of a little boy named Tintin.

And Then What Happened, Paul Revere?, by Jean Fritz
Jean Fritz has written a whole bunch of great biographies. Whether you have to do a report, or just want interesting reading, try one.

My Father's Dragon, by Ruth Stiles Gannett
Follow this great fantasy adventure to find out all about the wonderful dragon.

Jinx Gloves (series), by Matt Christopher
Every one loves this series of sports stories by Matt Christopher.

Mr. Popper's Penguins, by Richard and Florence Atwater
Add twelve penguins to Mr. Popper's house and see what happens.

THE FOURTH GRADE READING LIST

Here are some of the best books for a fourth grader to read. Many of the books are part of a series, so if you enjoy one, look for others in the same series.

Dear Mr. Henshaw, by Beverly Cleary
The story of Leigh Botts and his letters to a make-believe author Mr. Henshaw. Other great books by Beverly Cleary are the *Ramona* and *Henry Huggins* series.

Tales of a Fourth Grade Nothing, by Judy Blume
The wild adventures of Fudge and his fourth grade brother. If you love it, you'll want to read *Superfudge* and *Fudge-A-Mania* by Judy Blume as well.

Harriet the Spy, by Louise Fitzhugh
Harriet writes down everything she sees in a journal. The problem starts when her classmates find it.

Pippi Longstocking, by Astrid Lindgren
You may know Pippi—she's that crazy girl with the braids that stick straight out who walks half on the sidewalk and half on the street. She has lots of weird adventures.

Sideways Stories from Wayside School, by Louis Sachar
A series of hysterically funny books by Louis Sachar about a really silly school.

Harry Kitten and Tucker Mouse, by George Selden
Part of a series of Tucker books, this book is about two unlikely friends.

The Velveteen Rabbit, by Margery Williams
A classic story about a boy and his stuffed rabbit.

Thomas Jefferson, by Jim Hargrove
A fascinating story about our third president, the author of the Declaration of Independence.

Go Free or Die, by Jeri Ferris
The story of Harriet Tubman and the Underground Railroad is unbelievable. You might also like to look at *Aunt Harriet and the Underground Railroad* by Faith Ringgold.

Sarah, Plain and Tall, by Patricia MacLachlan
Sarah travels all the way from Maine to the Great Plains to become a wife and mother.

FROM *DEAR MR. HENSHAW* BY BEVERLY CLEARY

Dear Mr. Henshaw,

I bought a composition book like you said. It is yellow with a spiral binding. On the front I printed

DIARY OF LEIGH MARCUS
BOTTS
PRIVATE — KEEP OUT
THIS MEANS YOU !!!!!

When I started to write in it, I didn't know how to begin. I felt as if I should write, "Dear Composition Book," but that sounds dumb. So does "Dear Piece of Paper." The first page still looks the way I feel. Blank. I don't think I can keep a diary. I don't want to be a nuisance to you, but I wish you could tell me how. I am stuck.

Puzzled reader,
Leigh Botts

Help! I'm a Prisoner in the Library, by Eth Clifford
When two children get locked in a library in the middle of a blizzard, some very mysterious things begin to happen.

The Boxcar Children, by Gertrude Chandler Warner
This is a series of books about a group of runaway children who get involved in all sorts of mysteries.

The Chocolate Touch, by Patrick Skene Catling
John Midas gets the chocolate touch—anything he touches may turn to chocolate.

The Whipping Boy, by Sid Fleischman
The whipping boy is the boy who gets whipped whenever the prince misbehaves (you can't hit a prince, you know).

Norby and the Lost Princess, by Issac and Janet Asimov
Great science fiction from one of the great science fiction writers of our time, about a robot named Norby and his owner, Jeff.

Ben and Me, by Robert Lawson
Ben is Benjamin Franklin. Read this book to find out who "me" is.

Shiloh, by Phyllis Reynolds Naylor
This is a must-read for all dog-lovers.

Fat Men From Space, by Daniel Manus Pinkwater
William has a special tooth—it can detect the upcoming invasion of the Fat Men, who are heading our way for junk food.

S.O.R. Losers, by Avi
This is a special soccer team—the only members are kids who don't play any sports.

Sybil Rides for Independence, by Drollene P. Brown
Sybil rides to tell everyone that the British are coming.

The Fifth Grade Reading List

By fifth grade, you really have a choice of a ton of books to read. Everything from adventure, to mystery to real life stories. Try something new in fifth grade. There are many, many choices. Here are a few fifth grade favorites. How many have you read?

The Stinky Cheese Man and Other Fairly Stupid Tales, by Jon Scieszka and Lane Smith
A funny twist on some very familiar stories.

Sounder, by William Armstrong
A story about an African American boy and his dog in the south.

The Wizard of Oz, by L. Frank Baum
You've seen the movie—the book is even better. See if you can spot the differences in the stories.

The Incredible Journey, by Sheila Burnford
An unbelievable story of animals making their way back home to their masters.

My Side of the Mountain, by Jean Craighead George
The story of a boy who runs away from home to have a great adventure in the mountains of New York.

The People Could Fly, by Virginia Hamilton
These are African-American folk tales that tell you a lot about slave life.

Just So Stories, by Rudyard Kipling
How the rhinoceros got his skin; how the elephant got his trunk. Great stories to explain the strange things of everyday life.

From *Sixth Grade Secrets* by Louis Sacher

Mr Doyle was in the middle of teaching the class the difference between adjectives and adverbs. Gabriel understood the difference the first time it was explained.

He usually understood things the first time they were explained. That was one reason why he was always getting into trouble. He would get bored and have to find something else to do.

"What is Pig City?" he wondered. "Why does Kristin have to bring an extra pair of underpants?"

He looked at Laura. She sat three desks to the left of him. Her Pig City cap was pulled down tight over her long brown hair. He thought she had beautiful hair. He knew the story behind it, how she never told a lie. It made it even prettier to him. She was staring intently at Mr. Doyle, hanging on every word he said. Gabriel wished she would look at him like that someday.

If she asked me to answer yes or no, I'd say yes right away, he thought. I don't even care what the question is.

The problem was that whenever he tried to talk to her, his mind would

(continued)

(sixth grade Secrets, continued)

go blank on him. He could never think of anything to say except for "Oink oink." It was stupid. He knew it was stupid, yet he said it, anyway.

He opened his desk and took out a piece of paper and a pencil.

Dear Laura, he wrote.

He chewed his eraser, then continued.

I know all about Pig City. Don't worry, I promise not to tell anybody.

He smiled. He hoped it would trick her into telling him what Pig City was. Plus, she'd like him for not telling anybody. They could share the secret together.

You have pretty hair.

Love Gabriel

He read it over.

It was terrible. I practically told her I loved her! he thought.

The Way Things Work, by David Macaulay
A book filled with pictures to explain how everyday things work.

The Borrowers, by Mary Norton
Have you ever wondered what happened to that missing sock? This book will explain it all. If you love it, there are a bunch of sequels.

Freaky Friday, by Mary Rodgers
A girl and her mother switch places. For all of you who wish you were adults.

Hatchet, by Gary Paulsen
When a young boy is marooned in the middle of Canada with only a hatchet, an unbelivable adventure follows.

Danny, the Champion of the World, by Roald Dahl
Those of you who love Roald Dahl will love this gentle story of a boy and his father.

The Cricket in Times Square, by George Selden
A classic story about a cricket and a famous city—New York.

My Life with the Chimpanzees, by Jane Goodall
The life story of Jane Goodall, the famous naturalist, with photographs of her amazing chimps.

Missing May, by Cynthia Rylant
When May dies, Ob and Summer don't know what to do—they look for a sign from her to find the strength to keep on living.

Sixth Grade Secrets, by Louis Sachar
There are two secret clubs in sixth grade—Pig City and Monkey Town. This is another hysterically funny book by Louis Sachar.

Wilma Rudolph, by Tom Biracree
The story a woman who conquered polio as a child to go on to become the first woman to win 3 gold medals at the Olympics in track.

Tuck Everlasting, by Natalie Babbit
Would you want to live forever? Read this story.

Peter Pan, by J.M. Barrie
The story of a little boy who refused to grow up, the children who befriended him, the famous crocodile, and Captain Hook.

Scary Stories to Tell in the Dark, by Alvin Schwartz
This is the first in a series of Alvin Schwartz's very popular scary short stories that you may not want to read in the dark.

THE SIXTH GRADE READING LIST

Sixth grade is a time when you may be sharing books with adults and older brothers or sisters. The sixth grade list is made to reflect that.

A Wrinkle In Time, by Madeleine L'Engle
"It was a dark and stormy night . . ." So begins this wonderful book about time travel.

Island of the Blue Dolphins, by Scott O'Dell
A young girl lives alone on an island for eighteen years after her brother dies.

The Black Stallion, by Walter Farley
A wild black horse and a boy survive a storm. This is the story of how the boy tames the horse and they become friends.

FROM *THE PHANTOM TOLLBOOTH* BY NORTON JUSTER

"Our job," said the count, "is to see that all the words sold are proper ones, for it wouldn't do to sell someone a word that had no meaning or didn't exist at all. For instance, if you bought a word like ghlbtsk, where would you use it?"

"It would be difficult," thought Milo—but there were so many words that were difficult, and he knew hardly any of them.

"But we never choose which ones to use," explained the earl as they walked toward the market stalls, "for as long as they mean what they mean to mean we don't care if they make sense on nonsense."

"Innocence or magnificence," added the count.

"Reticence or common sense, " said the undersecretary.

"That seems simple enough," said Milo, trying to be polite.

"Easy as falling off a log," cried the earl, falling off the log with a loud thump.

"Must you be so clumsy?" shouted the duke.

"All I said was —" began the earl, rubbing his head.

"We heard you," said the minister angrily, "and you'll have to find an expression that's less dangerous."

The earl dusted himself off as the others snickered audibly.

"You see," cautioned the count, "You must pick your words very carefully and be sure to say just what you intend to say."

The Yearling, by Marjorie Kinnan Rawlings
The sad story of Jody, his pet fawn, and the difficult decisions Jody must make.

Are You There God? It's Me, Margaret, by Judy Blume
A moving story about a young girl trying to deal with a new school, a new city, changes in her body as she reaches adolescence, and her own religion.

The Hobbit, by J.R.R. Tolkien
Bilbo Baggins, the peace-loving dwarf, goes on a dangerous quest after being tricked by the Wizard. If you love this book, you may want to try *The Lord of the Rings* trilogy.

The Book of Three, by Lloyd Alexander
The chronicle of the fantastic land of Prydain and the adventures of Taran, the assistant pig-keeper. Continued in *The Black Cauldron,* and the whole series of Prydain books.

Anne Frank: The Diary of a Young Girl, by Anne Frank
Anne Frank was a young Jewish girl who lived in hiding during the reign of the Nazis. Her diary is one of the most famous ever written, and her story is one you will not forget.

Little Women, by Louisa May Alcott
The story of four sisters who grow up during the Civil War.

The Phantom Tollbooth, by Norton Juster
Milo is bored until he gets a mysterious package in the mail—a tollbooth, which he assembles and drives through. The next thing you know, "jumping to conclusions" takes on a whole new meaning.

The Dark is Rising, by Susan Cooper
The first in a series of wonderful books by Susan Cooper.

Bridge to Terabithia, by Katherine Paterson
This story deals with one of the most difficult topics there is—death.

Mrs. Frisby and the Rats of NIMH, by Robert C. O'Brien
Something's up at NIMH—find out what it is and what's happening to the rats.

The Sword and the Stone, by T.H. White
The story of young King Arthur and his famous sword, Excalibur.

From the Mixed-Up Files of Mrs. Basil E. Frankweiler, by E.L. Konigsburg
Claudia and her brother run away from home to The Metropolitan Museum of Art in New York City.

The Dream Keeper, by Langston Hughes
A beautiful book by one of the great writers of this century.

The Jungle Book, by Rudyard Kipling
Read about Mowgli, raised by the wolves, in this classic story.

The Call of the Wild, by Jack London
Another exciting adventure story by one of America's great writers.

Jesse Jackson, by Anna Kosof
This adult book is a biography of the African American minister who ran for president in 1984 and 1988.

The Devil's Arithmetic, by Jane Yolen
Hannah is unhappy about following Jewish traditions until she travels back to Nazi-occupied Poland.

TWENTY MORE GREAT BOOKS FOR GRADE SCHOOLERS OF ALL AGES

Charlie and the Chocolate Factory, by Roald Dahl
Five children get to visit the mysterious chocolate factory of Willy Wonka. The fantastic inventions and characters will win you over.

James and the Giant Peach, by Roald Dahl
Another classic from Roald Dahl, this is the story of James, who, while living with his aunts, comes across a fabulous giant peach.

The Chronicles of Narnia, by C.S. Lewis
There are seven books in this series. They tell of the adventures of a group of kids in the magical land of Narnia. Start with *The Lion, the Witch and the Wardrobe.*

Charlotte's Web, by E.B. White
Every kid should know the story of Fern, Charlotte, and Wilbur—"some pig," as Charlotte calls him.

Stuart Little, by E.B. White
"When Mrs. Frederick C. Little's second son was born, everybody noticed that he was not much bigger than a mouse." The adventures of Stuart—one of the coolest mice in children's lit.

Winnie-the-Pooh, by A.A. Milne
Don't get the abridged Disney version. Find the original edition with the illustrations of Ernest H. Shepard. A terrific group of stories that may be enjoyed on several levels.

Mary Poppins, by P.L. Travers
A wonderful book, a wonderful movie. Mary Poppins rocks. Chim-chim-charoo, dude.

Just So Stories, by Rudyard Kipling
From "How the Leopard Got His Spots," to "How the Elephant Got his Trunk," these are inventive, creative stories that all ages will get a kick out of.

Aesop's Fables
The Classics—like "The Grasshopper and the Ant," "The Tortoise and the Hare." Every kid should know the basic fables of Aesop.

The Wind in the Willows, by Kenneth Grahame
The story of Mole, Badger, Water Rat, and Toad and their lives along the banks of the river.

Chitty Chitty Bang Bang, by Ian Fleming
Even better than the movie version. The story, in case you don't know, of a magical car.

Treasure Island, by Robert Louis Stevenson
Pirates and treasure. Best read aloud to all but the most intrepid twelve-year-old readers.

Book of Greek Myths, by Ingri and Edgar Parin D'Aulaire
A great introduction to Greek myths. More advanced readers may want to try *Bullfinch's Greek Mythlogy* as well.

The Wizard of Oz, by L. Frank Baum
Dorothy, Toto, and the Wizard. Who doesn't know this story? Read the book if you've only seen the movie—it's worth it.

Andersen's Fairy Tales
These can be kind of intense. They're not at all like the washed-out Disney versions. "The Little Mermaid" doesn't have such a happy ending here. But all children should know "Thumbelina" and "The Ugly Duckling."

Grimm's Fairy Tales
From "Hansel and Gretel" to "Snow White and the Seven Dwarfs," many of our modern movies and stories started out as Grimm's Fairy Tales.

The Children's Bible
Even if you are not Jewish or Christian, these stories are part of much of American literature and film.

The Adventures of Tom Sawyer, by Mark Twain
A little difficult for younger readers, this book is best read aloud. The adventures of that crazy Tom and his friends never end.

Perrault's Fairy Tales
"Cinderella," "Puss In Boots," and "Sleeping Beauty"—some of the best tales of all time.

The Stories of Washington Irving
This collection includes classic American tales like "Rip Van Winkle" and "The Headless Horseman."

FIFTEEN GREAT RECORDINGS FOR GRADE SCHOOLERS

Symphony No. 5, by Beethoven
Beethoven's *Fifth Symphony* is the most famous classic of this most famous composer's repertoire. If you like it, try the *Ninth Symphony* with its beautiful "Song of Joy," or the quiet, lovely Sixth Symphony, sometimes called the "Pastoral Symphony."

Overture to "William Tell," by Tchaikovsky
If you've ever heard of the old Lone Ranger show, you may recognize this famous overture. When you listen to it, see if you can imagine a horse galloping along.

1812 Overture, by Rossini
This is one of the most fun songs you'll hear, with lots of booms and crashes. Imagine, if you will, great cannons going off as you hear each BOOM.

Peter and the Wolf, by Prokofiev
Peter and the Wolf is a great favorite of children everywhere. Get a recording that has the book with it and you can follow the story. In the music, each instrument is a different character.

Suite from "The Nutcracker," by Tchaikovsky
The Nutcracker is a favorite holiday ballet. It is the story of a Christmas long ago, and a little's girl's dreams. You'll certainly recognize the "Dance of the Sugar Plum Fairy" as soon as you hear it.

Pirates of Penzance, by Gilbert and Sullivan
Gilbert and Sullivan are a fun way to learn about operettas. In their day, they were as popular as the music you hear on the radio. "Pirates of Penzance" is one of their funniest compositions. See if

you can sing along with, "I am the very model of a modern major general."

Lullaby, by Brahms
Brahm's "Lullaby" has rocked babies to sleep for many hundreds of years. Take a trip down memory lane when you listen to this one. Or introduce it to a baby you might know.

Eine Kleine Nachtmusik, by Mozart
Mozart is one of the great composers of all time (maybe the greatest). You might recognize this piece. If you enjoy it and want to learn more about this wild character, rent the movie Amadeus.

American in Paris, by Gershwin
Gershwin is the premier American composer of the twentieth century. He combined traditional symphonic music with American jazz for a truly original sound.

Stars and Stripes Forever, by Sousa
If you've ever seen a fireworks display, you may have heard "Stars and Stripes Forever." It's one of those songs you'll hear on the Fourth of July or in a Memorial Day Parade.

The Weavers at Carnegie Hall, by The Weavers
Pete Seeger, Lee Hays, Ronnie Gilbert and Fred Hellerman came together in Greenwich Village, New York in the 1960s and performed this classic of American folk music at Carnegie Hall in 1961. It is considered to be one of the great performances of folk music.

The Beatles 1962-1966, and *The Beatles 1967-1970*, by The Beatles
These two Beatles albums, commonly called "the Red Album" and "the Blue Album," contain most of the Beatles's big hits. Check out a parent's collection—one may be hiding out there—and learn about what some call the greatest pop band ever.

Atlantic Rhythm & Blues 1947-1974, by Various Artists
A history of the evolution of African American Music. If you want to learn about rhythm and blues, you can't go wrong with any of the seven volumes in this set.

The Sun Story, by Various Artists
Early Johnny Cash, Carl Perkins, Jerry Lee Lewis, and a kid named Elvis on this absolutely great collection of country, rock-a-billy and early rock and roll. You gotta hear it to believe it.

The Harder They Come, by Various Artists
Jimmy Cliff and other reggae stars in the soundtrack from the movie. A fun introduction to reggae music, mahn.

FIFTEEN GREAT MOVIES FOR GRADE SCHOOLERS

The Wizard of Oz
Dorothy! Aunty Em! Scarecrow! And that little dog too. A true classic on videocassette and once a year on television.

Snow White and the Seven Dwarfs
Snow White was the first full length cartoon from Walt Disney. Now, so many years later, it still looks new and fresh—a real work of art. If you liked *The Lion King,* check this one out too.

Mary Poppins
A wonderful live action movie from Walt Disney (with a little animation thrown in). Julie Andrews as that strange and magical nanny and Dick Van Dyke plays a dual role (see if you can spot him in his second role—he's disguised).

Star Wars
Stars Wars revolutionized high tech science fiction movies and sent lines around the block almost 20 years ago. It's still a wild, fun ride. If you love it, see the sequels *Return of the Jedi* and *The Empire Strikes Back.*

E.T.
E.T., the story of a strange visitor from another planet, was one of the biggest films from movie maker Steven Spielberg. It's funny and sad and you'll be rooting for a wrinkly little alien by the end.

Duck Soup
You absolutely must see a Marx Brothers' movie—and this one is as good as any they made. You might also want to try *A Day and the Races* and *A Night at the Opera*.

National Velvet
Every kid at some point dreams about owning a horse. This is the ultimate—a young and beautiful Elizabeth Taylor and her famous horse.

The Court Jester/The Secret Life of Walter Mitty
These two movies by Danny Kaye will introduce you to one of the great film stars of all time. They're funny and silly. If you love them, also try Hans Christian Andersen.

The Sound of Music
The Sound of Music is considered by many to be the great movie musical of all time. In case you don't know, it's about a bunch of kids, and their nanny, and some songs they sing.

That's Entertainment
A ton of clips from old movie musicals. This is a fun way to see all the "best" parts of the movies your parents and grandparents keep telling you about.

Yellow Submarine
A fun introduction to the Beatles and this strange cartoony sort of thing that happened in the 1960s.

Old Yeller
A film about a boy and his dog. It's about farm life in 1859 Texas, and it's still one of Disney's best.

Swiss Family Robinson
Anyone who watches this movie and doesn't want to live in a tree-house is just plain lying. You see, this family gets shipwrecked. They build a modest little house in a tree. Pirates attack.What more could you want?

American Graffiti
High School in the fifties. You can laugh at the way they used to dress and talk, but the problems are not so different. Fun to watch, and great music as well. And, a little known Harrison Ford lurking in the background.

King Kong
A girl and her ape. Still fun to watch after all these years—and after it you may want to check out the classic *Mighty Joe Young*.

Index

Note: Italicized page numbers show main discussions. Definitions of words are shown by (def.).

plants, 259-260
Plato, 338
plot, 129
plural form, 56-58
Pluto, 232
Plymouth, 301
poetry, 106, *119-121*
poker, 111-113
poker face, 112(def.)
politicians, 293
Polk, James Knox, 349
Polka, 141
Pollock, Jackson, 145-146
polls, 319, 320
pollution, 240, *255-256*, 289
polygons, 161(def.)
population, 340(def.)
possessive form, 76-77
pot (poker), 112
precipitation, 268-269, 269(def.)
predicate, 67
prefixes, 81-82
prepositions, 89
present tense, 69-70
presidents, U.S., 123, 317-318
    current, 296
    election of, 297
    list of, 347-354
    slavery and, 134, 313
    Watergate scandal, 319-321
    in White House, 305-306
prices, 215-217
principal/principle, 62
prism, 256
proboscis monkeys, 254
prodigy, 133(def.), 134
Prodigy (computer service), 283
pronounce, 50(def.)
pronouns, 54(def.), 54-55, 88
    agreement with nouns, 94-95
    possessive form of, 76-77
pronunciation symbols, 50
proofreading, 85
proper nouns, 52
proportion, 225-227, 226(def.)
protostar, 278
pseudonyms, 62
puberty, 280, 281(def.)

punctuation, 46, 65-67, *77-79*, 78(def.)
Puritans, 304
Pyramid (game), 104-105
pyramids
    ancient, 336-337
    figures, 183
pyrophobia, 58

Q
queen, 109
quest, 130(def.)
question mark (?), 46, 65, 77-78
questions, 64-65
quizzes, by grade, 9-42

R
radiation, 330
rainbows, 256-257
raise, 112
RAM (random access memory), 272
range, 213(def.)
ratify, 332(def.)
rays, 210
Reagan, Ronald, 354
recipes, 246, 247, 269-271
rectangles, 161, 197-198, 205
recycling, 255
red giants, 279
red supergiants, 279
reduce, 186(def.)
referee, 114(def.)
reference books, 50-52, 58-59, 74, 84-85
reincarnate, 146(def.)
religions, *146-148, 299-300, 301(def.), 304, 333-334*
remainder, 184(def.)
Rembrandt, 144
Renaissance, 143
Reno, Janet, 343
representative democracy, 317
reproduction, 279-281
residence, 305(def.)
respiratory system, 274
responsibilities, 291, 292(def.)
rhetorical questions, 65
rhymes, 106, *119-121*
rhythm, 120(def.)
riddles, 118
right triangles, 228

Permissions Acknowledgements
(In order of appearance)

Fun and Games
The Bettmann Archive
The Bettmann Archive
UPI/Bettmann
Reuters/Bettmann
UPI/Bettmann
Reuters/Bettmann
UPI/Bettmann
Reuters/Bettmann
UPI/Bettmann

Humanities
UPI/Bettmann
UPI/The Bettmann Archive
UPI/Bettmann
The Bettmann Archive
The Bettmann Archive
The Bettmann Archive
The Bettmann Archive
The Bettmann Archive
UPI/Bettmann
The Bettmann Archive
The Bettmann Archive
UPI/Bettmann
The Bettmann Archive
UPI/Bettmann
The Bettmann Archive
The Bettmann Archive
The Bettmann Archive
UPI/Bettmann
The Bettmann Archive

Science
UPI/Bettmann
UPI/Bettmann
The Bettmann Archive
The Bettmann Archive
UPI/Bettmann
Reuters/Bettmann
The Bettmann Archive
The Bettmann Archive
The Bettmann Archive
The Bettmann Archive
UPI/Bettmann

UPI/Bettmann
The Bettmann Archive
UPI/Bettmann
The Bettmann Archive
The Bettmann Archive
The Bettmann Archive
The Bettmann Archive
The Bettmann Archive
The Bettmann Archive
UPI/Bettmann

Social Studies
Neg. No. 243367
Courtesy Department Library
  Services American Museum of
  Natural History
Reuters/Bettmann
The Bettmann Archive
Collection of the New-York
  Historical Society
The Bettmann Archive
The Bettmann Archive
UPI/Bettmann
UPI/Bettmann
UPI/Bettmann
The Bettmann Archive
UPI/Bettmann
Reuters/Bettmann
UPI/Bettmann
UPI/Bettmann
The Bettmann Archive
The Bettmann Archive
The Bettmann Archive
The Bettmann Archive
AP/World Wide Photos
The Bettmann Archive
UPI/Bettmann
UPI/Bettmann
Reuters/Bettmann
The Bettmann Archive
The Bettmann Archive
The Bettmann Archive
UPI/Bettmann
The Bettmann Archive
The Bettmann Archive
The Bettmann Archive

Reuters/Bettmann
UPI/Bettmann
UPI/Bettmann
The Bettmann Archive

The Presidents
The Bettmann Archive
The Bettmann Archive
The Bettmann Archive
The Bettmann Archive
The Bettmann Archive
The Bettmann Archive
The Bettmann Archive
The Bettmann Archive
UPI/The Bettmann Archive
The Bettmann Archive
The Bettmann Archive
The Bettmann Archive
The Bettmann Archive
The Bettmann Archive
The Bettmann Archive
The Bettmann Archive
The Bettmann Archive
The Bettmann Archive
The Bettmann Archive
The Bettmann Archive
The Bettmann Archive
The Bettmann Archive
The Bettmann Archive
The Bettmann Archive
The Bettmann Archive
Pach/Bettmann
The Bettmann Archive
Pach/Bettmann
The Bettmann Archive
The Bettmann Archive
Pach/Bettmann
The Bettmann Archive
UPI/Bettmann
The Bettmann Archive
UPI/Bettmann Newsphotos
UPI/Bettmann Newsphotos
UPI/Bettmann
UPI/Bettmann
The Bettmann Archive
UPI/Bettmann
UPI/Bettmann Newsphotos
Reuters/Bettmann
Reuters/Bettmann

ABOUT THE AUTHOR

Liz Buffa joined The Princeton Review in 1989. She is a graduate of Wellesley College and lives in Locust Valley, NY with her husband and two sons, David and Paul. This is her fifth book for The Princeton Review.